Studies in modern capitalism

Geopolitics and geocul

MW01046334

Studies in modern capitalism · Etudes sur le capitalisme moderne

This series is devoted to an attempt to comprehend capitalism as a world-system. It will include monographs, collections of essays and colloquia around specific themes, written by historians and social scientists united by a common concern for the study of large-scale long-term social structure and social change.

The series is a joint enterprise of the Maison des Sciences de l'Homme in Paris and the Fernand Braudel Center for the Study of Economies, Historical Systems, and Civilizations at the State University of New York at Binghamton.

This book is published as part of the joint publishing agreement established in 1977 between the Fondation de la Maison des Sciences de l'Homme and the Press Syndicate of the University of Cambridge. Titles published under this arrangement may appear in any European language or, in the case of volumes of collected essays, in several languages.

New books will appear either as individual titles or in one of the series which the Maison des Sciences de l'Homme and the Cambridge University Press have jointly agreed to publish. All books published jointly by the Maison des Sciences de l'Homme and the Cambridge University Press will be distributed by the Press throughout the world.

Geopolitics and geoculture

Essays on the changing world-system

IMMANUEL WALLERSTEIN

CAMBRIDGE
UNIVERSITY PRESS

Published by the Press Syndicate of the University of Cambridge
The Pitt Building, Trumpington Street, Cambridge CB2 1RP
40 West 20th Street, New York, NY 10011-4211, USA
10 Stamford Road, Oakleigh, Melbourne 3166, Australia
and Editions de la Maison des Sciences de l'Homme
54 Boulevard Raspail, 75270 Paris Cedex 06

First published 1991
Reprinted 1992, 1994

Printed in Great Britain by Athenæum Press Ltd., Newcastle upon Tyne

British Library cataloguing in publication data

Wallerstein, Immanuel, 1930–
Geopolitics and geoculture: essays on the changing world-system (Studies in modern
capitalism: Etudes sur le capitalisme moderne)
1. Political geography
I. Title   II. Series
320.12

Library of Congress cataloguing in publication data

Wallerstein, Immanuel Maurice, 1930–
    Geopolitics and geoculture: essays on the changing world-system/Immanuel
Wallerstein.
    p.   cm.   (Studies in modern capitalism = Etudes sur le capitalisme moderne)
    Includes index.
    ISBN 0-521-40454-1 (hardcover) – ISBN 0-521-40604-8 (paperback)
    1. Geopolitics.   I. Title.   II. Series: Studies in modern capitalism.
JC319.W25   1991
327.1'01—dc20   90-19644
                                                                          CIP

ISBN 0 521 40454 1 hardback
ISBN 0 521 40604 8 paperback
ISBN 2 7351 0401 X hardback (France only)
ISBN 2 7351 0402 8 paperback (France only)

GO

∾ Contents

✌ Acknowledgments

I am grateful to the original publishers for their kind cooperation in granting permission for publication here.

1 *SAIS Review*, no. 4, Summer 1982
2 *Millenium: Journal of International Studies*, vol. XVI, no. 3, Winter 1987
3 W.E. Hanreider (ed.) *Global Peace and Security* (Boulder, Colorado: Westview Press, 1987)
4 Bjorn Hettne (ed.) *Europe: Dimensions of Peace* (London: Zed Books, 1988)
5 *Theory and Society*, vol. XVIII, no. 2, Spring 1989
6 *Thesis Eleven*, no. 27, 1990
7 *Towards One World? International Responses to the Brandt Report* (London: Temple Smith, 1981)
8 *Review*, vol. II, no. 4, Fall 1988 (Fernand Braudel Center)
9 *Alternatives*, vol. XIV, no. 3, July 1989
10 *Millennium: Journal of International Studies*, vol. XIV, no. 2, Summer 1985
11 *Hitotsubashi Journal of Social Studies*, vol. XXI, no. 1, August 1989
12 A. D. King (ed.) *Culture, Globalization and the World-System* (London: Macmillan, 1991)
13 Numan V. Bartley (ed.) *The Evolution of Southern Culture* (Athens, Georgia: University of Georgia Press, 1988)
14 *Development: Seeds of Change*, nos. 1/2, 1986
15 *Thesis XI*, no. 25, 1990

✤ Introduction:
The lessons of the 1980s

The 1980s clearly ended with a bang and not a whimper. 1989 saw the dramatic collapse of Marxism-Leninism, both as a form of governance and as an ideological system and pole of political attraction. For the great majority of persons, the suddenness of the collapse (or even the very fact of a collapse at all) came as a surprise. For very many, the surprise was happy, signalling the triumph of liberty over despotism. For others, it was dismaying, signalling the end of illusions and the tempering (if not the disappearance) of revolutionary optimism.

The analyses that have been immediately forthcoming to explain these events have tended to suffer from being too episodic or event-oriented (*événementiel*, to use Braudel's distinction among three kinds of historical time), and insufficiently structural or cyclical (*conjoncturel*). Even big events, and 1989 was indeed a big event, cannot be understood intelligently if one analyzes them primarily in their own immediate context. If we try this, we tend not only to misread the events but, more importantly, to derive false lessons from them. This is what I fear is happening now: we are passing through a period (let us hope it is short) of drawing hasty and quite distorted implications from the events of 1989.

False conclusions are being drawn in the (ex-)Communist world, where the magic of the market is supplanting the magic of planning, whereas the market will by and large be no more efficacious an instrument of economic welfare for these states than had been planning, since the primary economic difficulties of these states derived (and derive) not from their internal economic mechanisms but from their structural location in the capitalist world-economy.

False conclusions are being drawn in the Western world, where the collapse of Leninism is being interpreted as the triumph of Wilsonian liberalism whereas, in fact, 1989 represents the demise not of Leninism alone but of both ends of the great ideological antinomy of the twentieth century, the Wilsonian versus the Leninist eschatologies. What we have been witnessing in eastern Europe has been far less the discovery of the spirit of 1776 or that of 1789 than the aftershock of 1968.

False conclusions are being drawn in the Third World, where the collapse of Leninism is being interpreted by many as a decisive weakening of these countries in their struggle against the economic domination of the North whereas, in fact, Soviet rhetoric of the past forty-five years had been of only marginal utility in the struggle of the countries of the Third World, and the weakness of their current position derives primarily from the continuing functioning of the capitalist world-economy, secondarily from the inefficacy of their strategies of "national development," and only tertiarily from the present inability (and unwillingness) of the USSR to sustain them. To accuse Gorbachev of "revisionism" is as event-oriented and irrelevant as to see Lech Walesa as Tom Paine.

This book is a collection of essays written in the 1980s. The most recent (chapter 6) was written in September 1989. Thus all were written before the most dramatic of the events in Eastern Europe (the collapse of the regimes in the German Democratic Republic, Bulgaria, Czechoslovakia, and Romania). Since the essays of Part I concern geopolitics, it may seem like a risky or dubious proposition to republish them. Yet, it is precisely because of the "end of the Communisms" that I have put together this collection – to argue that this is not a sudden unanticipated dramatic event but part of a larger process, the primary element of which is in fact, and not at all paradoxically, the end of the era of US hegemony in the world-system. Although many commentators have been hailing 1989 as the beginning of the Pax Americana, the thesis of this book is that, quite the contrary, it marks the end of the Pax Americana. The Cold War was the Pax Americana! The Cold War is over; thus the Pax Americana has now ended.

There are three basic vectors which need to be analyzed in order for us to make sense of the events of 1989. The first is the cyclical pattern of hegemonies within the modern world-system. The second is the blossoming between 1789 and 1968 of the ideological veneer(s) of the capitalist world-economy. And the third is the deep uncertainties of evolution, or how transitions from one historical system to another really occur. The description of each vector is a very large subject, and all I can do in this introduction is draw a vast and broad canvas, in the hope that it will enable the reader to pull together the detail that is found in the succeeding essays in this book (as well as elsewhere in my writings).

One of the basic structures of the capitalist world-economy is the cyclical rise and decline of "hegemonies" within the world-system. I have previously analyzed how I believe this structure operates.[1] The story of the third of the hegemonies, that of the United States, may best be started in 1873, the beginning of the so-called "Great Depression" of the nineteenth century, the moment after which one could say the era of British hegemony was over. Of course, Great Britain was still quite powerful, indeed still the most powerful and most wealthy country in the world-system. But it was no longer hegemonic. Its economic edge had disappeared. As of then, it faced the increasingly successful competition of both Germany and the United States, who became rivals for the succession. Great Britain was finding even French economic competition a renewed problem.

The geopolitical consequences were quite profound and quite immediate. Europe (or extended Europe, to include within this term both Russia and the United States) moved from a situation in which British political will was preeminent to one in which there was a revived balance of power, a situation of acute great-power rivalry, and an uncertain reshuffling of alliances. For about a half-century, this rivalry was to display itself primarily in the "extra-European" world, the peripheral and semiperipheral zones of the world-economy: the "scramble" for colonies in Africa, Southeast Asia, and the Pacific Ocean; the dismantlement

---

[1] See my "The Three Instances of Hegemony in the History of the Capitalist World-Economy," chapter 4 of *The Politics of the World-Economy*. Cambridge: Cambridge University Press, 1984, 37–46.

of the Ottoman and Chinese empires; the military interventions in Mexico, Central America, and the Caribbean. And it would be an incident in Sarajevo, a part of the periphery that intruded onto the European continent itself, which triggered the start of the First World War as the culmination of this interstate rivalry.

It was not, however, 1914 that was the symbolic year, but 1917. 1917 marked the October Revolution in Russia, to be sure – the coming-to-power by insurrection of the Bolsheviks. 1917 also marked, however, the entry of the United States into the war, the acknowledgment that the fundamental issue was not at all the fate of remote Balkan peoples, but the competition between the US and Germany to control the world-system in the next era.

Germany, of course, lost the First World War. But just as France refused to acknowledge its world-systemic defeat by Great Britain in 1763 and insisted on one further round of battle (which we would have from 1792 to 1815),[2] so Germany refused to acknowledge its world-systemic defeat in 1918 and insisted on another round of battle (which we would have from 1939 to 1945).

If we compare the last round of the US–German struggle of the long twentieth century with the last round of the British–French struggle of the long eighteenth century, there was one striking geopolitical similarity and one striking geocultural difference. All three hegemonic battles in the history of the modern world-system have been between sea powers and land powers. All three have been won by the sea powers, but each needed the crucial help of land forces of a continental power. Great Britain needed Russia's aid in the last round in order to defeat France, and the US needed the same Russia's aid in the last round to defeat Germany.

But here appears the geocultural divergence. France had a revolution in 1789, and this fact was of enormous geopolitical assistance to France in the last round. When French troops crossed European frontiers (under the Convention, the Directory, and the Empire) they came, at least at first, as triumphant

---

[2] For an analysis of the Franco-British struggle of 1792 to 1815, and the role therein of the French Revolution, see my *The Modern World-System, III: The Second Era of Great Expansion of the Capitalist World-Economy, 1730–1840s*. San Diego: Academic Press, 1989, ch. II, 55–126.

harbingers of a universalizing ideal. They incarnated the "revolu-tion" against the *ancien régime*.

Germany did not have a similar universalizing revolution before its last round. It almost did. The world "expected" it. The Russian Bolsheviks counted on it. But that revolution did not happen. Perhaps the Spartakists tried too soon. Perhaps they should have waited until 1933. By 1933, however, the Spartakists were out of the game, and the only revolution Germany could have was one that was anti-universalist in spirit. When German troops subsequently crossed frontiers (with the exception of Austria), they were not hailed, even at the beginning, as revolu-tionary heroes but rather as agents of darkness. This geocultural difference – the fact that it was Russia and not Germany which, after 1917, incarnated a universalizing ideal – led to a very curious and ambivalent geopolitical situation.

1917 was a turning-point in one further way. It was the moment of entry onto the world scene of the two great ideologues of the twentieth century – Woodrow Wilson and Nikolai Lenin. Wilson propagated Americanism, or the offer to "make the world safe for democracy." Lenin propagated Communism, or the offer to put the working class in power everywhere as the universal class. At the time, and right up to 1989, these two projects were presented as alternative and antagonistic ideologies. Yet they had more in common than either camp has been wont to admit. They shared the heritage of the Enlightenment, and the belief that humanity could rationally and consciously construct the good society. They shared the belief that the state was a key instrument of this construction as the locus of rational, conscious, collective decision-making. They shared a secular vision of the future. And, for the peripheral peoples of the world, they shared the ideal of the "self-determination of nations," nations that were all to be "equal." Finally they were both eschatologies. They shared this view that history was moving inevitably and ever more rapidly in the direction of their universalizing ideals which, in the end, they said, would exclude no one.

Of course, we need not exaggerate. There were many differ-ences between "Americanism" and "Communism," and the texts on both sides have explained these at length. Furthermore, in practice as well as theory there were differences too. But were their protagonists enemies? There was the rub, and the dilemma of the fact that it was Russia, and not Germany, which incarnated Leninism. For the geopolitical reality was that, in 1917 (and until 1945), the primary geopolitical antagonist of the United States remained Germany and, in 1917 (and until 1945), the United States would need the support of the Russian army to win its "Thirty Years' War." Hence, the US dilemma: how to conduct its Cold War with the USSR (begun in 1917, and not 1945, as André Fontaine reminds us[3]) while simultaneously fighting (or preparing to fight) a real war with Germany. And hence the complementary Soviet dilemma: how to pursue "revolutionary" Leninism, while defending itself against the more immediate danger of German military expansion. The USSR needed the US as much as the US needed the USSR for military reasons. Furthermore, the USSR retained the US as a technological model, if not as a model of economic organization. (Thus, Lenin's motto: "Communism equals Soviets plus electricity.")

It was the genius of Roosevelt and of Stalin to have found the formula, for good or ill, that would permit this collaboration of symbiotically linked presumed ideological enemies. The formula is what we have popularly called Yalta – not the particular formal agreements that were reached there, but the spirit that informed them, and from which, it should be underlined, Churchill did not dissent. Indeed Churchill's Fulton, Missouri speech in 1946 in which he coined the phrase, the "iron curtain," was not the denunciation of Yalta but its formal consecration.

In the grand construction of US hegemony after 1945, there were two military pillars. One was the erection of NATO which ensured that the US had the necessary military strength to pursue its political and economic objectives. The second was the arrangement with the USSR that ensured that this military force would never be needed in the one arena where war could not be won (even if it would not be lost) – nuclear war in Europe.

The enormous public attention that has been focused on the military components of this Cold War stalemate has masked the crucial politico-economic deal that underlay the European equilibrium of 1945–89. What the US offered the USSR and what the

---

[3] See André Fontaine, *Histoire de la guerre froide*, 2 vols. Paris: Fayard, 1969, 1971.

USSR was happy to accept was the creation of a Soviet *chasse gardée* in Eastern Europe, within which the USSR could set the political, economic, and cultural rules, provided that the USSR remained within those boundaries.

The advantages to both sides of this deal were very great; otherwise, it would never have been kept. For the USSR there were three principal gains. First, it permitted the USSR to exploit this zone economically, taking massive "war reparations" from it. Secondly, it offered the USSR a military shield against a resurgent Germany (which need derived essentially from a misreading, but a psychologically comprehensible one, of post-1945 geopolitical realities). Thirdly, and perhaps most significantly in the long run, it permitted the USSR to hold back (even suppress) revolutionary socialist tendencies in Eastern Europe, in Western Europe, and in the rest of the world. This latter effort was more successful in Europe (east and west) than elsewhere. But it was seen as crucial to the Soviet system, as Stalin had constructed it, that the USSR retain the monopoly of Communist discourse, and that no "adventurous" revolutions in the Third World undo the carefully constructed equilibrium with the US.

This makes clear the interest of the US in the arrangement. The USSR was in effect the subimperial power of the US for eastern Europe, and a quite efficient one at that. The 1948 purges eliminated any independent, "leftist" elements which were still around. Nor did this exhaust US advantage. The Soviet bloc was "unneeded" for the immediate economic expansion of the world-economy. The US had all it could handle with the economic "reconstruction" of western Europe and Japan. Hence, it was quite happy to be relieved for the moment of disbursive obligations to the Soviet bloc, knowing that it would be no problem later to pull the zone back into the commodity chains of the world-economy.

The final plus for the US was the replica of the final advantage to the USSR. Each ideological discourse sustained the other, and neither was plausible without the other. The Cold War permitted each side, in the name of Americanism and Leninism, to keep tight order in their camps, to clean house as they saw fit, and to reorient the mentalities of the future generations.

The US–USSR arrangement worked to the extent that US

hegemony in the world-system was relatively uncontested. But, of course, hegemonies breed their own undoing. The ways in which this took place is amply discussed in the essays that follow. The two main factors were the developing economic strength of Western Europe and Japan which turned them into economic competitors of the US and led to their increasing political independence; and the unwillingness of a number of Third World countries to accept the fate assigned to them by Yalta, which led to revolutions in China, Vietnam, Algeria, and elsewhere.

How these increasing difficulties led to the worldwide revolution of 1968 is also discussed in detail: the double role of 1968 as revolution against US hegemony and as rejection of the "Old Left"; its worldwide organizational suppression; its long-term success in undermining the ideological premises of the Old Left; and its continuing underground current of subversion of the world order.

The ways in which the US sought to slow down the consequences of its economic decline by utilizing the institutions of hegemony it had built – first via the low posture of the Nixon–Ford–Carter years, then via the machismo of the Reagan years – is also discussed, as are the reasons why neither tactic could do more than slow down the pace of decline.

Finally, when US power was sufficiently eroded, the USSR had no choice but to enter into the dangerous waters of Gorbachev's *perestroika* and *glasnost*, in the hopes that the USSR role as a great power (or at least Russia's role) could survive the wreckage of the Pax Americana.

Finally, in these essays, I argue the probable course of world geopolitical realignments in the coming world economic expansion of the first part of the twenty-first century.

In a sense, this whole discussion of the course of the US hegemonic era is dealing merely with a cyclical rhythm of the modern world-system. The events of 1989 need to be put as well into the context of the secular trends of the system and the structural limits of its linear curves.

The principal consequence for the capitalist world-economy of the French Revolution as a world-historical event was the cultural maturing of a value-system that would be most consonant with the

endless accumulation of capital. The events of 1789–1815 transformed the prevailing political consciousnesses, imposing upon
the general mentality the notion of the normality of change, and
the expectability of continuous evolution of the political mechanisms of the system. It was in response to this new *Weltanschauung* that the nineteenth century saw the emergence of the
three ideologies of the modern world-system – conservatism,
liberalism, and socialism – and the concurrent institutionalization
of the modes of translating these ideologies into empirical reality,
that is, the historical social sciences.[4]

In the struggle of the three ideologies against each other, which
in political practice often resulted in alliances of two of them
against the third, the lines that distinguished their positions were
very unsure. The three positions were far from fixed. They were
tonalities rather than dogmas, largely preferences about the
speed and extent of social change and the role therein of the state.
No two social analysts expressed these ideological positions in
precisely the same way. If there were three tonalities, there were
myriad specific philosophical stances.[5]

An analysis of the evolution of the three ideological expressions
reveals that after 1848 and until 1968, liberalism emerged as the
clearly dominant ideology. It was dominant in a very simple sense:
both conservatism and socialism increasingly defined themselves
in liberal categories, such that there seemed no longer a place for
pure liberalism at the very moment that liberalism could at no
point be put aside. After 1848, one could argue, there were in
practice only two ideologies: conservative liberalism versus socialist liberalism, with Marxism increasingly being absorbed by the
liberal attractor, first in its Bernstein version, then in its Kautsky
version, and finally in its Leninist version.

Liberalism had two strengths. It reflected the fundamental
trend of the system – endless expansion, continuous adaptation of
form but permanent reproduction of substance, along with the
prospect of universal participation in the good society, however

[4] For a discussion of these nineteenth-century developments, see my "The French
Revolution as a World-Historical Event," *Social Research*, LVI, 1, Spring 1989, 33–52.
[5] For a more developed explication of this argument, see my "Trois idéologies ou une
seule? Le problématique de la modernité," in E. Balibar and I. Wallerstein, eds., *Les Trois
idéologies* (forthcoming).

unequal it still was. This strength is well known, but a second strength is less frequently acknowledged. Indeed it is often denied. Liberalism is the only ideology that permits the long-term reinforcement of the state structures, the strategic underpinning of a functioning capitalist world-economy. Conservatism and socialism appeal beyond the state to a "society" which finds its expression in other institutions. Liberalism, precisely because it is individualistic and contractual, finds the ultimate resolution of conflicts in state decisions, the state alone being presumed to have no "interests" of its own but to be the vector of the majority compromise and consensus.

The state as arbiter is the strongest possible role for the state. That is why liberalism is reformist, and why reformism is state-enhancing. Liberalism legitimates the state whereas conservatism and socialism undermine it philosophically. But since the state-system is essential to the functioning of the capitalist world-economy, neither conservatism nor socialism could prevail within the capitalist world-economy in their pure form. They had to take the form of a blend: either conservative liberalism or socialist liberalism.

The great change of 1917 was not in this ideological antinomy, but in the fact that what we now call the North–South issue moved to the center of the stage for the first time. And it is this issue that accounts for the twentieth-century transposition of the late nineteenth-century antinomy into the form of Americanism versus Leninism. It was the peripheral zones of the world-economy that were the objects of Wilsonian "self-determination" and the countries that were to be made "safe for democracy." The Russian Revolution in turn occurred in the state that was the most "backward" of industrial Europe but, simultaneously, in fact the most "advanced" of the non-core states. If in 1917 Lenin still used a European workerist discourse, by the time of the Congress of the Peoples of the East in Baku in 1920, it was clear that Leninism had become the expression of socialist liberalism for the South – still called the East in 1920[6].

It is this intimate collusion of the Wilsonian and Leninist versions of universalizing liberalism that accounted for the ease

[6] The clearest theoretical appreciation of this was in the writings of M. Sultan-Galiev. See "The Social Revolution and the East," *Review*, VI, 1, Summer 1982, 3–11.

with which the US–USSR collusion could establish itself (behind the facade of enmity). It accounts as well for the ease with which (and the correctness with which) the rebels of 1968 could put the two regimes and the two ideologies in the same basket. 1968 reopened the ideological consensus that followed 1848.[7]

The Revolution of 1968 challenged the liberal verities, in all their manifestations. It challenged above all the belief that the state was a rational arbiter of conscious collective will. The revolutionaries of 1968 challenged not only those in power in the state structures themselves but all those in power in the "ideological apparatuses" of the state. They therefore challenged all the classical antisystemic movements, precisely because they had (in very many instances) already come to power, and were utilizing the myth of the state as the rational arbiter (or incarnation) of conscious collective will. To reduce the state to being merely one political "actor" among many was the implicit objective of the "new" antisystemic movements. It followed that the historical strategy of the "Old Left" – the seeking of state power – was no longer seen as the crucial strategy for the transformation of society; indeed, for many, it was counter-indicated entirely.

The rejection of liberalism as an ideology (both in its Wilsonian and Leninist forms) was no small episode. It represented a fundamental break with the intellectual premises of what I am calling the geoculture of the capitalist world-economy. Some describe the geoculture as the superstructure of this world-economy. I prefer to think of it as its underside, the part that is more hidden from view and therefore more difficult to assess, but the part without which the rest would not be nourished. I term it the geoculture by analogy with geopolitics, not because it is supra-local or supra-national but because it represents the cultural framework within which the world-system operates.

The challenge to the geoculture has, since 1968 (and especially in the 1980s), taken three major forms which are all, in fact, variants of the same theme, the rejection of the universalist pretensions of liberalism. The first form is the new intellectual focus on "culture" *as opposed to* a focus on the "economy" or on "politics." It is elementary to say that this comes out of disillu-

[7] See G. Arrighi, T.K. Hopkins, and I. Wallerstein, "1968: The Great Rehearsal," in *Antisystemic Movements*. London: Verso, 1989, 97–115.

sionment with the efficacy of transforming the world by altering its economic or political forms.

This disillusionment – the heart of 1968 – has led many to see "culture" as an alternative arena in which at last human action might be efficacious. Throughout the recent literature on "culture," the concept of "agency" constantly recurs as a theme. Against the so-called objective pressures that are said to come from the politico-economic realm, the acolytes of culture assert the intrusion of human agency – as intrinsic possibility, as source of collective hope. The people are oppressed (by the states, that is), but the people (and/or the intelligentsia) have the power (and exercise the power) of forging their own destiny. How it is then, using this analysis, that we are still living in the oppressive system that seems to persist is something of a mystery. But one need not be cynical. The concern with "culture" represents the search for ways out of the existing system, for ways out other than via the "classical" nostrums that seem to have failed. It thus sustains political activity.

The second mode of challenging the geoculture lies in the creation of the concepts of racism and sexism. These terms are not merely new clothing for old concerns. They are a belated recognition of a fundamental feature of the geoculture of the capitalist world-economy: the inherent and necessary existence of sexism and racism within its structures despite (or even because of) its universalizing pretensions. This challenge has taken both intellectual and organizational forms: the creation of new fields of study, the creation of new types of social movements. This second form of challenge both overlaps with and is more specific (and focused) than the generic concern with "culture." It therefore has had clearer political implications.

Nonetheless, the political implications are less than totally clear, since the debate about them still constitutes the major line of internal cleavage within the anti-sexist, anti-racist movements. The search for (and validation of) "identity" serves for some as the framework of an anti-universalist but worldwide alliance of struggles, with the promise ultimately of creating an entirely new geoculture. But this same search serves for others as a renewed separatist populism – and recent developments in the (ex-) Communist world show that these zones are no different in this regard – which can easily be recuperated within the framework of the universalizing liberalism of the capitalist world-economy.

And finally the challenge to the geoculture is to be found in the "new science," itself a direct attack on the oldest intellectual pillar of the modern world-system, Baconian–Newtonian science. The link of the "crisis in the sciences" to the crisis in the world-system and the crisis in the movements is argued in various of the essays of this volume. Here let me merely underline the link to the concerns with "culture" and with "racism-sexism." Physical scientists and mathematicians tend to live in a world remote from the "humanities" and even more remote from anti-racist, anti-sexist movements. These groups do not speak to each other for the most part. They do not read each other. Thus when the "new science" is "discovered" outside the closed walls of the scientific academy, it tends to be interpreted in a very romantic fashion, and thereby loses its intrinsic power as an analytic tool. The deep strength of this rebellion against the centrality of linear, equilibrium processes in scientific analysis and against the theoretical possibility of total precision lies not in any rejection of the basic scientific enterprise – the optimal comprehension of material reality – but in the rapprochement of the scientific method (reinterpreted as the attempt to interpret complexity rather than the attempt to reduce complexity to minimalism) with intelligent work in the social sciences and the humanities. It is precisely the denial of the concept of the "two cultures" – science and/versus the humanities – which is the essential thrust. The concept of the two cultures served the same purpose (indeed was essentially the same thing) as the distinction between nomothetic and idiographic epistemologies in the social sciences – as pillar of the geocultural system of the capitalist world-economy. The "new science" has fatally eroded the premises of Baconian–Newtonian science, and is therefore a fundamental element in the post-1968 challenge to the geoculture, however little aware of this some of the "new scientists" may themselves be.

And thus we come to the last element needed in the analysis of 1989, the crisis of the system, or the uncertainties of evolution. One of the most extraordinary misunderstandings of 1989 is to see it as somehow a reinforcement of the system. The regime changes of 1989 were, we have said, the outcome of the latent, continuing revolt of 1968. That its local expression was most naturally directed against the local previously dominant discourse (and praxis) of Leninism does not make it any the less a rebellion against liberalism. That momentarily, and in desperation, the new governments are seeking salvation in the "market" and other IMF formulas is no more significant, and probably no more beneficial, than it has been for Tanzania, Brazil, or the Dominican Republic. This will be very clear for the populations of these countries very soon.

The model of evolution of the world-system being used here is derived from the "new scientific" modes of analysis, as suggested in many of these essays. In brief, it is that the capitalist world-economy constitutes an historical system, which thereby has an historical life: it had a genesis; it has a set of cyclical rhythms and secular trends that characterize it; it has internal contradictions which will lead to its eventual demise.[8] The argument is that the short-run contradictions lead to middle-run solutions which translate into long-run linear curves approaching asymptotes.[9] As they approach these asymptotes, the pressures to return to equilibria diminish, leading to ever greater oscillations and a bifurcation. Instead of large random fluctuations resulting in small changes in the curve, small fluctuations will result in large changes.

The imminence of bifurcation, brought about by the fact that middle-run solutions to short-run contradictions are no longer readily available, is disastrous for the system. The collapse of Leninism is very bad news indeed for the dominant forces of the capitalist world-economy. It has removed the last major politically *stabilizing* force within the world-system. It will not be easy to put Humpty-Dumpty together again.

This fact is not *necessarily* good news for the opponents of the system. Bifurcations are unpredictable in their outcomes. What will replace the capitalist world-economy eventually may be better, but it could be worse. Thus we have reason neither for

---

[8] This was originally argued in 1974 in "The Rise and Demise of the World Capitalist System: Concepts for Comparative Analysis," reprinted as chapter 1 of *The Capitalist World-Economy*. Cambridge: Cambridge University Press, 1979, 1–36.

[9] The case is made in most detail in my "Crisis as Transition" in S. Amin et al., *Dynamics of Global Crisis*. New York: Monthly Review Press, 1982, 11–54.

despair nor for celebration. Nonetheless, there is one fundamentally encouraging element. The outcome will be the result of our collective effort, largely as expressed in the work of the new antisystemic movements. Whereas before large fluctuations resulted in small changes (hence the "determinism," hence the disillusionment with the outcomes of reformism, even when called "revolution"), now small fluctuations will result in big changes (hence the opening for true "agency," hence the responsibility we all bear).

The world-system is in mutation now. This is no longer a moment of the minor, constant cumulation of cycles and trends. 1989 is probably a door closed on the past. We have perhaps arrived now in the true realm of uncertainty. The world-system will continue, of course, to function, even function "well." It is precisely because it will continue to function as it has been functioning for 500 years, in search of the ceaseless accumulation of capital, that it will soon no longer be able to function in this manner. Historical capitalism, like all historical systems, will perish from its successes not from its failures. Exit Lenin. Exit Wilson.

Part I
Geopolitics: post-America

1 ✿ North Atlanticism in decline

The end of NATO is near. That is not the same thing as the end of the world. It will rather be one step in a gigantic restructuring of world alliances that may take thirty years to crystallize fully and whose implications for the twenty-first century are surely hard to discern in any detail.

The economic roots of the restructuring are very straightforward. Since I have analyzed this elsewhere,[1] let me simply summarize my views here. US global hegemony, a brief phenomenon, as have been previous such hegemonies, was based on a temporary dramatic edge in the efficiencies of US productive, commercial, and financial enterprises. This period is now over. Enterprises in Japan on the one hand and in Western Europe (with France and Germany at its heart) on the other are genuinely competitive with US-based enterprises, and the trend is in their favor rather than against them. The continued relative decline of US economic enterprises, and of the politico-military power of the US state (though one should remember that the decline is slow and is, for the moment, only a *relative* decline), can only render more acute the competitive atmosphere. In the 1980s, when the world-economy will still be in the throes of its stagnation phase, this competition will center around the fiscal crises of the states and the attempts of the major industrial powers to export unemployment to each other. In the 1990s, when the world-economy will probably be on the upturn, the competition will

---

[1] "Friends as Foes," Foreign Policy, No. 40, Fall 1980, 119–31; and "Crisis as Transition" in S. Amin et al., *Dynamics of Global Crisis*. New York: Monthly Review Press, 1982, 11–54.

center around the rate of expansion of the new growth-industries (microprocessors, biotechnology, etc.).

Japan seems to be playing the same role today *vis à vis* the United States that the United States played *vis à vis* Great Britain in the late nineteenth century. Unburdened in the short run by the level of politico-military expenditures of the old leading power, unburdened also by the high rent that economic cadres of the old leading power extract from the accumulation process, unburdened by as much existing antiquated plant (in the broadest sense of this term), Japan presents the figure of lean, aggressive, confident economic growth. To be sure, Japan lacks the immense internal resource-base upon which the nineteenth-century United States could count. But a Sino-Japanese economic symbiosis could remedy that.

Far from tweaking the nose of the United States, Japan is trying to emulate US policy toward Great Britain in the late nineteenth century: turn the old leader gently and gradually into the junior partner. No doubt there are acute difficulties in such a project, not least of which is the cultural distance, but it is not an inherently unfeasible objective. No doubt, also, Japan eventually will have to assume a military posture consonant with such a role, but there is no rush. Remember the slow transformation of the US military from 1873 to 1945.

Against this Pacific Rim geopolitical alliance, whose pioneer was none other than Richard Milhous Nixon (as he more or less constantly reminds us, most recently on *The New York Times'* Op Ed page of February 28, 1982), Western Europe has nowhere else to turn in order to survive economically but in the direction of a similar geopolitical alliance with the USSR. Nothing illustrates this more clearly than the French signing of the gas-pipeline arrangements with the USSR precisely when French public opinion was more angrily anti-Soviet than at any other moment in recent history because of the developments in Poland. The *raison d'état* of Charles de Gaulle is the *raison d'état* of François Mitterrand, as indeed it had been that of Valéry Giscard d'Estaing.

Lest I be accused of being the latest cynical prophet of realpolitik, let me indicate immediately where ideology comes in. In this context, we shall discuss Poland, but first let us review the politics and ideology of the post-1945 period. The first great ideological faultline was East–West: the Cold War. The issues were stated in different terms by the two protagonists, but each side basically believed, in John Foster Dulles's words, that "neutralism is immoral." This was the ideological base of US hegemony and of the parallel existence of a *chasse gardée* called the Soviet bloc. It was this basic division of the world that underlay the construction of NATO. This ideological fissure in the world-system still exists. Ronald Reagan may shout the most loudly but it would be a grievous error of judgment to believe that Brezhnev, Mitterrand, or Schmidt are any less committed to the views they and their parties have historically expressed on these ideological issues. Bonn–Paris–Moscow cooperation will not be built on overcoming ideological differences, but on ignoring them.

It would be wrong, however, to see the ideological arena of the post-1945 period as occupied only by the East–West divisions. There have been three other ideological debates that have played a role. One is the now equally stylized North–South split. Once again, it was defined differently on both sides. The South strongly asserted that the advanced industrialized countries of the North must give priority to North–South issues rather than to those deriving from the East–West split. This view has never been accepted in the North. It is clear, however, that the end of US hegemony has eroded the material base for the priority assigned to the East–West conflict.

A third ideological conflict has been that of reform vs. revolution within the world's antisystemic movements. Central to world politics in the 1917–39 era, this division in the world's workers' and nationalist movements seemed to blend in readily with the East–West fissure of the post-1945 period, with the reformists becoming identified with the West and the revolutionaries with the East. However, a curious slippage occurred. A hydra-headed monster known as "revisionism" began to overtake the world's Communist parties in power. One has only to read Stalin on Tito, Mao Zedong on Khrushchev, or Enver Hoxha on Mao Zedong to realize that purity of intent seems to vanish like snow precisely as springtime brings change. One post-revolutionary regime after another has come up against the winds of external constraint imposed by the interstate system and the world-economy's law of value, and one after another has bent wisely with the wind. (If it did not, it was broken like Kampuchea.) Once again, the end of US hegemony has seemed to hasten this process.

Finally, there has been one other ideological split, though less clear. There has been a growing struggle "against the system" in ways that could be fit into none of the standard ideological boxes, although its protagonists identified themselves at various points with one side or another of these other debates. Fifteen years ago the spokesmen for this new ideological fissure were called the New Left or the counterculture. Later, they were located in the Green movement, the women's movement, or the movement for decentralization. They reemerged as antinuclear demonstrators in Western Europe in 1981. That this thrust has been neither coherent nor well-organized does not make it less powerful. It was this group against all the rest, who were indiscriminately seen as the Establishment. The single most important feature of this ideological thrust has been its implicit (and often explicit) rejection of the primacy (sometimes even the relevancy) of all the other ideological divisions.

Poland illustrates the interplay of these four ideological debates and the resulting ideological confusion. It also illustrates exactly the degree to which these ideological factors are and are not playing a role in the present conjuncture. It is clear that for many inside and outside Poland, on both sides, the challenge of Solidarity to the regime was a classic expression of East–West divisions. Yet, for others it was the North–South dimension that mattered. Poland's economic difficulties reflected the standard "debt-trap" dilemmas of a semiperipheral power, and the Western banks reacted to the crisis in ways hard to distinguish from their reactions to potential defaults in, say, Zaire.

The fact that Poland had fallen into a debt trap and has not been the only Communist regime to court such dangers (*vide* North Korea, Romania, and Hungary, for example), is itself the most striking example of the operations of the constraints of the world-system leading to a dramatic blurring of the reformist-revolutionary fissure. What, it has frequently been asked of late (not least of all in Poland itself), represents a "Left" position inside a Communist country? Finally, the constant search by Solidarity to pursue its goals without seeking responsibility in the state apparatus was, in part, a tactic, taking account of Soviet views on "limits," but it was also an expression of the profound fear of "cooptation" within the movement, which represented a variant, and outgrowth, of 1960s New Leftism.

The immediate Polish political struggle is ongoing. There has been no resolution. We are witnessing at the moment (March 1982) a very shaky temporary equilibrium with which no side, inside or outside of Poland, is in the least content. And this is precisely because the present equilibrium meets none of the ideological demands of either side on any of the four faultlines. Furthermore, it is clear that nearly everyone, inside and outside of Poland, is uncertain where to move next.

It seems likely that the Polish-style political situation, one in which there is much ideological confusion and where great passions are tempered by tactical uncertainty, is something we shall see considerably more of in the years to come, even where the particular historical circumstances are quite different from those of Poland.

In such circumstances, ideology tends to lose much of its braking power on the thrust of economic forces. This is the primary reason why I believe that the fierce and rather anarchic phase of intracapitalist worldwide competitive struggle we are now witnessing (and will continue to witness for a good while) will press "objectively" towards geopolitical realignments, despite the degree to which such realignments will contradict ideological commitments.

Let me be clear. It is not that ideology will play no role. But it will play a subordinate role. Any arrangement between Western Europe and the Soviet Union that eventually would occur will resemble the current arrangement between the French Socialist and French Communist parties – a *mariage de convenance*, based on mutual suspicion and mutual interest, but a *mariage* nonetheless. This is, after all, the kind of arrangement that has been developing between the United States and China. Such arrangements may go through many tumultuous periods, and they are scarcely engraved in stone, but if they have a secure material base, they will persist.

Reagan, Schmidt, and Mitterrand have been making ritual speeches of late about how they wish to preserve, even strengthen, the Western alliance. What this really means is that no one is anxious to have a precipitous break. But, neither are they willing to draw back from protecting their economic flanks against the others. The recent Wasserman cartoon expressed it most aptly. It showed Schmidt explaining the joint plan of action on Poland that he and Reagan had worked out: "The United States will not import natural gas from the Soviets, and we won't sell them any grain." Of course, if the situation in Poland leads to considerably increased internal violence, this will delay this process of geopolitical realignment. But nothing short of nuclear war is likely to derail it entirely.

Such a fundamental shift in the interstate system and the attendant ideological confusion is not in the long run an adverse development from the perspective of those who stand for radical social transformation in the world. There are several positive consequences for the system as a whole. In the short run, it probably reduces rather than increases the likelihood of world war, although it increases rather than decreases the prospect of multiple local wars and civil wars. Nuclear war remains a possibility, but the uncertainties of planning and of alliances should lead to additional prudence until the situation becomes much clearer, especially because, under the circumstances, military leaders feel they are dealing with soft political underbellies at home. Witness Defense Secretary Weinberger's caveats on Central American intervention.

Second, the disintegration of the ideological crusts makes it possible for there to be continuing, active evolution of the class struggle *within* post-revolutionary states. This is what I take to be the most important lesson of Solidarity, which has not, in my view, been defeated in the way that previous such movements have been. I believe we shall have one, two, many Solidarities, and within the Soviet Union itself.

Finally, I believe that we shall move towards new structures of trans-national antisystemic movements that will link together *for the first time* liberation movements in the Third World, radicalized workers' movements in the West, and a new breed of revolutionary movements in all the Socialist countries. This will represent a healthy reshuffling of movements and may succeed in removing the albatross of the Second International, the Third International, and the decolonization movements whose collective errors have plagued the mission of the world's antisystemic forces. Thus unburdened, the way will be open for clearer ideological formulations of the world-wide "party of movement" in the struggle against the worldwide "party of order."

In this light, it is hard to feel that the fading-out of the particular client relationship that Western Europe had with the United States during the era of US hegemony is particularly unfavorable for anyone. Nor is it likely that there will be any forces, radical or conservative, that will do very much to revive "North Atlanticism" in the two decades to come.

The end of NATO is near. So is an acute depression.

2 ✤ The Reagan non-revolution, or the limited choices of the US

At the end of the Second World War, the United States was the strongest economic center of the world-economy. It alone had emerged from the war with a very advanced and efficient industrial network that had been unscarred by wartime destruction. The productivity of its agriculture was very high. It had in place by far the best, in some ways the only significant, set of institutions for research and development.

Its major rival of 30, if not 80, years – Germany – was in ruins. Its political allies (but economic rivals) in Western Europe were in almost as bad a shape. Japan seemed to have been set back severely in its drive to industrial strength. As for the USSR, it seemed literally exhausted economically by its wartime efforts and sacrifices.

The moment of US hegemony in the world-system had clearly arrived. But hegemony requires more than the economic underpinnings – the ability to outproduce and outsell major rivals in their home settings. It requires also a set of primarily political structures to lock economic advantage into place and make it function smoothly. The US needed to establish such institutions to handle the four principal geographic arenas of the world, as seen from a Washington perspective after 1945: the other major industrial countries; USSR and its zone of influence; what would come to be called the Third World; and, not least, the US itself.

In hindsight, it is easy to see what the problem was in each arena and how it was handled by the successive US governments. The immediate problem with the other major industrial countries was that they had suffered too much destruction during the war, and were too poor in current production to serve as significant markets for US peacetime exports. The US could produce what they needed cheaply enough, and needed them as customers if it was not to relapse into the Depression's underconsumption pattern. Europe (and Japan) were eager to buy. But they had no dollars. *Ergo*, the Marshall Plan, and related programs of "reconstruction."

In addition, the US faced only one opponent of significance in the world-system, and that not in the economic arena. The USSR, while weak economically, was strong militarily, politically, and ideologically. The US needed to "shore up" Western Europe, particularly since France and Italy, at least, had powerful Communist parties, *Ergo*, NATO and related programs of alliance-building. Both the economic and political programs were successful in that by the early 1950s the US was the clear leader of a political-military bloc of major industrial nations who were recovering their economic vitality.

The problem in the second arena was how to "handle" the USSR. There were three alternatives available: permit Soviet influence and/or "Communism" to spread; go to war to destroy the USSR; do something in between. It is quite apparent today that the US did neither of the first two. But what was the "something in between"? The two code words often used to describe it, and not incorrectly, are "Yalta" and "containment".

On the one hand, Yalta represented symbolically what its detractors have charged, a "division of the world." When Winston Churchill declared in Fulton, Missouri in 1946 that there was an "iron curtain" from Stettin to Trieste, he was actually giving the final legitimation to a clear demarcation line in Europe between the "Communist world" and the "free world" (or, in other language, between the "socialist camp" and the "capitalist camp").

Since that time, in Europe, the relation between the two camps has been one of tension, separation, and mutual abstention from military interference in each other's zones. The West came to call this "containment," and that it was. But it is important to note that "containment" was not, was never, "rollback." In other words, there has been an implicit, and unviolated, agreement to maintain the political *status quo* in Europe despite the many moments of turbulence that could have reopened the question (from the Berlin airlift and the Tito–Stalin break to the suppression of Solidarity).

The third arena was the Third World. It was not yet called that in 1945 for the very simple reason that it was not yet taken seriously enough politically. What the US saw were vast geographic zones with sectors of considerable strategic importance and of considerable mineral wealth, but zones for the most part too poor to be much of an immediate market for export goods. The US worried, however, that these zones were politically volatile and hence subject to the "spread" of Communism. Indeed, after the so-called "fall" of China in 1949 with the proclamation of the Chinese People's Republic, the US began to fear a rapid diffusion of what it clearly thought of as a sort of contagion. Thus was born the famous "dominos" analogy.

The US evolved a three-part formula to deal with this arena. It consisted of one dose of concessions to the natives (favoring "decolonization" or "popular regimes," provided they were "moderate"), one dose of the iron fist (intermittent military or covert operations when necessary, e.g., Guatemala in 1948, Iran in 1952, Lebanon in 1956), and one dose of rhetoric masking largely benign (economic) neglect (Truman's "Point Four" program, Kennedy's "Alliance for Progress").

But none of this would have worked, had the US government not been able to contain internal US social conflict. It must be remembered that the 1930s was a period of very acute domestic strife in the US, on two fronts. There was class conflict between labor and capital, which centered around the attempt to create union structures in the major industries. The CIO (Congress of Industrial Organizations) was organizing workers in the automobile, steel, electricity, and chemical sectors, plus the major extractive industries. In 1936, Walter Reuther was still getting his head battered in the wake of a famous sitdown strike.

The second arena of internal US conflict was primarily among the middle classes (indeed, some would argue, among different segments of big capital). The disagreement centered on whether the US should continue to look inward economically (and hence politically and militarily) or should orient its economy to world trade. This was the famous isolationist-interventionist debate which was passionate, bitter, and prolonged. It was, of course, the reason why the US was the last major power to enter the Second World War.

In 1945, many commentators expected both struggles (which had been largely put aside by considerations of wartime unity) to resume, and in full force. And, indeed, there were signs that they would. It was the isolationist-interventionist struggle that was buried first. One of the political leaders of the isolationist camp. Senator Arthur Vandenberg, "capitulated." His call for a "biparti-san foreign policy," one based on the US "assuming its responsibi-lities" in the world, was quickly embraced by Roosevelt and Truman. The concept that politics should "stop at the water's edge" has been a basic pillar of the mainstream consensus of US politics ever since. The US was now committed to an activist role in world politics, one in which it had a position on everything everywhere, and was ready to support this position politically, economically, and militarily.

The class struggle was a little more difficult to contain. In 1946 the workers at General Motors went on a lengthy strike which seemed to revive the spirit of 1936. The strike, however, was finally settled by an accord based on a significant wage and benefits increase for the workers against the following counter-parts: increased productivity, a no-strike pledge during the contract, and the right of management to raise prices (which affected US non-unionized and foreign workers more than US union members). This formula came to be standard for all major industries. The deal also presumed the purge of Communists and "leftists" from union structures. The result was relative labor peace and a rising standard of real income for US unionized workers for the next 25 years.

There was one last arena of social conflict in the US, its most perennial: Black oppression. Blacks had gotten very little out of the Second World War. But they had become far more urbanized in the twentieth century and seemed ready to organize seriously. This action was headed off for a while by a series of major "concessions." In 1948, President Truman integrated the armed forces (still segregated, even during the war) and began to use the federal system to move against "discrimination." In 1954, the Supreme Court made its historic ruling in Brown vs. Board of

Education, declaring segregation unconstitutional. The basic legal battle had now been won. Thus it was that, in the new era of hegemony, the US could face the world as its dominant force with a united front at home: East Coast and Middle West, Labor and Capital, Black and White. Or more or less.

This institutionalization of US hegemony worked marvellously well in the 1950s, the Eisenhower days. The world-economy was steadily expanding and the US was economically flourishing. The standard of living of almost all strata was rising. Internal dissent was first crushed, then co-opted out of existence. On the world scene, the US construction of its alliance network and its containment of the USSR was translated into the very visible automatic majority on everything in the United Nations.

There was, to be sure, a nasty war in Korea, but it was a draw and could be seen as the last part of the phase of constructing the hegemonic institutions, not really a challenge to them. Decolonization had gotten off to a splendid start in the British, Dutch, and US empires – the British being the largest and most important – and to a somewhat weaker start in the French. Generally speaking, despite Bandung, US "benign neglect" of the Third World seemed to be working.

Nonetheless, by the 1960s, cracks began to appear in the by now well-oiled structures. Between European recovery in general and the German "miracle" in particular on the one hand and Japan's striking development on the other, the major allies of the US were suddenly transformed from junior partners and beneficiaries to potential, even actual, competitors.

The death of Stalin in 1953 turned out quickly to mark the end of an era of Soviet "monolithism". Within a very short time there was the beginning of "de-Stalinization" in the USSR and "de-satellitization" in the socialist bloc. Khrushchev's "secret report" to the Twentieth Party Congress was speedily diffused to the entire world, courtesy of the CIA, but it is not clear that these developments worked entirely in US favor. The true "Cold War" period, roughly 1946–55, was a period of enormous political stability and ideological rigidity. Now there was to be less of each, and political maneuvering required a great deal more subtlety and sophistication. Enter the era of Kennedy.

The Third World, furthermore, was getting out of hand. With

the admission of a large number of Third World countries in the UN, the automatic US majority disappeared. By the end of the 1960s it had become virtually an automatic US minority. True, it was only a matter of toothless resolutions, but it began to be annoying, even vitiating for the US. The Cuba of the nationalist victory of the 26th of July Movement came to be transformed into the Cuba that inspired socialist revolutions everywhere in the Americas. True, US ineptitude played a large part in this further turn of the screw, but suddenly "subversion" seemed to be located in the US "backyard." And in Asia, the Indochina "arrangement" of 1955 came very unstuck and President Johnson escalated the US into full-scale involvement in a second and far less winnable Asian land war.

Finally, at home, the 1960s would become the era of revolt on many fronts. Vietnam gave rise to a serious antiwar movement that started with "teach-ins" and progressed to marchers chanting "Ho Ho Ho Chi Minh." The social reality of continued segregation after the legal victory of 1954 led first to Rosa Parks and the Montgomery bus boycott, then to Freedom Marches in Mississippi, and culminated in the assassination of Martin Luther King and of Malcolm X and the rise of the Black Power Movement. And what started as mild counterculture among college students blended with antiwar, anti-imperialist, and antiracist sentiments to explode across the country from Columbia in 1968 to Kent State and to the almost nationwide strike because of the Cambodia bombings in 1970.

All of this was taking place just as the Kondratieff long wave phase of expansion was beginning to turn down. The fabulous ascent of the 1950s, the easy new prosperity of the 1960s, would become the era of financial squeeze, inflation, oil price rise, and serious unemployment of the 1970s. In short, the economic foundations of US hegemony had been sapped by its very successes: the economic growth everywhere, and in particular in Western Europe and Japan, the rising benefits for the US working class, the monumental expansion of the salaried professional strata, especially (but not only) in the US. Suddenly times were difficult. The debate shifted from who would get what share of an expanding world-economy to who would bear the brunt of the cutbacks caused by a stagnating one.

Faced with this new, less rosy situation, the US presidents of the 1970s – Nixon, Ford, Carter – tried a new strategy. It might be called the search for the low posture, or how to minimize the losses. In the emerging West–West conflict, the US sought to alleviate west European and Japanese unhappiness with America's previous somewhat authoritarian leadership of the alliance by offering a new and more equal status within the framework of "trilateralism."

Faced with the reality of socialist states that were scarcely any longer a monolithic bloc, the US decided to develop a differentiated strategy, which was the Nixon–Kissinger combination of the spectacular re-establishment of relations with China and the simultaneous pursuit of *détente* with the Soviet Union.

In the wake of the withdrawal of the US from Vietnam in 1973 and the successful coup of the Portuguese Armed Forces Movement in 1974, the US decided to try a different kind of Third World strategy: one of a sharp reduction in the level of political interventionism against "radical" movements: the Clark amendment forbidding CIA involvement in Angola, non-intervention when the Shah fell in Iran, support for the Lancaster House talks on Zimbabwe, non-support of Somoza towards the end of his regime. To be sure, this attitude was in part the consequence of the strength of popular forces, in part the result of the so-called Vietnam syndrome in US public opinion. But there was also the belief in US government circles that the US might benefit by "playing it cool" with Third World revolutionary movements.

Finally, at home, the US moved from confrontation with the Black Power and the women's movements to the institution of "affirmative action." Instead of denouncing counter-culture, the Establishment tried to co-opt its practitioners via the acceptance of new dress codes and liberalized sex and drug mores precisely among the future elites – the young upwardly mobile professionals – or yuppies. The 1970s, with Nixon chased from office and the Church committee exposing the CIA, seemed a far cry from McCarthyite anti-Communist hysteria or even the self-assured liberal interventionism of the Kennedy days.

All these changes of the 1970s were no doubt the result of a transformed geopolitics and a shaky world-economy. My point, however, is that the US government tried to respond by effecting some reduction in its arrogance quotient, playing for time, reducing immediate damage. It was as though the leaders believed that, even if the US was declining in the long run, the long run could be a very long time. And meanwhile US life, even if somewhat troubling, did not have to be that bad.

Needless to say, this is the kind of policy that can only work with a great deal of patience. And a weakening economy was not well-suited to maximize patience. Rather it rendered more acute internal tensions. Hence, when the Ayatollah Khomeini decided to take over the US embassy and hold hostages for a whole year, he quickly strained US popular patience. Unable to overthrow Khomeini, the US voters overthrew Carter and elected Ronald Reagan. Reagan's appeal, and the basis of his subsequent political strength, was in his denunciation of the entire Nixon–Ford–Carter stance of "adjustment to new world realities" and the recognition of the "limitations" of US power. Reagan argued that the problem lay not in objective world reality but in the subjective response to it of US leadership during the 1970s. Reagan argued that if the US were tough (again), the world would respect the US (again). He wanted to be tough with the USSR, tough with US allies, tough with the Third World, and tough with all the liberals, deviants, and delinquents in the US itself.

Or so he said. That is to say, Reagan's rhetoric was *machismo* down the line. But what was his practice? Therein lies a tale, as any US "conservative" can attest. Once again, let us review what the US government actually did in its four arenas: the West, the East, the South, and at home.

The Reagan administration tried "toughness" on two major economic issues with its Western European allies. In the early 1980s it tried to prevent them from entering into an agreement with the USSR to build a gas pipeline across Europe. The US argument was military and ideological. The response of its allies, even faithful and Tory Mrs Thatcher, was that the issue was strictly economic. Later on, a similar debate occurred over the building of a West European airbus. In both cases, the US was totally incapable of dissuading Western Europe from pursuing its direct economic interests. The same had quite clearly been the case with Japan in the interminable trade talks of the two countries. In this arena, Mr Reagan has been a paper tiger.

The Reagan administration has certainly played it tough with the "evil empire." It has spent incredible and unprecedented amounts of money on the military. But what has it thereby accomplished militarily, or politically, that is different in any important way from the *status quo ante*? Has the USSR changed its geopolitical stance on any major issue? Is it politically less powerful in the world-system? Unless Mr Reagan wishes to take immediate credit for the political emergence of Gorbachev, it is hard to see what he can use to demonstrate that *machismo* has made a difference.

In the Third World to be sure Reagan can show some startling achievements: the US military unseated the government of Grenada, where a politically unfriendly regime commanded the resources of a population of just over 100,000 people. The US has also managed to bomb Libya – once! What the US manifestly has not been able to do is to keep marines in Beirut, intimidate Khomeini, or overthrow the Sandinistas in Nicaragua.

The last is the most interesting non-action, since it has clearly been extremely high on the Reagan agenda, and would have been the clear evidence of "success" in this arena. If Reagan has not been able to invade Nicaragua, the reason seems clear enough. The US public seems ready to tolerate maximally the loss of a handful of lives in an action that is over in three days (Grenada), but not the loss of 200 lives in a situation of indefinite further loss (Beirut), and surely not the prospective loss of tens of thousands of lives in a far-off warfare zone (Nicaragua). Call it the Vietnam syndrome, or what you will, but the fact is that it has become a political reality so clear that *even* Reagan has not dared go against it directly. This is the simplest explanation of the inefficacious convolutions of the Iran-Contra fiasco.

Well, then, surely at home Reagan has made a difference? He has tried to intimidate the Democrats by a distorted reading of the "bipartisan" foreign policy. While the Democrats in Congress win few medals for bravery in their foreign-policy disputes with Reagan, the fact is that they have dragged their feet on more issues than at any previous time. One cannot say intimidation has more than slowed down the rate of Democratic defection from their previous automatic Cold War reflexes.

Mr Reagan has broken the labor-capital arrangements in a big way, both by busting unions (PATCO, during the air traffic controllers' strike) and by leaning on the real wage income of the unionized working class (tax-cut redistribution to the wealthy). He has no doubt made the poor poorer. But a revolution in the system established by the New Deal? Scarcely. Everything is in place to rebound, when labor gets ready to be militant again, which should be soon.

Mr Reagan has also sought to break the "affirmative action"-style thrusts of the 1970s. He certainly has been unfriendly in every possible way, and neither minorities nor women will think of the Reagan years as a moment of advance. But how far have they been pushed back *politically*? An honest response would be: a lot less than they feared. As for the so-called "social agenda" – issues like abortion, prayer, pornography – one only has to listen to the current screams of right-wing groups devoted to these issues to realize that they are screams about Reagan's betrayal (that is, inefficacy) on these issues.

The lesson of the Reagan era is that *machismo* as a response to US decline is certainly not more, and probably a lot less, effective than the Nixon–Ford–Carter "realist" approach. Objective reality sets limits on policy-makers. One can defer negatives, minimize losses, maneuver to retain some (if less) advantage, but one cannot command the waves to halt.

3 ❧ Japan and the future trajectory of the world-system: lessons from history?

We are in the middle of economic and political changes in the world-system that are widely perceived to be important. Many people consider the possible impact of these changes as disquieting or uncertain; some regard them as undesirable. The current period follows a period of US hegemony, which I date from 1945 to 1967. That earlier period, by contrast, was one of relative stability (if not tranquillity) in the world-system.

The stability of the postwar period was based on overwhelming US power — economic power, political power, military power, cultural power. This power was unquestioned not only among its allies but essentially even by the USSR (which merely tried to carve out a largely autarkic zone whose autonomy would be tolerated by the United States — the essence of the so-called Yalta agreement). The economic strength of the United States during that period was constructed out of its "efficiencies" of production in virtually all fields. And these US efficiencies were the motor of an expansion of the capitalist world-economy unparalleled in its history, one that resulted in an upsurge in the volume of production everywhere in the world. As for US political power, we are inclined to forget today just how great it was. One simple item will show the contrast with the 1980s. In the 1950s, the United States was pleased that it had obtained UN endorsement of its military action to support the Republic of Korea but realized that this had been possible only because of the temporary and never to be repeated absence of the USSR from Security Council sessions. US Secretary of State John Foster Dulles therefore arranged the passage of the so-called Uniting for Peace resolution that accorded some new authority to the UN General Assembly in case of a future Soviet veto of a similar action. The assumption, of course, was that a future US resolution would easily pass the General Assembly. This was in fact true in the 1950s. Who could imagine this would be true in the 1980s? Certainly not the US government, whose entire current attitude towards the UN is predicated on the assumption that the United States tends to be on the losing side of every major General Assembly debate.

US power had been significantly diminished by the 1970s; the United States was forced to withdraw from Vietnam; the world-economy was in a serious downturn, a Kondratieff B-phase. Industries in Western Europe and Japan were by and large fully competitive with US industries on the world market, and indeed in many cases the former had become more "efficient" than US industries. The political relations of the various major powers in the world presented a far more complex mosaic than previously; the political positions of Western Europe and Japan could no longer be taken for granted by the United States. This situation led to the creation of the Trilateral Commission. Simultaneously, however, the so-called socialist bloc was in disarray. Chinese and Soviet foreign policy was at odds. The USSR's relations with its East European allies had become difficult. Militarily, there was more parity in US–Soviet firepower than previously, but the ability of either power or both to control military conflicts outside the European arena had enormously diminished.

The ideological reflection of this new situation could be found in two continuing political discussions that have thus far been indecisive. One revolved around the codification of so-called East–West issues in terms of reciprocal military alliances of the North Atlantic Treaty Organization (NATO) and the Warsaw Pact. Many argued that this confrontation was somehow outdated; yet everyone seemed to hesitate to change the framework significantly. The second was the debate about so-called North–South relations (under the rubric of a discussion on a new international economic order). This debate too has thus far been largely rhetorical and inconclusive.

The widespread disquiet is thus easily understandable. The objective basis of existing world political and economic institutions is no longer there, but the institutions continue as though it were. This situation clearly cannot go on for very long, and fears about some sort of collapse are not without basis. Yet no one seems willing to take any very serious steps to push for change, as though matters were too delicate to touch. In fact, of course, all sorts of changes are in the making or have begun, and it is not too difficult to outline the major directions of these prospective economic and political realignments based on a reading of the past history of the capitalist world-economy.

Before I turn to the analysis of the near future in the light of the past history of the system, let me lay out three fundamental premises about how the capitalist world-economy works. First, it is an historical system; that is, it has rules and structures and it has an historical development with a beginning and, eventually, an end. One ideological product of this system, in which we are living, has been the dubious epistemological tenet that there exist three different and empirically separable realms of human activity – the economic, the political, and the social and/or cultural – that are in effect subsystems with autonomous logics and/or sets of actors and/or motivations. I do not believe this to be any more true of the capitalist world-economy as an historical system than it was of any previous historical system. Economy, polity, and society are analytic abstractions that perhaps on occasion serve heuristic purposes but are not to be reified, much less compartmentalized in any concrete discussion. In practice, the imbrication is total, constant, and reciprocal.

The material analyzed under the separate headings of the economic, the political, and the sociocultural frequently does reflect a real existential dilemma – the contradictions between the pursuit of interests in the multiple social times of the short run, the middle run, and the long run. In particular, the solutions to the problems caused by middle-run concerns seem to cause long-run problems. Therefore, the other two premises of my analysis have to do with the middle run and the long run.

The middle run of any historical system is cyclical. We call it a system because it contains feedback mechanisms that maintain it within certain parameters, and hence the measured diachronic descriptions take the form of curves that go up and down with some regularity. The cyclical tension that most immediately concerns us in the analysis of the world-economy is the tension caused by the constant thrust for monopolistic position within an economic structure mediated by market transactions and commodification. To the extent that a market is totally competitive, the rate of profit by definition has to be low. On the other hand, anyone who can achieve an even partial monopolistic advantage in any market can by that fact automatically retain more of the surplus flowing through the circuit of commodities. Hence all participants in all markets are always seeking to promote monopolies for themselves and to break the monopolies of others.

In the short run some participants in markets are always successful in creating some monopolies. The achievement of an even partial economic monopoly is always a political phenomenon reinforced by sociocultural mechanisms. The available political mechanisms are manifold and include direct or indirect state measures to limit entry into a market (or to prevent other states from undertaking antimonopolistic measures), the direct transfer of resources that permit price undercutting, guarantees of various ownership rights (e.g. patents), the socialization of some costs (e.g. infrastructure, research and development), the physical destruction of competitors, and so on. The sociocultural mechanisms to reinforce monopolies include socialization processes to facilitate transactions in certain channels, stratified recruitment patterns of personnel, ideological constraints on market behavior, the hidden persuaders of marketing, and so on.

Wherever monopolies are created, there is high profit. This in itself creates a sector under assault by others who seek entry. Over time, in the middle run no monopoly can last in the capitalist world-economy precisely because there is no overarching political structure and no singular cultural system to maintain a frozen division of labor. Hence the cycle we observe is the consequence of the constant shifting of monopolistic locations in the world-economy. There are three such cyclical shifts. The first is in the location of core-periphery links in commodity chains. We mean by corelike processes the ones in which partial monopolies exist; peripheral processes are ones in which market competition is maximal (and profit levels low). As particular economic processes shift from being corelike to being peripheral (from being monopolistic to being competitive), there are frequently concomitant locational shifts.

The second shift is between A- and B-phases of Kondratieff long waves. A-phases are moments in which the overall world-economy has a high dosage of monopolistic sectors. Consequently, accumulation rates are higher and everything pushes towards economic expansion. B-phases are moments in which markets are saturated with too much competition. Consequently, accumulation rates are lower, and everything pushes toward contraction but also, of course, towards the search for the creation of new monopolistic sectors. The third shift, over much longer periods of time, is one between moments of hegemony in the interstate system and periods of rivalry (the so-called balance of power). True hegemony is the achievement by one strong state of a high concentration of economic monopolies, which then undergird other kinds of power. Maximal rivalry occurs when these concentrations are fairly evenly divided among a series of strong states. My second premise about the middle run of social time thus manifests itself in these cyclical patterns of shifts in monopolies.

The third premise has to do with the long run – with the secular trends of the historical system that eventually account for its historical demise. The long-run problem of the capitalist world-economy is essentially that it undermines its *raison d'être* by its successes and that it breeds its own ever more efficacious opposition. Let us consider first how it undermines itself by its successes. If the unending accumulation of capital is the *raison d'être* and the monopolistic advantages make possible high capital accumulation, the completion of the process of the commodification of everything will in fact undo the ability to create monopolistic constraints by maximizing the ability of multiple actors to compete in multiple markets. It should follow then that capitalists, far from having pushed towards the full freedom of the factors of production, should have been dragging their feet (as has been the case historically). Nevertheless, the competitive antimonopolistic struggles, causing cyclically economic downturns, require repeated partial increases of commodification precisely in order to relaunch economic expansion after cyclical downturns. After 500 years (the period that this has been going on) we have begun to reach a relatively high degree of commodification in the world-economy, a process whose configuration logically approaches an asymptote. As the process approaches the asymptote it becomes more and more difficult to solve middle-run problems; this kind of process has created the long-run so-called structural crisis that involves a long period of transition in which historical choices are wide open.

We should take note of a second secular trend. Concomitant with the secular process of commodification – resisted by or reluctantly but relentlessly acceded to by the principal beneficiaries of the system – is the secular process of the contractualization of political processes (sometimes referred to as bureaucratization, as democratization, and as the strengthening of the state structures within an ever more codified interstate system). This process has also been resisted by or reluctantly acceded to by the principal beneficiaries of the system, but this process too has been relentless. And this process is also reaching an asymptote where it becomes more and more difficult to solve the middle-run problems that therefore create the long-run structural crisis.

We should briefly review the politics of this contractualization process over the history of the capitalist world-economy. On the one hand, those excluded from the benefits of the partial monopolies have from the beginning sought increased political contractualization (the codification of rights) as a major means of ensuring a diminution of the negative effects of these monopolies. Hence, they have tended to push for the strengthening of formal state structures. Although those who control old and declining monopolistic sectors are, of course, opposed to such further contractualization, those who have sought to create new monopolistic sectors, particularly in times of economic stagnation, have also sought to use state structures, which were thereby strengthened. This combination led almost all actors to center their attention on the state structures as the key political agencies in the modern world.

In the nineteenth century, we finally saw a major development in this process – the emergence of formal, bureaucratized antisystemic movements, in the form originally of labor and socialist parties on the one hand, and nationalist movements on the other. In the short run, these movements were antagonistic to the basic principles of the world-system and mobilized political energy against it, indeed with increasing success over time. In the middle run, however, by the very achievement of their intermediate goal (accession to state power) these movements have become part of the cyclical renewal of the capitalist world-economy. In the long run, however, by furthering the world-wide process of contractualization and pushing it towards its asymptote, they have contributed to the structural crisis of the system, which includes a questioning by new movements of the very role the older movements have played in the middle-run stabilization of the world-system. This last phenomenon has been expressed in the rise of the new social movements in the Organization for Economic Cooperation and Development (OECD) countries, the repeated emergence of antibureaucratic movements in the socialist countries, and the emergence only recently of postnationalist movements in the Third World.

Let me therefore review where we are in this discussion. The present period defined narrowly (say from 1970 to 1995) can be described, in the terminology of the middle-run cyclical rhythms of the world-system, as a Kondratieff B-phase. This B-phase or economic contraction of the world-economy is simultaneously the first part of the post-US hegemonic era. In terms of these cyclical rhythms, we can fairly easily foresee where we are heading. But the present period defined less narrowly (say from 1914 to 2050) can be described, in the terminology of the long-run secular trends of the world-system, as a period of structural crisis whose outcome we cannot easily foresee.

The scenario on the basis of the middle-run cyclical rhythms is familiar, as it should be if it is cyclical. The present Kondratieff downturn is a moment of acute economic competition between enterprises in the three strong concentrations of quasi-monopolistic activities: the United States, Western Europe, and Japan. Each is trying in the very short run to export profit loss and unemployment to the other. The ball in this regard has been shuttling back and forth for the past 15 years and will probably continue to do so for the next 10. The game is played in terms of the major variables we read about in the newspapers: the zig-zagging of energy price levels, the rates of exchange of major currencies, comparative inflation rates, internal reshufflings of tax structures, relative degrees and forms of protectionism, and so on. This part of the competition, however, is very short run and is heavily political, in that one of the key objectives is the maintenance of state-level political stability in these economically central states. The score in this regard is, in my view, fairly even among the big three.

A more important short-run game than the export of unemployment is the competition to control the major potential new zones of monopolistic production: microprocessing and all its potential product packaging, biogenetics, and new energy sources. Everyone anticipates that these economic sectors will be the heart of the next Kondratieff upturn, beginning somewhere between 1990 and 2000 and promising to be even more spectacular than that in 1945–67. Here the struggle concerns the control of key technology through research and development on the one hand and organizational concentration on the other. Transnational enterprises pursue this game through internal development, industrial espionage, mergers, and cartel-like arrangements. The governments get into the act primarily by channeling vast public sums into these arrangements (Reagan's Star Wars package is perhaps the most ambitious of these attempts) and by cornering potential markets via rather traditional zone-of-interest diplomacy.

In this race, it is my impression that Japan is inching steadily ahead, primarily because it is less burdened than the United States (and to a lesser extent than Western Europe) by the enormous economic drain of capital to the middle strata (via government social welfare programs, private enterprise's swelled middle-management rosters, and enormous consumption in the tertiary sector) and, of course, less burdened by the politico-military expenditures occasioned by the defense of past advantages. No doubt the difference in this regard between Japan and the other two powers may disappear over the next 30 years, but by then the new advantages will have been consolidated. Although the United States is still the world's strongest power and will no doubt remain so for some time, Japan's real competitor in the long run is less the United States than a revitalized Western Europe, which should not be underestimated despite its atmosphere of cultural pessimism and the slownesses caused by the absence of a single state structure.

This kind of worldwide economic reshuffling of the location of leading sectors should lead to a reconstruction of interstate alliances. We have seen this happen twice before, at the end of Dutch hegemony in the mid to late seventeenth century and at the end of British hegemony in the last third of the nineteenth century. In each case, as now, the economic strength of the hegemonic power had been undermined by decreasing economic efficiencies and increasing social drainages as a result of taxes levied to sustain the politico-military costs of political hegemony and the consumption levels of the middle strata. In each case, there were two successor claimants (for the Dutch, the English and the French; for the British, the Americans and the Germans). In each case, the declining hegemonic power had originally been militarily a sea power and had begun to invest in land forces only as it became hegemonic. In each case, of the two successor claimants, one was land-based (the French following the Dutch era; the Germans following the British era), and one was sea-based, or later sea/air-based (the English following the Dutch era; the Americans following the British era). And, in each case, the sea power was the winner. For one thing, its overhead was less. In each case, the former hegemonic power joined forces, economically and politically, with the future hegemonic power, first as senior partner, then as junior partner (the Dutch with the English, and the British with the Americans). It took a very long time until the successor hegemonic power actually became hegemonic and, without exception, this required a world war with the rival (the Franco-British wars of 1792–1815, the German-American wars of 1914–1945).

If we drew a simple analogy from these two past cycles of the swing from one hegemony to another over a long period of great power rivalry, we could see Japan and Western Europe as the two successor candidates, Japan as the sea/air-based candidate and Western Europe as the land-based one. We would then anticipate a US–Japan economic-political alliance, with the United States first as the senior partner, then as the junior partner. (We see the beginning of this in new links between US and Japanese transnationals.) We could anticipate other zones of the world being pulled into this vortex. If China were to be brought fully into a US–Japan economic zone, then Western Europe would have no choice but to try to join forces with the USSR and Eastern Europe.

The Third World would obviously be a zone of contest for the two new grand alliances, with the likelihood of a Middle East link to the Europe–USSR zone and a continued Latin America link to the now Pacific-based US–Japan zone. And, to be sure, in this scenario there might be a world war, *circa* 2050 – not primarily between the United States and the USSR but between Japan and Western Europe which, by analogy, Japan should win.

But you will say, and you should, that this scenario is absurdly simplistic. It only takes into account the middle-run cyclical rhythms and omits the long-run secular trends and therefore the structural crisis of our historical system, which is also occurring now. Even for the middle-run scenario, there is one major problem. Each previous shift of hegemony, and hence each previous alliance of the old hegemonic power and its successor (the Dutch and the English, the British and the Americans), was intra-European. A long-term alliance between the United States and Japan poses cultural problems of another order, and it is uncertain how these will be navigated. However, I do not consider this a fundamental obstacle to the fulfillment of expectations; culture has a marvelous plasticity when necessity requires it.

The fulfillment of this middle-run hegemonic cycle is complicated by the fact of structural crisis. One facet of the incredible expansion of the role of antisystemic movements is the rejection of the Europe-based universalistic ideology propagated in the nineteenth century. The reassertion of non-European civilizations is a major political reality today and will be even more so in the century to come. The economic rise of Japan fits in symbolically with this reassertion; however, it cannot be its centerpiece because the very point of this civilizational reassertion is its multiplicity. This civilizational reassertion in its multiplicity has been a part of interstate relations since the conference of Bandung. Its diplomatic efficacy has perhaps been limited thus far, but its strength in the popular ideology is not to be doubted.

Even so, the crucial issue is not the decline of the West following its rise; it is the transformation of our current world-system into a different form (or forms) of historical system. Here I must first insist on some general processes of transition before we can appreciate our own concrete dilemmas. Three things should be noted about structural transitions. First, when structural transitions begin, the processes of the old historical system do not thereupon cease. In fact, precisely the opposite occurs: the old processes continue and intensify, which is exactly what is provoking and intensifying the structural crisis. Capitalists will not cease to be capitalists, nor state managers to be state managers. In the next 75 years we shall have even more commodification, even more contractualization, and even more production, productivity, and technological innovation. Those who wish to stress, for ideological reasons, the rosy side of the picture will have many arguments they can use. It is very important to realize that a transition, a demise of an historical system, is less its breakdown than its fulfillment.

Nevertheless, eventually there is breakdown in one very crucial area: there comes to be a slow squeeze on the process of accumulation. As this becomes acute, it magnifies the normal intra-elite competition into continuous destructive internecine struggle. When this occurs (and it has not yet occurred in our historical system) it opens the path for more serious, less co-optable breakdowns of political order – something the antisystemic movements had been prematurely predicting for 150 years. The cause of their inaccurate forecasts is that they always predicated the moment from the actions of the underclasses, whereas the true cause of the breakdown of order in historical systems is the collapse of the spirit of the guardians of order.

However, when, in a transition, one approaches the stage of the breakdown of order, and it becomes obvious that a new historical system or systems will come into being, the real struggle begins, and only then. When change (truly fundamental change) is unavoidable, everyone or virtually everyone embraces it, and this is the dangerous moment. The breakdown of order becomes simultaneously the breakdown of ideology. When everyone talks the language of change, it is hard to distinguish the sheep from the goats, the tenants of old privilege from their opponents, the heralds of more egalitarianism from the proponents of less egalitarianism. This phase now lies before us, and it is coinciding precisely with the normal cyclical process of the decline and renewal of hegemony within the present existing historical system. In the next 75 years we shall see a totally confused mix of continuity/repetition of existing social forms and simultaneously the adoption on all sides of change in social forms as their guiding principle.

The politics of such a situation are by no means clear. But because the stakes are very high, we must try to see as clearly as we can. And it is best to start perhaps by locating the arena of true battle of this struggle. Let us start with where it will not be. It will not be in interstate struggles, neither East versus West, North versus South, nor the European cultural zone versus the non-European cultural zone. Many people will insist that the real struggle is there; they do now. But these arguments are purely an ideological veil in which many are interested precisely because it diverts us from clarifying the issues in the true arenas of battle.

In other words, East–West and North–South are arenas of battle of the processes we are calling the cyclical rhythms of the capitalist world-economy. But the arenas of battle of the structural transformation of this world-economy into something else, the result of the secular trends, lie elsewhere: first, within the broad family of movements, of all those movements that lay claim in some way to being antisystemic; and, second, within the ideational realm of science (in the broad sense of all efforts to understand social reality). And the struggle in both realms is not about the existing historical system but about its successor or successors. There are basically two possibilities for succession: a new historical system (or several) which, though different from the capitalist world-economy, is similarly inegalitarian in basic structure; or a new system that is largely egalitarian, that is largely libertarian, since it is impossible to distinguish the two.

In terms of antisystemic movements, the difficulty for the egalitarian faction in this struggle is whether it can develop some strategy of transformation other than the nineteenth-century approach of seeking state power, which has failed because it has succeeded. The problem is that it is not clear that any other strategy can be organizationally efficacious. In terms of the debates of science, the difficulty is whether one can truly bridge the false debate of the particular and the universal, of the idiographic and the nomothetic, with a methodology that can effectively describe diachronic systems that have an "arrow of time" (what I have been calling for the social world "historical systems"). Once again, as in the case of the movements, it is easy to see that old strategies have failed precisely because they have succeeded. It is less certain, however, that any other strategy can be organizationally efficacious.

To return to our starting point, insofar as the capitalist world-economy pursues its ongoing cyclical rhythms, Japan is destined to play an increasingly central role in this system. Insofar, however, as the capitalist world-economy is in the midst of a structural transformation, this hegemonic cycle may never quite fulfill itself. In any case, it may be only marginally relevant to the debate – the struggle over the construction of a replacement system or systems. I have tried in this description of the future to be neither optimistic nor pessimistic. I am firmly convinced that, during the moments of transition from one historical system to another, human will has wide scope and therefore historical choices are real and not manipulated. The successor historical system or systems of 2050 or 2100 will be ones we construct, but it is not certain which one we will choose to construct.

4 ❧ European unity and its implications for the interstate system

One of the most remarkable features of the contemporary world is that the continent which, since 1945, has seen the least amount of violence (interstate or intrastate) is Europe. There has been some violence of course, but compared to Asia, Africa, and Latin America very little. And yet the two world wars of 1914–18 and 1939–45 were fought largely on the European landmass and resulted in enormous physical destruction, loss of lives, and political upheaval there.

If one asks why this is so, there is no doubt that to a considerable extent Europe has been in the shelter of the Cold War. This may sound paradoxical. However, the reality of "mutual deterrence" has meant that both the US and the USSR were frightened that any small outbreak of violence in Europe could escalate rapidly into full-scale nuclear war. They have clearly been less frightened that this would happen if violence occurred elsewhere. I cite four arenas in which violence has occurred or is occurring without (as yet) such escalation: Iran–Iraq, Cambodia–Vietnam, Ethiopia–Somalia, Honduras–Nicaragua. The explanation for the violence in each arena is different. The degree of direct influence of the US and the USSR varies greatly. I wish in no way to suggest that these conflicts are the same, or even similar, except in one respect: they have gone on for some length of time without resulting in nuclear war. It is hard to believe this would be true in the very unlikely case that armed conflict were to commence between, for example, West Germany and Czechoslovakia.

On the other hand, of all the regions of the world, Europe has also experienced the least political change since, say, 1947, by which time the present political arrangements seemed more or less to have been consolidated. To be sure, Greece, Spain, and Portugal have undergone some important constitutional changes. But, even so, it would not be hard to defend the case that Europe has been more politically stable than Asia, Africa, or Latin America. If one asks why this is so, once again a large part of the explanation lies in the Cold War. By 1947, it was clear on which side of the Cold War various governments were located. This has been institutionalized in NATO and the Warsaw Pact. There are some states outside these frameworks but, in each case, there are tacit understandings about the ways in which these states will conduct both their foreign and internal affairs. When we use the code word of Yalta, we are referring to this reality, whatever was or was not actually agreed upon at the Yalta meeting itself.

Elsewhere, more political change has occurred. In part, this has been because the US and/or the USSR was not always able to block such changes. Vietnam represents the most stunning example of the limits of US power. But it would falsify analysis if we only considered the variable of indigenous roots of change. A second factor was that, for all the verbiage of their leaders, the US and USSR governments have shared one geopolitical assumption: in Europe was located the vital core of their "interests." They might "tolerate" changes elsewhere, however reluctantly, but they could not tolerate them in Europe.

Their devotion to Europe has not been a source of unmitigated joy to Europeans, either west or east. But it has been a fact of life, with which Europeans have learned to live and from which they have drawn certain advantages. At the same time, they have squirmed under the disadvantages of this *mise en tutelle*, for it has been nothing less, but thus far we have seen no real rebellion. In a recent article in *Le Monde*, André Fontaine, who is always judicious, wrote:

The French disagree amongst themselves about many things, but there are some points, and more than is generally realized, on which they all agree. The management of the country's affairs in the light of the international crisis and the dedicated selfishness of our American ally is increasingly an element in this consensus.

The "sacred egoism" of the superpowers is a heavy burden for

Europeans to bear. Europeans chafe under them, demonstrate against them, but suffer them largely because they have no real choice. I do not wish to exaggerate. Many west Europeans are happy to think of themselves as the allies of the US and many east Europeans think likewise of the USSR. But presently there is no real way by which to measure how large a group would remain happy were all constraints to disappear. Since they will not disappear in any near future, perhaps we will never know.

One last reality about Europe should not be ignored. This UNU conference on European security took place in May 1985 on the eve of the 40th anniversary of the defeat of Europe's then most powerful, most centrally located country, Germany. One lasting legacy of that defeat was the creation of two German states, each attached very firmly to a different side of the Cold War. German reunification has been only a minor issue in post-war politics. Perhaps careful studies of the collective psychology of Germans in the two states would find that reunification was not even a high priority for many of them. But it is such a powerful latent rallying-point in this present epoch – the heyday of nationalisms – that it will again be on the political agenda in the near future. If, however, once again one asks why this has not yet been the case, again the main explanation must be the Cold War. Neither superpower would tolerate for a moment the possibility that "their" ally would be swallowed up by the other side's ally. And probably neither would they tolerate even the idea that their "ally" would be the one doing the swallowing, since it would then become a much more powerful and intractable ally – a fear shared by most other European countries. Hence everyone throws cold water on any thought of German reunification, and the Germans thus far have had no choice but to go along as graciously as possible. (This is not to deny that there are not many Germans who themselves are opposed to reunification, fearing its political implications.)

The relative absence of violence in Europe, combined with the relative political stability, makes Europe the exception rather than the rule of the post-1945 world. Will this continue? Since I have explained these phenomena as being in large part a consequence of the Cold War, the question is whether the Cold War will continue for much longer. Reading the newspapers of the last five years, one has the impression that the Cold War, after having flagged somewhat in the late 1960s and 1970s, has been revitalized and determines more than ever the course of European history. And yet, of course, we know that there are a number of objective factors underlying this conflict which are in the process of changing radically.

One is economic conjuncture. Since 1945, the capitalist world-economy has been in one of the expansive phases of its regular long cycles – indeed the biggest single economic expansive period in the history of the world-economy, in terms of absolute production, productivity, mechanization, urbanization, and proletarianization worldwide. We are wont to talk of an industrial revolution in the late eighteenth century. But, in fact, if ever there were a moment to be called an "industrial revolution," meaning by that making the manufacturing sector the central pivot of world economic activity, it is probably this post-1945 period which really merits the title. During it, manufacturing became so widespread that it ceased to be the mark *per se* of economic advantage. Manufacture has become commonplace in the world-economy.

This extraordinary expansion was, however, able to sustain itself no longer than previous such expansions, that is, *circa* a quarter of a century. It was to be followed, as had happened so many times before, by a long period of relative economic stagnation (the so-called "crisis" of popular denomination), in the middle of which we find ourselves at present. Europe, both west and east, had flourished in the period of expansion. From the ruins of war a phoenix-like reconstruction and technological transformations took place. We talk of "economic miracles" in Western Europe and of very high growth rates in Eastern Europe. The basic reality was not all that different between the two parts of Europe, although the level of economic activity and well-being was higher in the west. No doubt other areas of the world experienced the advantages of economic expansion as well, but none (except for Japan) quite to the extent of Europe in the 1950s and 1960s. This economic well-being certainly did not disturb the relative political tranquillity of which I have been speaking.

There was a second structural feature to this first postwar period. Within the framework of an expanding capitalist world-economy, the role of US economic enterprise was at first overwhelming. In 1950, the US could outproduce all other zones of the world-economy in all domains. And, on this basis, American enterprises were able not merely to dominate world trade but to expand individually in size and space (that is, transnationally) to an extraordinary degree. Of course, when one produces so very well, one is sometimes caught short by a lack of customers. The US had to create customers, concentrating on Western Europe (and Japan). This was so for purely economic reasons; but it was also for political reasons – once again the Cold War. Thus it was, however, that by 1970, when the world-economy had already entered its B-phase of stagnation, the greatly expanded basic productive plant of western Europe and Japan had in many ways caught up to and, in some ways passed beyond, US structures. The overwhelming US economic advantage of 1950 had become much slimmer by 1970.

These two changes – the shift of the world-economy from an A- to a B-phase, and the shift from a situation in which the US was economically a giant amidst Lilliputians to one in which she was one strong power among several – were part of the same process, the normal entropy of monopolistic advantage within capitalism.

The fact that such a relative economic decline of the US in the world-economy was in some sense normal did not make it less a shock for the world-system. America's role in the world-system from 1945 to *circa* 1967 was special. It was the hegemonic power. Its unquestioned economic competitive advantage in all fields, plus its exceptional military power, allowed it almost always to obtain its will in the political arena. To be sure, the USSR was able to carve out what might be called a zone of non-interference. And some national liberation movements in the peripheral areas were able to pursue their paths despite fierce US opposition – most notably, in China and Vietnam. Yet, by and large, US word was fiat in this period.

With the ending of the expansionary phase, and the frittering of the US monopolistic advantages (especially *vis-à-vis* Western Europe and Japan), this ceased to be true. The automatic US majority in the United Nations was transformed virtually into the opposite, an automatic anti-US majority. US ability to contain national liberation movements it considered unfriendly was severely undermined. Iran provides the most spectacular example.

And, less obviously, but perhaps more importantly, US political leverage in Western Europe declined considerably. No doubt Reagan foreign policy was designed to reverse this political downturn, but it has at most only slowed the process. From the standpoint of the US, the halcyon days of the 1950s and early 1960s are gone, never to return.

There is a fourth factor of structural change, a change in the ideological structures, the mentalities, of the world-system. At a purely ideological level, the Cold War was the culmination of a nineteenth-century intellectual battle between "liberalism" and "Marxism." The real history of these two ideologies is rich and complicated. What is to be noted is that one correlate of the early Cold War was the crystallization of each ideology into a particular, relatively simplified, form which was dogmatic (in the sense that intellectual variance was not well-tolerated politically), rigid (in the sense that intellectual activity was largely confirming rather than reorganizing activity), and consequently brittle.

That which is brittle is bound to crack. There were two big cracks, which reinforced each other, and which can be symbolized by two dates: 1956 and 1968. 1956 was the year of the XXth Party Congress of the CPSU. Khrushchev's report had a major impact, not so much because of what it said, but because it was said at all. This self-criticism, however limited, not of an individual, but of the leading party in the Communist world movement, reversed long-standing truths and apologias, and therefore permanently legitimated skepticism. The corrosive effects of such skepticism on the internal social structures of the USSR, on the relations between the USSR and other socialist states (China, Eastern Europe), on the functioning of the world Communist movement have been great and are far from exhausted today. One half of world verity had been opened to reorganization.

The other half could not be too far behind. What 1968 represented was the institutionalization of a deep skepticism about the liberal consensus that had previously dominated all the cultural, intellectual, and political institutions of the Western world and, indeed, of large parts of the periphery. There too what was important was less what was said than that it was said. What had been self-evident became debatable, and the group who had the right to enter the debate was no longer restricted to a small number of specialists. Debate had become open to informed "amateurs."

In all these arenas – economic, political, ideological – it would be a mistake to exaggerate the structural changes of the last 15 years. But it would be a mistake as well to underestimate them. For it is in the nature of these structural changes that they will continue, and will have greater import as the years go by. Eventually they should shake the relative stability of the European scene, the phenomenon with which we began this analysis. In each of the three arenas, an element has been set in movement whose outcome is uncertain.

Economic reorganization is going on in the world-economy. The 1970s and the 1980s mark the period in which considerable reshuffling – of location of economic activity, of sectoral profitability, of world economic structures – is occurring. The real question, however, is where this reshuffling is going to come out in the 1990s and beyond. We may anticipate that it is likely that the world-economy will enter into a new expansionary phase, perhaps not quite as spectacular as the last but quite real nonetheless. We may anticipate that informatics, biotechnology, and new energy forms will serve as the leading industry sectors. But who will be able to gain monopolistic edges that will guarantee the direction of flows of surplus? This is not at all certain, but clearly it must be of concern to Europe that she might come a poor second in the race. We see this in the current maneuvring concerning the SDI.

There is a reorganization underway also in the interstate system. The principal political structures of the Cold War still stand – the two military alliances. But important elements have changed. China is no longer a Soviet ally. The political leverage of Western Europe and Japan *vis-à-vis* the US has increased enormously. And the actual military strength of a number of countries in Asia, Africa, and Latin America is more significant than it once was. Instead of a crisp bipolarization, there is a fuzzy one, with many players more equal to each other. This means that a reshuffling of alliances is a political possibility, which it was not before. Were there to be a reshuffling, it is not clear who would end up where. What is clear is that there is no advantage in being the last to move. And this must be of concern to Europe.

Finally, if the crystalline versions of the two nineteenth-century ideologies have been cracked, they have not been shattered. Several ideological developments are possible. Both ideological systems could take advantage of the new flexibility forced upon them and reproduce themselves in more sophisticated forms. Or, only one of the systems might do this. Or, neither would do it, and then we would have one of two main possibilities: a long period of confusion and the erratic emergence of new mysticisms; or a more rational *Aufhebung* of the ideological superstructure. Europe, which gained an ideological monopoly on world thought four centuries or so ago, is under severe and efficacious attack from the multiple civilizational renewals elsewhere. Once again, Europe's concern is no doubt whether it will put itself in a purely reactive position (and hence, ultimately, a marginal position) or whether Europe can participate actively in the new processes of intellectual analysis.

What are the chances, therefore, that Europe will take significant initiatives in the process of economic, political, and ideological reorganization of the world-system, initiatives in the next 25 years or so? The most spectacular initiative would be a move in the direction of European unity, one that would heal the division of Europe which is a fundamental legacy of the Second World War. Is this in the realm of the possible, or mere *kaffeeklatsch* fantasy?

It is easy to see the factors which make this seem remote, indeed fantastic. There are two fundamentals. The first is that there are genuine, deep-seated ideological and political differences between Western and Eastern Europe. If one has doubts about this, one has only to look at how people and governments thought about, talked about, and reacted to the rise and fall of Solidarność between 1980 and 1982. By post-1945 standards, the struggle between Solidarność and the Polish government was a relatively civil and muted one – in terms of violence and ideological screeching. Yet the issues were clearly drawn and strongly felt, and that throughout Europe. These differences will not disappear suddenly. The ability of the US and the USSR, as the official champions of the contending ideologies, to utilize calls to ideological basics as tactical weapons in controlling their allies has repeatedly been shown to be real and efficacious. That is to say, both these countries have power beyond the strictly economic, military, and political realms. There are still many people in other countries who act in terms of these internalized ideologies, and accept the legitimacy of the ongoing ideological leaderships the US and the USSR give. In hard ideological terms, unity between Western and Eastern Europe seems to imply that one or the other or both yield serious ideological ground, and on both sides this breeds very strong resistance.

There is a second fundamental difficulty about European unity. I have stressed previously certain economic parallels (seen from a world perspective) of European economic developments in the 1950s and 1960s, but we should be careful not to overstate these similarities. At the moment, the unification of Europe into some common economic structure would pose the same problem, multiplied several times, of the incorporation first of Greece, now of Spain and Portugal, into the EEC. We have seen the political stability of the EEC very stretched in this process. It is not clear it could survive an attempt to widen membership further, especially as long as the world-economy remains in its stagnation phase.

Frankly, the two factors – the ideological rift and the economic disparities – are enough for most analysts to dismiss further discussion of European unity as politically irrelevant. I wish, however, to pursue the subject at least one step further, speculating on what kinds of developments might alter the situation sufficiently that the present barriers to unity would weigh less in the picture. I think the initial shock would probably have to come from outside.

Suppose, first, that US–Japanese relations changed suddenly from their present carefully articulated minuet of fierce but gentlemanly economic competition, combined with the political low posture of the Japanese, to one in which there was open, dynamic economic collaboration, to the exclusion of Western Europe. This would involve interlocking directorates of US and Japanese transnational corporations, and relatively coordinated investment processes. This no doubt would be politically dangerous and fly in the face of deep cultural resistances. But look at some of the economic advantages of such an economic flight forward. From a situation in which the countries with the two leading R & D loci for the leading industries of the 1990s are cutting each other's throats, and therefore their eventual profits, the two combined could quickly gain that kind of unquestioned transitory monopoly on the world market that would make possible a quite extraordinary capital accumulation. It would give the Japanese instantly an economic lead they might otherwise have to struggle hard for with less certain, more partial results. It would, however, give American corporations a cushion that would guarantee a long period of lucrative activity, with the side bonus for the ordinary American of making economic decline much slower and less perceptible. Certainly, US corporations (and corporate executives) might feel they were accepting an eventual formally junior role, but this could be hidden for quite a while. Such executives have already learned how to accept their greying hair by combining it with slim bodies and a little *dolce vita*. This lesson could be applied to new world economic alliances. Furthermore, such a scenario is not pure invention. The arrangements between Toyota and General Motors, for example, are the first steps in this direction.

Of course, such an alliance between transnationals would have very clear political consequences. One would be over relations between the US and Japanese states. The latter would probably have to play a bigger military role than it does now. It would be reluctant to do so, first because of the internal political tensions this might stimulate and, secondly because this is expensive and, in the short run, economically damaging. It is exactly for this reason, however, that the US government would be pressing it to play (and pay) its "fair share," since this would then relieve the US burden, with consequent world economic and internal political advantage.

The second political consequence might be to shift the internal political balance within the US establishment. There has been a long-standing debate about geopolitical strategy in the US between Europe-firsters and advocates of a Pacific Rim strategy. This is a complicated picture of strange internal alliances and motivations. The key fact, however, is that the US establishment – industrial, financial, and political – has, for the most part and for obvious reasons, been Europe-firsters. This has been, therefore, US strategy, and we have already spoken of its consequences for Europe. A genuine intermesh of American and Japanese transnationals could alter the US internal political balance and make possible, for the first time, the triumph of a Pacific Rim strategy.

Finally, China might have to precipitate decisions in matters about which she has wanted to move slowly. China's geopolitical strategy since 1949 – whoever has been in power – has been very long run. The main emphasis has been on pursuing an internal structural transformation within relative isolation until the economic base would become strong enough for China to play the world role that seems appropriate to her. But a Japanese–American flight forward could upset the calculations of such a prudent strategy. Both the temptations of joining such a winning alliance early and the economic risks of holding back might lead to the decision that an early commitment might optimize China's ability to rise within the new alliance, and *vis-à-vis* its partners, with relative rapidity.

Suppose then – we are only speculating. I remind you – the US–Japan–China triumvirate (of say 1995 or 2000) were to reason, with some plausibility, that the optimal policy to pursue in the interstate system *vis-à-vis* the peripheral zones of the world – the "South" – was not the repressive one of opposition to their national liberation movements, but a *selective* cooperation with such movements in power in the stronger Southern semiperipheral states, or even just with some of them. This would have to involve some redistribution of world surpluses, but given that I am postulating a significant increase in the accumulation of capital, there would be plenty of profit to spread around. One does not even have to assume that this policy would succeed everywhere in defusing political explosions. A partial and limited success might be seen as sufficient justification for such a policy.

Now look at such a picture for Europe's standpoint. Threatened by economic retrogression *vis-à-vis* a new multi-state, multi-national network which would seem to have "harnessed" the market potential of China and, perhaps increasingly, of some large, important, politically solid (because nationalist) zones of the South, western Europe might conceivably come to feel as does the USSR that it was "surrounded" by a potentially hostile world. And Eastern Europe might feel in danger of becoming the backwater of a declining world zone. Attitudes could conceivably drastically change in western Europe, eastern Europe, *and* the USSR.

Let me postulate one last possibility. For quite different reasons, it is conceivable that both the US and the USSR could see a steep increase in internal disorder. Again we do not need to exaggerate. I am not postulating civil wars, or even overthrows of governments. I am merely suggesting the existence of social unrest sufficient for the two governments to be forced to concentrate considerable energy and money in resolving these internal situations.

The course of such unrest in the US is quite clear. In fact, in some sense, the social unrest has already begun. The two central stimulants of such US unrest are the "Third World within" and the victims of economic reorganization. The existence, repression, and rebellion of the "Third World within" is an old story in US history. There is one difference today. The present main groups involved (Blacks and Hispanic-speakers) represent for the first time a really large demographic mass, concentrated in the major urban centers, more politically sophisticated than ever before, and somewhat linked emotionally (and even politically) to a worldwide network of liberation movements.

The US already had a major explosion in the 1960s which was defused only by some political concessions and considerable economic transfers. Economic decline, however, makes further transfers unlikely. And it even makes political concessions more difficult. This is because the decline, while no doubt disproportionately hurting the minorities, also hurts important segments of the ethnic majority. The latter also demand state action on their behalf and, increasingly, see state action in favor of minorities as competitive with their own demands. We could conceivably, therefore, see in the US both "left-wing" and "right-wing" strong social movements, each fighting the establishment and each other.

The position in the USSR is, of course, quite different. Politically, the great problem is the heavy hand of a complicated set of bureaucratic structures (state plus party) which is resistant to streamlining and processual change. Furthermore, this is not merely a matter of mentalities but of economic interest. The inefficiencies of this structure are rewarded by excessive privileges. No doubt various leaders at the top of the structure are aware of these problems and, supported by certain cadres, want to reform the situation. But will they be able to do so? The world economic situation also places constraints on the USSR in terms of how much surplus is at their disposal to reallocate. Furthermore, the Cold War (especially in its current renewed intensity) places enormous economic constraints, as well as constraints of human energy, on the USSR.

Two further elements complicate the picture. Nationalism within the USSR has been remarkably well contained over the past 60 years. In that sense, the Soviet system has worked relatively well. Still there are strains that are not negligible. The currents of "Muslim" nationalism are very strong in the world today and diffusion across the frontiers cannot be discounted. Western-zone and Caucasian nationalism may well be fed by strains coming from Eastern Europe. And finally there is the sleeper of Russian nationalism, the one nationalism thus far most suppressed in the USSR.

This is compounded by the absence of genuine workplace trade-union rights which, in the advanced industrial structures of the USSR, cannot but mean that they are a hotbed of latent protest. If, in the interest of streamlining these structures, some pressure is placed on the extensive featherbedding which is today one of the chief rewards of the Soviet industrial working class, the situation could breed still more discontent and consequently unrest. And this unrest could then take the form either of trade-unionism or Russian nationalism, either of which could be explosive.

In any case, I am not trying here to examine in detail the internal structures of either of the superpowers. I merely want to suggest some reasons why extensive social unrest is possible. And the significance of this for our purposes is that such unrest would normally force the governments to turn inward, and therefore to some extent away from Europe. I realize it is more complicated than this. First of all, one classic solution for internal social unrest is external aggressivity. Secondly, in the case of both the US and the USSR, especially the latter, neglecting external situations could permit developments on their frontiers which could stimulate still further internal social unrest. Nonetheless, Europe might acquire more autonomous "space."

What I have done is try to develop a series of circumstances that are not too implausible and which might create conditions in which steps towards European unity, West and East, might seem one viable political option. Consider, given the circumstances I have been outlining, how the situation might look from the point of view respectively of Western Europe, the Soviet Union, and Eastern Europe.

For Western Europe the advantages in some kind of economic arrangement among these three zones would be several. They could see it as strengthening their position in the world-economy in important ways. It would directly enlarge their market at a moment when our presumed Japanese–US temporary monopolistic advantage was excluding them from much of the world. Indirectly, if Western Europe were to get the political support of the USSR, it might then have greater political success in getting access to some markets in the periphery from which the Japanese–US combine was seeking to exclude them. And politically, Western Europe might see this as a big step in "recuperating" Eastern Europe in cultural terms, since the political "liberalization" of the Eastern European countries might be considered to be part of the package.

The Soviet point of view would be quite different from that of Western Europe. The USSR might also see, however, various kinds of advantage in the arrangement. First, loosening the ties of Western Europe and the US (even if NATO were not disbanded) has long been a major objective of Soviet foreign policy, and they might see this as one inevitable side-effect of new economic arrangements with Western Europe. Secondly, the USSR wants some guaranteed access, at least over the next 20–30 years, to various kinds of advanced technology, and such an arrangement would offer such a guarantee. Third, the USSR might feel that one way to contain internal unrest would be both to improve the immediate economic situation and to obtain the political umbrella of a link with Western Europe, thereby undermining some of the "radicalism" of the opposition. Fourth, the USSR might entertain the hope that this would help the long-range prospects of political parties sympathetic to her.

As for Eastern Europe, such an arrangement might be almost all gain. It would permit an "opening" to the west which would not be interpreted as "opposition" to the Soviet Union. They would draw many of the same economic advantages as the Soviets. It would contain their own internal unrest. In any case, Eastern Europe has no better alternative to its present impasse than such a development.

Finally, the one advantage all parties to such an arrangement might see in common would be that it could provide an elegant "solution" to the division of Germany, permitting a sort of informal reunification that, from the point of view of neighbors, west and east, would seem non-threatening.

All this has been an exercise in geopolitical speculation. I have not yet indicated whether and for whom this is good or bad. From the perspective of the world-system as a whole, I see one enormous negative to the whole development compensated perhaps by three positives.

The negative is that, if everything I have described were to occur, this would breathe considerable new life into the existing capitalist world-economy by creating relative stabilities where they do not now exist and by recreating a relatively even balance of forces in the world-system. Of course, for some this would not be a negative. But for me, one must realize that, in the reworked system I have been picturing, a large portion of the world's population would still be outrageously exploited, perhaps more than ever.

Nevertheless, I offer my three positives. First, such a reorganization of the interstate system would reduce the likelihood of nuclear war, both by creating a better balance of forces and, paradoxically, by dethroning Europe from its position as the key arena of the Cold War. Europe's stability has since 1945 always been under the sword of Damocles. This might cease to be so.

The second great advantage is in the realm of ideology. What I have described as possible is ideologically absurd. Remember, I am *not* positing any change in the dominant ideology of any significant actor in this situation. Coming in the wake of all the skepticism that already exists about the traditional dominant ideologies, this "theatre of the absurd" might be the culminating blow in forcing a genuine intellectual *Aufhebung* which, in my view, is desperately needed – the dethronement not only of nineteenth-century social ideologies but of Baconian–Newtonian physical science as well.

The third great advantage is that such an intellectual revolution might make possible a genuine re-evaluation by the world's antisystemic movements of their strategic options so that they might get out of the historic cul-de-sac in which they have found themselves more and more in the post-1945 period, which is that the seizure of state power by these movements is simply not a sufficient condition to permit the passage from a capitalist world-economy to a socialist world order. It will take time, energy, and thought to rework fundamental strategy. The postulated shifts in the interstate system might provide the time and, by the intellectual dethroning, the incentive to organizational rethinking. And all this together might make possible the genuine fundamental change these movements have been seeking, thus far with only partial success.

5 ❧ 1968, revolution in the world-system

Theses and queries

Thesis 1: 1968 was a revolution in and of the world-system

The revolution of 1968 was a revolution; it was a single revolution. It was marked by demonstrations, disorder, and violence in many parts of the world over a period of at least three years. Its origins, consequences, and lessons cannot be analyzed correctly by appealing to the particular circumstances of the local manifestations of this global phenomenon, however much the local factors conditioned the details of the political and social struggles in each locality.

As an event, 1968 has long since ended. However, it was one of the great, formative events in the history of our modern world-system, the kind we call watershed events. This means that the cultural-ideological realities of that world-system have been definitively changed by the event, itself the crystallization of certain long-existing structural trends within the operation of the system.

Origins

Thesis 2: The primary protest of 1968 was against US hegemony in the world-system (and Soviet acquiescence in that hegemony)

In 1968, the world was still in the midst of what has come to be called in France the "thirty glorious" years – the period of incredible expansion of the capitalist world-economy following the end of the Second World War. Or, rather, 1968 immediately followed the first significant evidence of the beginning of a long world-economic stagnation, that is, the serious difficulties of the US dollar in 1967 (difficulties that have never since ceased).

The period 1945–67 had been one of unquestioned hegemony of the United States in the world-system, whose bedrock was the incredible superiority in productive efficiency of the United States in all fields in the aftermath of the Second World War. The United States translated this economic advantage into a world-wide political and cultural domination by undertaking four main policy initiatives in the post-1945 period. It constructed around itself an "alliance system" with Western Europe (and Japan) characterized as the leadership of the "Free World," and invested in the economic reconstruction of these areas (the Marshall Plan, etc.). The United States sought thereby both to ensure the role of Western Europe and Japan as major economic customers and to guarantee their internal political stability and international political clientship.

Secondly, the United States entered into a stylized Cold War relationship with the USSR based on reserving to the USSR a small but important zone of political domination (Eastern Europe). This so-called Yalta arrangement enabled both countries to present their relationship as an unlimited ideological confrontation, with the important proviso that no changes in the East–West line were to occur and no actual military confrontations were to ensue, especially in Europe.

Thirdly, the United States sought to achieve a gradual, relatively bloodless decolonization of Asia and Africa, on the assumption that this could be arranged via so-called moderate leadership. This was made all the more urgent by the victory of the Chinese Communist Party in China, a victory (be it noted) that was achieved despite the counsels of the USSR. Moderation was defined as the absence of significant ideological links of this leadership with the USSR and world Communism and, even more, the willingness of the decolonized states to participate in the existing set of international economic arrangements. This process of decolonization under the control of moderates was abetted by the occasional and judicious use of limited US military force.

Fourthly, the US leadership sought to create a united front at home by minimizing internal class conflict, through economic concessions to the skilled, unionized, working class on the one hand, and through enlisting US labor in the worldwide anti-Communist crusade on the other hand. It also sought to dampen potential race conflict by eliminating blatant discrimination in the political arena (end of segregation in the armed forces, constitutional invalidation of segregation in all arenas, Voting Rights Act). The United States encouraged its principal allies to work in parallel ways toward maximizing internal unity.

The result of all these policy initiatives by the United States was a system of hegemonic control that operated quite smoothly in the 1950s. It made possible the continuing expansion of the world-economy, with significant income benefits for "middle" strata throughout the world. It made possible the construction of the United Nations network of international agencies, which at that time reflected the political will of the United States and ensured a comparatively stable world political arena. It contributed to the "decolonization" of large parts of what came to be called the Third World with surprising rapidity. And it ensured that, in the West, generally, the 1950s was a period of relative political quietude.

Nonetheless, by the 1960s, this pattern of successful "hegemony" had begun to fray, in part because of its very success. The economic reconstruction of the US's strong allies became so great that they began to reassert some economic (and even some political) autonomy. This was one, albeit not the only, meaning of Gaullism, for example. The death of Stalin marked the end of a "monolithic" Soviet bloc. It was followed, as we know, by a (still ongoing) process of de-Stalinization and de-satellitization, the two major turning-points of which were the Report of Khrushchev to the XXth Party Congress in 1956 and the Sino-Soviet split in 1960. The smoothness of the decolonization of the Third World was disturbed by two long and draining anti-colonial wars in Algeria and Vietnam (to which should be associated the long Cuban struggle). Finally, the political "concessions" of the 1950s to "minority groups" in the United States (and elsewhere in the Western world) accentuated expectations that were not in fact being met, either in the political or the economic arenas, and hence in actual practice stimulated rather than constrained further political mobilization.

The 1960s began with the tandem of Kennedy and Khrushchev, who in effect promised to do things better. Between them, they succeeded in lifting the heavy ideological lids that had so successfully held down the world in the 1950s without, however, bringing about any fundamental reforms of the existing system. When they were removed from power, and replaced by the tandem Johnson–Brezhnev, the hopes of the early 1960s disappeared. However, the renewed ideological pressures that the powers attempted to reapply were now being placed on what was a more disabused world public opinion. This was the pre-revolutionary tinderbox in which opposition to US hegemony, in all its multiple expressions, would explode in 1968 – in the US, in France, in Czechoslovakia, in Mexico, and elsewhere.

Thesis 3: The secondary, but ultimately more passionate, protest of 1968 was against the "old left" antisystemic movements

The nineteenth century saw the birth of two major varieties of antisystemic movements – the social and the national movements. The former emphasized the oppression of the proletariat by the bourgeoisie. The second emphasized the oppression of underdog peoples (and "minorities") by dominant groups. Both kinds of movements sought to achieve, in some broad sense, "equality." In fact, both kinds of movements used the three terms of the French revolutionary slogan of "liberty, equality, and fraternity" virtually interchangeably.

Both kinds of movements took concrete organizational form in one country after another, eventually almost everywhere, in the second half of the nineteenth and the first half of the twentieth century. Both kinds of movements came to emphasize the importance of obtaining state power as the indispensable intermediate achievement on the road to their ultimate objectives. The social movement, however, had an important worldwide split in the early twentieth century concerning the road to state power (parliamentary versus insurrectionary strategies).

By 1945, there existed three clear and separate networks of such movements on the world scene: the Third International

Communist parties; the Second International social-democratic parties; and the various nationalist (or national liberation) movements. The period 1945–68 was a period of remarkable political achievement for these three networks of movements. Third International parties came to power, by one means or another, in a series of countries more or less contiguous to the USSR (Eastern Europe, China, North Korea). Second International parties (I use the term loosely, including in this category the Democratic Party in the United States as Roosevelt reshaped it) came to power (or at least achieved *droit de cité*, that is, the right of *alternance*) in the Western world (Western Europe, North America, Australasia). Nationalist or national liberation movements came to power in most formerly colonized areas in Asia, the Middle East, Africa, the Caribbean and, in somewhat different forms, in long-independent Latin America.

The important point for the analysis of the revolution of 1968 was that the new movements which emerged then were led largely by young people who had grown up in a world where the traditional antisystemic movements in their countries were not in an early phase of mobilization but had already achieved their intermediate goal of state power. Hence these "old" movements could be judged not only on their promises but on their practices once in power. They were so judged and, to a considerable degree, they were found wanting.

They were found wanting on two main grounds. First, in their efficacy in combating the existing capitalist world-system and its current institutional incarnation, US hegemony. Secondly, in the quality of life they had created in the "intermediate" state structures they presumably controlled. Thus it was that, in the words of one famous 1968 aphorism, they were no longer to be considered "part of the solution." Rather, they had become "part of the problem."

The anger of the US SDS against "liberals," of the *soixante-huitards* against the PCF (not to speak of the Socialists), of the German SDS against the SPD was all the more passionate because of their sense of fundamental betrayal. This was the real implication of that other 1968 aphorism: "Never trust anyone over the age of 30." It was less generational at the level of individuals than generational at the level of antisystemic organizations. I take it as no accident that the major outbreak in the Soviet bloc was in Czechoslovakia, a country with a particularly long and strong Third International tradition. The leaders of the Prague Spring fought their struggle in the name of "humanist Communism," that is, against the betrayal that Stalinism represented. I take it also as no accident that the major outbreak in the Third World was in Mexico, the country that had the oldest national liberation movement continuously in power, or that particularly important outbreaks occurred in Dakar and in Calcutta, two cities with very long nationalist traditions.

Not only was the revolution of 1968 directed, even if only secondarily, against the "old lefts" throughout the world, but these "old lefts" responded, as we know, in coin. The "old lefts" were first of all astonished at finding themselves under attack from the left (who us, who have such impeccable credentials?), and then deeply enraged at the adventurism that the "new lefts" represented in their eyes. As the "old lefts" responded with increasing impatience and hostility to the spreading "anarchism" of the "new lefts," the latter began to place greater and greater emphasis on the ideological centrality of their struggle with the "old lefts." This took the form of the multivariate "Maoisms" that developed in the early 1970s in all parts of the world, including, of course, in China itself.

Thesis 4: Counterculture was part of revolutionary euphoria, but was not politically central to 1968

What we came to call in the late 1960s "counterculture" was a very visible component of the various movements that participated in the revolution of 1968. We generally mean by counter-culture behavior in daily life (sexuality, drugs, dress) and in the arts that is unconventional, non-bourgeois, and Dionysiac. There was an enormous escalation in the quantity of such behavior directly associated with activism in the "movement." The Woodstock festival in the United States represented a kind of symbolic highpoint of such movement-related counterculture.

But, of course, a counterculture was not a particularly new phenomenon. There had been for two centuries a "Bohemia" associated with youth and the arts. The relaxation of puritanical sexual mores had been a steady linear development throughout the twentieth century worldwide. Furthermore, "revolutions" had often previously been the occasion of countercultural affirmation. Here, however, two models of previous revolutions should be noted. In those revolutions that had been planned, organized, and involved long military struggle, revolutionary puritanism usually became an important element of discipline (as in the history of the Chinese Communist Party). Where, however, revolutionary circumstances included a large measure of spontaneous activity (as was the case in the Russian Revolution of 1917 or the triumph of Castro in Cuba), the spontaneity involved a breakdown in social constraints and hence was associated, at least initially, with counterculture (for example, "free love" in post-1917 Russia). The revolution of 1968 had, of course, a particularly strong component of unplanned spontaneity and therefore, as the thesis says, counterculture became part of the revolutionary euphoria.

Nonetheless, as we all learned in the 1970s, it is very easy to dissociate counterculture from political (revolutionary) activity. Indeed, it is easy to turn countercultural trends into very profitable consumption-oriented life-styles (the transition from yippies to yuppies). While, therefore, the counterculture of the new left was salient to most of these forces themselves, as it was to their enemies, in the final analysis it was a minor element in the picture. It may be one of the consequences of 1968 that Dionysiac life styles spread further. It is not one of its legacies. It is to the political legacies that we must now turn.

Legacies

Legacies of watershed events are always complex phenomena. For one thing, they are always ambiguous. For another, they are always the object of a struggle by various heirs to claim the legacy, that is, the legitimacy of a tradition. Please note that there already exists a tradition of 1968. Traditions are rapidly created, and the "tradition" of the Revolution of 1968 was already functioning by the early 1970s. And in 1988 there are many celebrations, many books, and many attempts at recuperation as well. This should neither surprise us nor dismay us. World-historic events have lives of their own and they resist any kind of simple capture. 1968 is no different. Having thus warned you against myself, I shall nonetheless put before you what I think are the two principal legacies of 1968.

Thesis 5: Revolutionary movements representing "minority" or underdog strata need no longer, and no longer do, take second place to revolutionary movements representing presumed "majority" groups

1968 was the ideological tomb of the concept of the "leading role" of the industrial proletariat. This leading role had long been challenged, but never before so massively and so efficaciously. For in 1968 it was being challenged on the grounds that the industrial proletariat was and would always structurally remain just one component among others of the world's working class.

The historic attitude of both varieties of "old left" movements (the socialist and the nationalist) was that they represented the interests of the "primary" oppressed – either the "working class" of a given country or the "nation" whose national expression was unfulfilled. These movements took the view that the complaints of "other" groups who saw themselves as being treated unequally – the unfulfilled nationalities for socialist movements, the working class for nationalist movements, women for both kinds of movements, and any other group that could lay claim to social or political oppression – were at best secondary and at worst diversionary. The "old left" groups tended to argue that their own achievement of state power had to be the prime objective and the prior achievement, after which (they argued) the secondary oppressions would disappear of themselves or at least they could be resolved by appropriate political action in the "post-revolutionary" era.

Needless to say, not everyone agreed with such reasoning. And the socialist and nationalist movements of the world often quarreled fiercely with each other over precisely this issue of priority of struggle. But none of the "old left" movements ever ceded theoretical ground on this issue of strategic priorities in the struggle for equality, although many individual movements made tactical and temporary concessions on such issues in the interests of creating or reinforcing particular political alliances.

As long as the "old left" movements were in their pre-revolutionary, mobilizing phases, the argument about what would or would not happen after their achievement of state power remained hypothetical. But once they were in state power, the practical consequences could be assessed on the basis of some evidence. By 1968, many such assessments had been made, and the opponents of the multiple "other" inequalities could argue, with some plausibility, that the achievement of power by "old left" groups had not in fact ended these "other" inequalities, or at least had not sufficiently changed the multiple group hierarchies that had previously existed.

At the same time, a century of struggle had begun to make clear two sociological realities that had great bearing on this debate. The first was that, contrary to prior theorizing, the trend of capitalist development was not to transform almost all the world's laboring strata into urban, male, adult, salaried factory workers, the ideal-type of the "proletarian" as traditionally conceived. The reality of capitalism was far more occupationally complex than that. This ideal-type "proletarian" had represented a minority of the world's laboring strata in 1850, of course. But it had then been thought this was merely transitional. However, such ideal-type "proletarians" remained a minority in 1950. And it was now clear that this particular occupational profile would probably remain a minority in 2050. Hence, to organize a movement around this group was to give priority – permanent and illegitimate priority – to the claims of one variety over other varieties of the world's laboring strata.

Analogously, it had become clear that "nationalities" were not just there in some form that could be objectively delineated. Nationalities were rather the product of a complex process of ongoing social creation, combining the achievement of consciousness (by themselves and by others) and socio-juridical labeling. It followed that for every nation there could and would be sub-nations in what threatened to be an unending cascade. It followed that each transformation of some "minority" into a "majority" created new "minorities." There could be no cut-off of this process, and hence no "automatic" resolution of the issue by the achievement of state power.

If the "proletariat" and the "oppressed nations" were not

destined to transform themselves into uncontested majorities, but would forever remain one kind of "minority" alongside other kinds of "minorities," their claim to strategic priority in the antisystemic struggle would thereby be grievously undermined. 1968 accomplished precisely this undermining. Or, rather, the revolution of 1968 crystallized the recognition of these realities in the worldwide political action of antisystemic movements.

After 1968, none of the "other" groups in the struggle – neither women nor racial "minorities" nor sexual "minorities" nor the handicapped nor the "ecologists" (those who refused the acceptance, unquestioningly, of the imperatives of increased global production) – would ever again accept the legitimacy of "waiting" upon some other revolution. And since 1968, the "old left" movements have themselves become increasingly embarrassed about making, have indeed hesitated to continue to make, such demands for the "postponement" of claims until some presumed post-revolutionary epoch. It is easy enough to verify this change in atmosphere. A simple quantitative content analysis of the world's left press, comparing say 1985 and 1955, would indicate a dramatic increase of the space accorded to these "other" concerns that had once been considered "secondary."

Of course, there is more. The very language of our analyses has changed, has consciously and explicitly been changed. We worry about racism and sexism even in arenas once thought "harmless" (appellations, humor, etc.). And the structure of our organizational life has also changed. Whereas prior to 1968 it was generally considered a desideratum to unify all existing antisystemic movements into one movement, at least into one movement in each country, this form of unity is no longer an unquestioned desideratum. A multiplicity of organizations, each representing a different group or a different tonality, loosely linked in some kind of alliance, is now seen, at least by many, as a good in itself. What was a *pis aller* is now proclaimed as a "rainbow coalition" (a US coinage that has spread).

The triumph of the Revolution of 1968 has been a triple triumph in terms of racism, sexism, and analogous evils. One result is that the legal situations (state policies) have changed. A second result is that the situations within the antisystemic movements have changed. A third result is that mentalities have changed. There is no need to be Polyannish about this. The groups who were oppressed may still complain, with great legitimacy, that the changes that have occurred are inadequate, that the realities of sexism and racism and other forms of oppressive inequality are still very much with us. Furthermore, it is no doubt true that there has been "backlash" in all arenas, on all these issues. But it is pointless also not to recognize that the Revolution of 1968 marked, for all these inequalities, a historic turning-point.

Even if the states (or some of them) regress radically, the antisystemic movements will never be able to do so (or, if they do, they will thereby lose their legitimacy). This does not mean that there is no longer a debate about priorities among antisystemic movements. It means that the debate has become a debate about fundamental strategy, and that the "old left" movements (or tendencies) are no longer refusing to enter into such a debate.

Thesis 6: The debate on the fundamental strategy of social transformation has been reopened among the antisystemic movements, and will be the key political debate of the coming twenty years

There exist today, in a broad sense, six varieties of antisystemic movements. (a) In the Western countries, there are "old left" movements in the form of the trade-unions and segments of the traditional left parties – labor and social-democratic parties, to which one might perhaps add the Communist parties, although, except for Italy, these are weak and growing weaker. (b) In the same Western countries, there is a wide variety of new social movements – of women, "minorities," Greens, etc. (c) In the socialist bloc, there are the traditional Communist parties in power, among whom a strain of persistent antisystemic virus has never been extinguished, which gives rise to renewed (and "feverish") activity from time to time. The Gorbachev phenomenon, insofar as it appeals to "Leninism" against "Stalinism," can be taken as evidence of this. (d) In this same socialist bloc, a network is emerging of extra-party organizations, quite disparate in nature, which seem increasingly to be taking on some of the flavor of Western new social movements. They have, however, the distinctive feature of an emphasis on the themes of human rights and anti-bureaucracy. (e) In the Third World, there are segments of those traditional national liberation movements still in power (as, for example, in Algeria, Nicaragua, and Mozambique) or heirs to such movements no longer in power (although "heritages" such as Nasserism in the Arab world tend to fritter). Of course, in countries with unfulfilled revolutions (such as South Africa or El Salvador), the movements, still necessarily in their mobilizing phase of struggle, have the strength and the characteristics of their predecessors in other states, when they were in that phase. (f) And, finally, in these same Third World countries, there are new movements that reject some of the "universalist" themes of previous movements (seen as "Western" themes) and put forward "indigenist" forms of protest, often in religious clothing.

It seems clear that all six varieties of movements are far from uniformly antisystemic. But all six varieties have some significant antisystemic heritage, some continuing antisystemic resonance, and some further antisystemic potential. Furthermore, of course, the six varieties of movements are not entirely limited geographically to the various zones as I have indicated. One can find some trans-zone diffusion, but the geographical segregation of varieties holds true, broadly speaking, for the moment.

There are, I believe, three principal observations to make about the relation of these six varieties of (potentially, partially, historically) antisystemic movements to each other. First, at the time of the Revolution of 1968, the six varieties tended to be quite hostile to each other. This was particularly true of the relation of the "old" to the "new" variety in each zone, as we have already noted. But it was generally true more widely. That is, any one of the six varieties tended to be critical of, even hostile toward, all five other varieties. This initial, multifaced mutual hostility has tended to diminish greatly in the subsequent two decades. Today, one might speak of the six varieties of movements showing a hesitant (and still suspicious) tolerance towards each other, which is, of course, far short of being politically allied with each other.

Secondly, the six varieties of movements have begun tentatively to debate with each other about the strategy of social transformation. One principal issue is, of course, the desirability of seeking state power, the issue that has fundamentally divided the three "old" from the three "new" varieties of movements. Another, and derived, issue concerns the structure of organizational life. These are, to be sure, issues that had been widely debated in the 1850–80 period and, at that time, more or less resolved. They have now been reopened, and are being discussed again, now, however, in the light of the "real-existing" experience of state power.

Thirdly, when and if this debate on global strategy will be resolved, even if the resolution takes the form of merging the six varieties of movements into one grand worldwide family, it does not follow that there will be a unified antisystemic strategy. It has long been the case, and will continue ever more to be so, that these movements have been strongly penetrated by persons, groups, and strata whose essential hope is not the achievement of an egalitarian, democratic world but the maintenance of an inegalitarian, undemocratic one, even if one necessarily different in structure from our existing capitalist world-economy (currently in its long structural crisis). That is to say, at the end of the debate among the movements, we shall most probably see a struggle within the possibly single family of movements between the proponents of an egalitarian, democratic world and their opponents.

Lessons

What lessons are we to draw from the Revolution of 1968 and its aftermath? What lessons indeed are we to draw from more than a century of worldwide, organized antisystemic activity? Here I think the format of theses is not reasonable. I prefer to lay out the issues in the form of queries. These are queries, I hasten to add, that cannot find their answers in colloquia alone, or in the privacy of intellectual discussion. These are queries that can be answered fully only in the praxis of the multiple movements. But this praxis of course includes, as one part of it, the analyses and debates in public and in private, especially those conducted in a context of political commitment.

Query 1: Is it possible to achieve significant political change without taking state power?

I suppose the answer to this depends first of all on how one defines "significant." But the question is a real one nonetheless. If the Marxists won the political debate with the Anarchists in the nineteenth century, and the political nationalists won their parallel debate with the cultural nationalists, the explanation was the compelling force of one assertion that they made: those with existing privilege will never cede it willingly, and will use their control of state violence to prevent significant change. It followed that ousting the privileged from state power was the prerequisite to significant change.

It seems quite clear that even today, in some countries (say, South Africa), there are governments representing privileged minorities that are resolutely unwilling to cede their privilege. In these countries it seems very implausible to suggest that any significant political change could occur in the absence of vigorous, and almost inevitably violent, political activity. South Africa is no doubt a quintessential instance of a state in which the majority of its citizens have never had *droit de cité* and have therefore never felt that the government was "theirs" in any sense whatsoever.

But today there is a large number of states in which the majority of the population believe that, in some sense, the government is "theirs." Most "post-revolutionary" regimes by and large enjoy this fundamental sense of popular support. This is no doubt true of the USSR, of China, and of Algeria. But if of Algeria, is it not also true of India? And is this not true of Sweden, where fifty years of Social-Democratic regimes have "integrated" the working class into political life? And what about France, or Germany? One could go on. Each national case has its specificity. But it is surely clear that there is a very large number of states in which popular support for the state is widespread, and where, therefore, a struggle for the primary accession to state power has little resonance. It is probably not very useful to suggest therefore that some of these state structures are "post-revolutionary," implying that the others are "pre-revolutionary." Most of them are in the same boat in terms of degree of popular support (and popular cynicism). To repeat, this is not true in states such as South Africa, where accession to state power by the majority still remains the primary political issue. But such states today are a minority.

Indeed, is not the prime issue in many states, and perhaps most especially in those that are self-consciously "post-revolutionary," the question of achieving the control by the "civil society" over the state? Is this not the heart of the internal political debate not only in the "socialist countries" but also in Latin America, and Southern Europe, and Southeast Asia, and Black Africa? "More democracy is more socialism," says Mr Gorbachev. But, if so, what is the function of an antisystemic *movement* in the USSR?

Query 2: Are there forms of social power worth conquering other than "political" power?

Obviously, there are other forms of social power – economic, cultural (Gramsci's "hegemony"), power over self (individual and "group" autonomy). And, obviously, individuals, groups, and organizations constantly seek such kinds of power. But how does the effort to attain this articulate with the *political* activity of antisystemic movements? In what sense will the achievement of more economic power, or more cultural power, or more power over self in fact contribute to a fundamental transformation of the world-system?

We are here before a question that has beset antisystemic movements since their outset. Is fundamental transformation the consequence of an accretion of improvements that, bit by bit and over time, create irreversible change? Or are such incremental achievements very largely a self-deception that in fact demobilize and hence preserve the realities of existing inequities? This is, of course, the "reformism-revolution" debate once again, which is larger than the constricted version of this debate symbolized by Eduard Bernstein versus Lenin.

That is to say, is there a meaningful strategy that can be constructed that involves the variegated pursuit of multiple forms of power? For this is what is suggested, at least implicitly, by a lot of the arguments of the new social movements that emerged in the wake of 1968.

Query 3: Should antisystemic movements take the form of organizations?

The creation of bureaucratic organizations as the instrument of social transformation was the great sociological invention of nineteenth-century political life. There was much debate about whether such organizations should be mass-based or cadre-based, legal or underground, one-issue or multi-issue, whether they should demand limited or total commitment of their members. But, for over a century, there has been little doubt that organizations of some kind were indispensable.

The fact that Michels demonstrated a very long time ago that these organizations took on a life of their own that interfered quite directly with their ostensible *raisons d'être* did not seem to dampen very much the enthusiasm to create still more organizations. Even the spontaneous movements of 1968 became transformed into many such organizations. This no doubt had consequences that made many of the post-1968 generation very uncomfortable, as may be seen in the acerbic debates between Fundis and Realos in the German Green movement.

The tension between the political efficacy that organizations represent and the ideological and political dangers they incarnate is perhaps unresolvable. It is possibly something with which we simply must live. It seems to me, however, that this is a question that has to be dealt with directly and debated thoroughly, lest we simply drift into two pointless factions of the "sectarians" and the "dropouts." The numbers of individuals throughout the world who are "ex-activists" and who are now "unaffiliated" but who wish in some way to be politically active has, I believe, grown very sharply in the wake of the post-1968 letdown. I do not think we should think of this as the "depoliticization" of the disillusioned, though some of it is that. It is rather the fear that organizational activity is only seemingly efficacious. But, if so, what can replace it, if anything?

Query 4: Is there any political basis on which antisystemic movements, West and East, North (both West and East) and South, can in reality join hands?

The fact that there are *six* varieties of antisystemic movements, an "old" and a "new" variety in each of the three different zones, seems to me no passing accident. It reflects a deep difference of political realities in the three zones. Do there exist any unifying political concerns that could give rise to a common worldwide strategy? Is there any evidence that, even if this wasn't true in the period following 1945, it is beginning to be true in the 1980s, and might be even more true in the twenty-first century?

Here we need more than pieties and wishful thinking. There has never existed heretofore international (that is, interzonal) solidarity of any significance. And this fact has given rise to much bitterness. Three things seem to me important. First, the immediate day-to-day concerns of the populations of the three zones are today in many ways strikingly different. The movements that exist in these three zones reflect their differences. Secondly, many of the short-run objectives of movements in the three zones would, if achieved, have the effect of improving the situation for some persons in that zone at the expense of other persons in other zones. Thirdly, no desirable transformation of the capitalist world-economy is possible in the absence of trans-zonal political cooperation by antisystemic movements.

This trans-zonal cooperation would have to be both strategic and tactical. It might be easier (albeit still not easy) to establish the bases of tactical cooperation. But strategic? It is probable that strategic collaboration can only be on the basis of a profound radicalization of the objectives. For the great impediment to trans-zonal strategic collaboration is the incredible socio-economic polarization of the existing world-system. But is there an objective (and not merely a voluntaristic) basis for such a radicalization?

Query 5: What does the slogan, "liberty, equality, fraternity" really mean?

The slogan of the French Revolution is familiar enough to us all. It seems to refer to three different phenomena, each located in the three realms into which we are accustomed to divide our social analyses: liberty in the political arena, equality in the economic arena, and fraternity in the socio-cultural arena. And we have become accustomed as well to debating their relative importance, particularly between liberty and equality.

The antinomy of liberty and equality seems to me absurd. I don't really understand myself how one can be "free" if there is inequality, since those who have more always have options that are not available to those who have less, and therefore the latter are less free. And, similarly, I don't really understand how there can be equality without liberty since, in the absence of liberty, some have more political power than others, and hence it follows that there is inequality. I am not suggesting a verbal game here but a rejection of the distinction. Liberty-equality is a single concept.

Can then fraternity be "folded into" this single concept of liberty-equality? I do not think so. I note first that fraternity, given our recent consciousness about sexist language, should now be banned as a term. Perhaps we can talk of comradeship. This brings us, however, to the heart of the issues raised by sexism and racism. What is their opposite? For a long time the lefts of the world preached one form or another of universalism, that is, of total "integration." The consciousness of the Revolution of 1968 has led to the assertion by those who most directly suffered from racism and sexism of the political, cultural, and psychological merits of building their own, that is separate, organizational, and cultural structures. At a world level, this is sometimes called the "civilizational project."

It is correct to assert that the tensions between universalism and particularism are the product of the capitalist world-economy and are impossible to resolve within its framework. But that gives us insufficient guide for future goals or present tactics. It seems to me that the movements after 1968 have handled this issue the easy way, by swinging back and forth on a pendulum in their emphases. This leaves the issue intact as a permanent confusion and a permanent irritant. If we are to think of a trans-zonal strategy of transformation, it will have to include a fairly clear perspective on how to reconcile the thrust for homogeneity (implied in the very concept of a trans-zonal strategy) and the thrust for heterogeneity (implied in the concept of liberty-equality).

Query 6: Is there a meaningful way in which we can have plenty (or even enough) without productivism?

The search for the conquest of nature and the Saint-Simonian moral emphasis on productive labor have long been ideological pillars not only of the capitalist world-economy but also of its antisystemic movements. To be sure, many have worried about excessive growth, and waste, and resource depletion. But, as with other such rejections of dominant values, how far can we, should we, draw the implications of the critiques?

Once again, it is easy to say that jobs versus ecology is a dilemma

produced by the current system and inherent in it. But once
again, this tells us little about long-term objectives or short-term
tactics. And once again, this is an issue that has profoundly
divided the antisystemic movements within zones, and even more
across the zones.

Concluding note

One of the principal implicit complaints of the Revolution of 1968
was that the enormous social effort of antisystemic movements
over the prior one hundred years had yielded so little global
benefit. In effect, the revolutionaries were saying, we are not
really farther along than our grandparents were, in terms of
transforming the world.

The criticism was a harsh one, no doubt a salutary one, but also
an unfair one. The conditions of the world-systemic revolution of
1968 were entirely different from those of the world-systemic
revolution of 1848. From 1848 to 1968, it is hard to see,
retrospectively, how the antisystemic movements could have acted
other than they did. Their strategy was probably the only one
realistically available to them, and their failures may have been
inscribed in the structural constraints within which they necessarily worked. Their efforts and their devotion were prodigious.
And the dangers they averted, the reforms they imposed probably offset the misdeeds they committed and the degree to which
their mode of struggle reinforced the very system against which
they were struggling.

What is important, however, is not to be a Monday morning
quarterback of the world's antisystemic movements. The real
importance of the Revolution of 1968 is less its critique of the past
than the questions it raised about the future. Even if the past
strategy of the "old left" movements had been the best possible
strategy for the time, the question still remained whether it was a
useful strategy as of 1968. Here the case of the new movements
was a far stronger one.

The new movements however have not offered a fully coherent
alternative strategy. A coherent alternative strategy is still today to
be worked out. It will possibly take ten to twenty more years to do
so. This is not a cause for discouragement; it is rather the occasion
for hard collective intellectual and political work.

6 ❧ Marx, Marxism-Leninism, and socialist experiences in the modern world-system

Marx and his ideas are flourishing, stand up better today than those of any other nineteenth-century analyst, and promise to remain central to social life in the world-system in the twenty-first century. Marxism-Leninism as a strategy and an ideology has played out its historic role and has become marginal to the ongoing political economy of the world-system. Socialist experiences in the modern world-system, if we can call them that, are in great disarray and may or may not survive in any form that will be recognizable as "socialist."

I propose to analyze Marxism-Leninism as an historical phenomenon of the modern world-system from its origins to today, in terms of responses to six questions: (1) why Leninism? (2) why a Leninist revolution in Russia first? (3) why Stalinism? (4) why a Soviet empire? (5) why de-Stalinization? (6) why *perestroika* and *glasnost*?

(1) Leninism or Bolshevism is conventionally said to have come into organizational existence in 1902 with Lenin's counter-draft to the text of Plekhanov for the Second Congress (the so-called Unification Congress) of the All-Russian Social-Democratic Labor Party that was held in the summer of 1903. As we know, the Congress resulted in a split of the party. Lenin proved himself an excellent political in-fighter and he emerged with control of a party that assumed (somewhat dubiously) the appellation of Bolsheviks.

Today it is commonplace to simplify the history of world socialist movements as the story of an historic split between two tendencies, one symbolized by Eduard Bernstein and one by Lenin, consecrated in organizational form after 1921 by the existence of two Internationals, the Second and the Third. This is equally simplified as the division between reform and revolution. One can always attack the simplism of simplifications, but for the first half of the twentieth century, this classic formulation seems to me essentially correct.

The key arguments of the "revisionists" derived from a straightforward and rather economistic understanding of the evolution of the world-system. They saw a process of inevitable technological advance bringing into existence an ever-larger industrial working class. They presumed it would have the political consequence of the inevitable extension of political rights (especially suffrage), presumably under the joint pressure of capitalist rationality and working-class struggle. They reasoned that, over the course of time, the industrial working class would dominate numerically the political arena, and thus they could quite simply vote themselves into power. Once that occurred, they could legislate an end to capitalism and the establishment of a socialist society. It followed from this reasoning that the optimal political tactic was to organize, politically and socially, as large a part of the working class (as well as their sympathizers) into a mass party.

The reasoning was clear and, to many, persuasive. The scenario, in reality, turned out to be only partially true. There was continued technological advance, and the size of the industrial working class did increase. Universal suffrage did become a reality. However, it was not true that the industrial working class came to represent a large majority of the voting population. Nor was it true that all workers voted for the socialist party. Second International parties did come to power in a whole series of countries. They did not however legislate an end to capitalism. They legislated, rather, the so-called welfare state.

Why was Lenin resistant to this reasoning? It was because he intruded other variables into the scenario. The first and most important variable upon which he insisted was the strength with which the capitalist strata would resist their liquidation. He presumed they would use their existing control of the state apparatuses to struggle by any means (fair or foul) to preserve their position. He thus thought that the concept that they could be voted out of power was totally chimerical. He insisted, therefore, that the only way the working class would come to power was by revolution, that is, by insurrection. He saw such struggles as politico-military and therefore insisted, quite plausibly, that an essential ingredient of success was a highly disciplined organization. His views on party structure followed quite logically. Since the bourgeoisie would use any means to stay in control, and since a politico-military struggle required a disciplined organization, the party should be composed of dedicated and more or less full-time cadres, and should operate, at least partially, underground. In this way, he reasoned, when the moment was ripe, the party could seize power and install a so-called dictatorship of the proletariat. However, his vision of what would happen once they came to power was not too different from that of the revisionists. The new government would legislate the end of capitalism and the establishment of a socialist society.

This reasoning also was clear, and also was persuasive to many. In point of fact, this scenario too in reality turned out to be only partially true. Insurrections were successful in only a few countries. Indeed, the Russian case itself can be thus described only partially. In fact, the case that most approximated Lenin's scenario would turn out to be that of China, where indeed a disciplined cadre party did organize a long politico-military struggle and did eventually seize power, installing a dictatorship of the proletariat. It is true that, wherever Third International parties came to power (by whatever means), they did legislate more or less the end of capitalism (in the narrow sense of the abolition of private property in most productive enterprises). Whether they established socialist societies has been a matter of controversy for some 70 years now, and never more so than in the last few years.

Lenin had an unspecified premise in his reasoning. He was struggling in Russia, and Russia was not Germany, *a fortiori* not Great Britain. That is to say, Russia was a country in which the technology was "backward" with reference to that of Western Europe and North America. Furthermore, Russia was a country which, except for the briefest of periods, did not even have a parliamentary system, much less the expectation that it would move to universal suffrage within a reasonable length of time. In any case, there were very few industrial workers even if there had been universal suffrage. The great majority of the population were rural workers and peasants. Hence, the revisionist scenario seemed totally irrelevant to the Russian situation, and one must admit that Lenin was essentially correct in that assessment. It seemed to him, therefore, that the only viable alternative was his own program. Whether this was correct or not is difficult in hindsight to assess, since everywhere the socialist movement moved in one or the other direction, either towards revisionism or towards Leninism (often but not always Marxism-Leninism).

(2) It is well known that the Russian Revolution of 1917 was a surprise in the sense that virtually everyone in the world socialist movement expected that the "first" socialist state would be Germany. This expectation was that of the Bolsheviks as well, even Lenin. Why no one, as of say 1900, believed that Great Britain, Marx's own candidate, would be the first socialist state is a question worth pursuing, but I cannot do it here. It does demonstrate, however, that in the reasoning of both revisionists and Leninists there were other hidden premises.

As we know, Lenin had a hard time persuading his colleagues to try to seize power in October 1917. And, in any case, everyone seemed to feel that the aberration of Russia preceding Germany would soon be corrected. Indeed, of course, many argued that the new Soviet state could not survive unless something occurred rapidly in Germany. We know this expectation was never fulfilled, and after about five years was finally abandoned.

Still, why did the expectation go awry? E.H. Carr, in trying to place the Russian Revolution in historical perspective, argues:

The same ambivalence which ran through Russian 19th century history marked the Bolshevik revolution. In one aspect it was a culmination of the westernizing process, in another a revolt against European penetration.[1]

In 1914, Russia was a European country, a great military power, and a country with a significant industrial sector. But, as an industrial country, it was clearly the weakest of the European states. In 1914, Russia was simultaneously a non-European (or

---

[1] Edward Hallett Carr, *The Soviet Impact on the Western World*. New York: Macmillan, 1947, p. 105.

non-Western) country, as well as primarily an agricultural country. But, as an agricultural country, it was clearly the strongest of the non-Western states. Hence, in our current language, Russia was either the weakest power in the core or the strongest in the periphery. It was, of course, both and was virtually the exemplar of what we today call a semiperipheral country.

I would argue that a Leninist strategy could succeed only in a semiperipheral country. Therefore, retrospectively, it is not at all surprising that the first socialist "revolution" occurred in Russia. It was probably the only place in which it was truly possible in that epoch. This was clear for three main reasons. Firstly, such an insurrection was not possible within core zones of the capitalist world-economy because the working class had too many options that seemed more attractive to them in the short run without their taking the enormous risks of insurrectionary activity. This has become clear beyond doubt in the years since 1917. It may not have seemed so obvious then.

Secondly, we have come to understand that the mobilization of mass support for an insurrectionary movement is not likely on the basis of class appeals exclusively. There must be added to the class appeals a strong dose of nationalist sentiment, what subsequently we have called anti-imperialism. But, in the core zones, a sense of nationalist achievement was for most of the countries behind them. Only in Germany and Italy could this possibly have been a major factor and, of course, these were as a consequence the two main loci of fascist movements in the interwar years.

Finally, a successful insurrection requires some significant sector of urban human infrastructure, a working class and an intelligentsia of some size and consciousness. Most peripheral zones did not yet have this in 1917, but Russia did. Thus, Marxism-Leninism emerged as the efficacious ideology for anti-systemic activity in the semiperiphery in the beginning of the twentieth century, as its subsequent history has demonstrated.

(3) Why Stalinism? Again it seems obvious in retrospect. The revolution was the work of a cadre party, by definition a small group. It started from the perspective that its task was politically very difficult since it presumed the relentless opposition of the local and the world bourgeoisie to its efforts. And, indeed, this presumption was confirmed by the experience of the Soviet

Union, not only in the first few years after 1917 but subsequently.

As a result of civil war and foreign intervention, Russia was a war-devastated country whose economic strength was not all that great in the first place. Just holding the state together was a monumental task, especially since Russia was an empire and not a nation-state. The rapid trend towards a one-party state, towards a mercantilist policy of "socialism in one country," and towards the conversion of the Third International into a worldwide support system for the beleaguered "first socialist state" are certainly not surprising outcomes of the situation.

What is the big question-mark, if one retraces Soviet history today, is whether the Bolsheviks would not have been better served by a different attitude towards the peasantry. Clearly, forced collectivization was a critical decision and a turning-point, creating a situation which still has repercussions today. But was it inevitable, or even wise? Marxist culture had certainly ill-prepared socialists anywhere to develop a politically intelligent stance towards the peasantry. They were, in the famous and infamous phrase of Marx, "a sack of potatoes." Lenin, one might have thought, could have done better. He was, after all, the author of an excellent analysis of the development of rural social relations in late Tsarist Russia. He had at least studied the peasantry, unlike Marx. But he was too caught up in the manipulative politics of a professional revolutionary to translate his somewhat academic study into lessons for political tactics. Did even Lenin really believe in NEP?

The fact is that Russia was a semiperipheral country, and its leadership (and here there is a continuity from von Witte to Stalin) defined its world-economic priority as the rapid industrialization of the country. Lenin's slogan that "Communism equals soviets plus electricity" continued to hang in big banners in Moscow until a very few years ago. The whole leadership believed in the "socialist accumulation of capital," and would boast, up to the 1980s, about their great success in pursuing this objective. If steel factories are the be-all and end-all of socialist planning, then there cannot be too much sympathy for the plight of a peasantry that was being confiscated and proletarianized. An occasional tactical retreat, yes; a basic accommodation, never!

It is easy to be a Bukharinite today. It is less clear that

Bukharin's moderate policies were politically feasible. In any case, they did not prevail. I believe the fundamental reason they did not prevail is that the majority of politically active elements in the 1920s were not really persuaded that the Soviet state could truly survive if they pursued his policies. But, of course, the forced collectivization created conditions which led directly (if not perhaps inevitably) to the terror and the purges.

Stalinism was further abetted by geopolitics. In the 1933–41 period, it was clearly the case that both Germany and the Western trio (US, UK, France) were maneuvering to see if there were some way they could destroy the Soviet state. Stalin's argument that his policies were defensive against an external and powerful enemy, and were the only possible way to defend the Soviet state, may not have been correct, but they persuaded many and in an important sense gave Stalinism some popular legitimacy. The period of the Great Patriotic War of course reinforced this legitimacy mightily.

Furthermore, there was a second external support we should not forget. We all presume too blithely that there was a shift in US policy towards the USSR from the accommodation of Roosevelt to the Cold War hostility of Truman and his successors. I disagree. It seems to me US policy was a continuous one, behind the change in rhetoric. The US wanted a Stalinist USSR with a mini-empire, provided it remained essentially within the 1945–48 borders. Stalinism served the US as ideological justification of and cement for its hegemony in the world-system. Stalinism was a moderating, not an exacerbating, influence on worldwide antisystemic forces. Stalinism guaranteed order in a third of the world, and the USSR could, in that sense, be thought of as playing the role of a "subimperialist" power for the US. From a US point of view, everything about the USSR has been going downhill since the death of Stalin. Witness the current deep embarrassment that the Gorbachev phenomenon is causing the US.

(4) Why did the USSR create an "empire" after 1945? Let us look carefully at what they did. There is no question that the USSR and the occupying Red Army brought to power Communist parties in six states where they could not have made it otherwise, either by elections or by insurrection. The six are, of course, Poland, Bulgaria, Romania, Hungary, Czechoslovakia, and the German Democratic Republic.

I think the explanation of these actions is simple and even mundane. First, the USSR feared a possible US military action against it and a resurrection of Germany, and wished to strengthen its military position. This was in fact a total misreading of US strategy, but it was nonetheless believed. Secondly, the USSR wished (and economically needed) war reparations, and felt that the only way they could be sure to get them was by taking them. And thirdly, the USSR actually feared the potential strength (and therefore independence) of indigenous Communist movements, and wished to ensure that the east European parties would be satellite parties.

Of course, this mode of installing Communist parties in power was bound to uproot whatever legitimacy they had as of 1945. The only possible (and temporary) exception was Czechoslovakia, where the Communist party had some genuine local strength. The purges of 1948–49 were indeed anti-nationalist, not anti-bourgeois-nationalist, but anti-Communist-nationalist. With the purges, the fig leaf was off, and it was only a matter of time that nationalist (and therefore anti-Soviet) sentiment would resurface in politically efficacious form.

By contrast, the USSR and the Red Army had nothing to do with the coming to power of Communist guerilla movements in Yugoslavia, Albania, and China. And it is, therefore, no accident that all three Communist governments had rather spectacular open breaks with the USSR in the postwar period. None of the three were ever satellites, and could not be said to have been part of a Soviet "empire." For a short while, they were allies, but no more. Stalin understood that from the beginning. That is why he advised the Chinese CP to come to terms with the Kuomintang, advice that was ignored. That is why he scotched the beginnings of a Yugoslav–Bulgarian federation that Dimitrov was trying to promote. And that is, of course, the reason why Soviet troops withdrew from Northern Iran in 1946 and the USSR scuttled the Greek Communist insurrection in 1947. Stalin was not merely not in favor of, but positively opposed to, the coming to power of indigenous, nationally legitimate Communist parties.

To be sure, the "empire" has turned out to be burden as well as benefit, but not a burden of which the USSR could so easily divest itself. After 1968 and the invasion of Czechoslovakia, we have come to talk of a Brezhnev doctrine, meaning the immutability of satellite status. Should we not rather call it the Brezhnev–Johnson doctrine? Did not Lyndon Johnson give Brezhnev the necessary assurances? And if so, why? The answer seems to me clear. The US wanted the USSR to continue to assume (for both good and ill) the burden of empire, and certainly did not wish to take the risks of disorder and the economic costs of assistance of successful de-satellitization. Johnson delayed the inevitable for 20 years. George Bush is squirming today before the difficulties caused by a de-satellitization at last in process.

(5) Why de-Stalinization? It seems a crazy question today. Who likes Stalinism? Obviously, everyone would want to change it. We have to remind ourselves that, as recently as the mid-1980s, there were many analysts outside and within the socialist countries that thought this was an impossible idea. There were even people who argued that Khrushchev's speech and the Sino-Soviet split were mere tricks or illusions. In 1953, Isaac Deutscher began to write in the weeks after Stalin's death a book forecasting "a break with the Stalin era." As he tells us in the Foreword: "My friends, among them eminent students of Soviet affairs, shook their heads skeptically."[2] The heart of Deutscher's prognosis lay in one sentence: "The economic progress made during the Stalin era has at last brought within the reach of the people a measure of well-being which should make possible an orderly winding up of Stalinism and a gradual democratic evolution."[3]

Deutscher should get enormous credit for the basic vision, but he turned out to be only partially right. What Deutscher had predicted came into practice as Khrushchevism, and Khrushchevism was a failure. Khrushchev was a failure not because he had an excitable temperament, but because he was still wedded to and believed profoundly in the developmentalism that had always been the basis of Soviet economic policy. We will bury you by the year 2000, he told Americans. It seems farcical now. It did not, however, seem farcical then, and we should analyze why. The remark was made during the period of incredible expansion of the capitalist world-economy that ran from *circa* 1945–67. Every-

---

[2] Isaac Deutscher, *Russia, What Next?* New York: Oxford University Press, 1953, p.v.
[3] *Ibid.*, p. 221.

one was "developing" then, but some were doing better than others. The growth rates in the Comecon countries were remarkable, and projected forward the USSR might have "caught up" with the US, if not by 2000, then a decade or two later.

These growth rates, furthermore, were not only high in comparison to the countries in the core, but looked particularly good when matched against countries in the Third World. Of course, Japan also had remarkable growth rates, but in the 1950s few noticed this. Soviet developmentalism therefore was not merely a source of pride to the Communist parties in power but a beacon for the national liberation movements of the Third World. In the 1950s, belief in the Soviet Union as a model of economic development was widespread, albeit, of course, never universal. And the explanation given for this success, particularly but not exclusively in the Third World, was the efficacy of Leninism. I say Leninism rather than Marxism-Leninism because, partly out of expediency partly out of cultural resistance, many Third World movements preferred to import the Leninism (particularly the party structures and the state planning) without importing the Marxism (particularly the concept of an internal class struggle and the Europocentrism).

Khrushchev was not innovating in being a developmentalist; he was, in fact, continuing the legacy of Stalin and Lenin. His innovation came in seeking to represent the interests of the cadres of the Soviet system who wanted two things: assurances against terrorism, and increased consumerism. His naïveté in the end was to think that one could control the process of loosening the reins without reforming the basic political structure. Khrushchevism represented a fundamental underestimation of the sociological transformation of the USSR as well as misreading of the functioning of the modern world-system. Khrushchevism represented in a way a belief in Soviet rhetoric, a sin of which Stalin was never really guilty.

The senior cadres who wanted what Khrushchev had to offer were appalled once they saw that they might be letting a genie out of the bottle. Brezhnevism represented the attempt to put the genie back in – always as we know, a futile attempt. The two elements that Khrushchev did not take into account were the degree of urbanization and transformation of the labor force of the USSR, and the cyclical rhythms of the capitalist world-economy.

When he opened the possibilities in the USSR (and hence in the Comecon countries as well) of some political liberalization and some consumerism, Khrushchev vastly underestimated the demand. It has long been a truism of sociological analysis that it is easier for a state to be totally repressive than to offer a small but inadequate amount of space for political and cultural pluralism. Opening a small space whets the appetite without satisfying it, and emboldens the demand for more. How much space is needed before political calm returns is difficult to estimate, but it is clear Khrushchev offered too little. The Brezhnev solution was obviously to move in reverse direction without, however, installing a directly life-threatening terror that would have cast the senior cadres back into fear. Such a reverse policy can work for a while, and did so under Brezhnev, both in the USSR and in Eastern Europe.

But the even greater error of Khrushchev was to be unaware of how the capitalist world-economy really works. The impressive growth rates were based primarily on an inefficient base of extensive growth with high labor-intensivity. For a while, and as long as the world-economy was expanding, this could result in a growth of GNP, even of GNP per capita. But the inefficiency of the methods meant that they reached a cap, and the increase in standard of living always lagged behind the increase in the core zones in the same period, if not behind that of most peripheral zones. Sooner or later, the socialist economies could not meet the expectations of improvement of an ever-larger stratum of persons who were sufficiently well-informed to be aware of the discrepancies. Of course, this was less severe in more efficient economies like the GDR and Czechoslovakia, but even there it was but a matter of time for there to be insufficient surplus to meet politically real demand.

When the downturn in the world-economy came, the economic processes in the socialist countries were not all that different from that of the Third World. In the 1970s, some countries benefited from oil rent, and the USSR was among them. Western financial institutions pressed loans upon all these countries in order to maintain world effective demand, and not a few socialist countries became among the largest per capita debtors, to suffer in the 1980s from a radical inability to service the debt, much less to repay it (or, if to repay it, to do so at the incredible human and social cost that Romania has incurred). And socialist countries, no less than Third World countries, found themselves in great difficulty trying to sell their products on the world market, to be "competitive" in the current jargon. Hence, the socialist countries no less than the Third World countries suffered from inflationary pressures and a declining standard of living. Like most of the Third World countries, the socialist countries began to seek refuge in (were pressed to seek refuge in) a liberalization of their markets. And, like most Third World countries, the increased opening to the market by the socialist countries has at best only slightly alleviated their economic difficulties.

(6) We can regard *perestroika* and *glasnost* as a conjunctural response to a general dilemma, and indeed I have just in effect described it in this way. But it is more than that. In the guise of a return to Leninism, it is an attempt by the elites to regroup in the wake of the collapse worldwide of (Marxism-)Leninism as an ideology and a strategy. In the process, the USSR is at last decolonizing (not only within the socialist camp but also within its own frontiers).

Everyone speaks of Gorbachev's dilemmas: the dilemma of a *perestroika* that isn't working yet; the dilemma of a *glasnost* that has not yet gone far enough to satisfy most people but has gone far enough to result in considerable internal turmoil; and, finally, the dilemma of a decolonization *octroyée à la de Gaulle*, without the favorable world economic climate from which de Gaulle bene-fited. All this is true, but in my view secondary. Gorbachev's main dilemma is that he hasn't got an alternative ideology and strategy to substitute for the defunct Marxism-Leninism. He is to be sure an excellent tactician. He is indeed liquidating the Cold War singlehandedly, and thereby doing more to guarantee world and Soviet evolution in a positive direction than any other contem-porary leader. But, in the end, what has happened to the socialist project?

I believe that we must reassess the socialist experiences conduc-ted under the aegis of Marxism-Leninism, seeing them primarily as an historically comprehensible but transient phenomenon in the historical development of the modern world-system. It is not that they have failed. The term "failure" assumes that there were plausible historical alternatives. I believe there were no such plausible alternatives to the social-democracy that emerged in the Western world, the Marxism-Leninism that took hold in the USSR and China at least, and to the national liberation movements that came to power in the Third World. This whole process can be said to cover a period of a century or so between the 1870s when these movements were in reality born, up to 1968, which I take as the symbolic turning-point in the history of these movements.[4]

The three kinds of movements represented, in fact, merely three variants of a single strategy: the seizure of state power by a party claiming to incarnate the popular will, and using state power to "develop" the country. This strategy has proved unworkable, but it was not possible to appreciate this in 1870 or even in 1945. The movements should not be faulted for being products of the historical limitations of their times. But we are now living in a different climate. René Dumont has said: *Finis les lendemains qui chantent*.[5] I do not believe myself however that utopianism is at an end. Quite the contrary. Perhaps it is only now that we can invent utopian utopias.[6]

The construction of socialism in this world, if it is to occur, is still before us – as an option, but scarcely as a certainty. The so-called real existing socialist experiences can teach us much by negative example and a little by positive example. It is well to

[4] See my "1968, Revolution in the World-System: Theses and Queries," reprinted here as chapter 5.
[5] Paris: Seuil, 1983.
[6] I have previously discussed the relation between Marxisms and utopias in my "Marxisms as Utopias: Evolving Ideologies," *American Journal of Sociology*, XCI, 6, May 1986, 1295–308. In that article, I argued:
   "Utopias are always ideological. Here Engels (and Marx) was right, provided one remembers that they were wrong in the implicit utopia involved in believing that there could ever be an end to history, a world in which ideologies no longer existed. If we are to make progress, it seems to me we have not only to accept contradiction as the key to explain social reality but also to accept its enduring inescapability, a presumption alien to orthodox Marxism. Contradiction is the human condition. Our utopia has to be sought not in eliminating all contradiction but in eradicating the vulgar, brutal, unnecessary consequences of material inequality. This latter seems to me intrinsically a quite achievable objective" (p.1307).

remember that in the end Marxism-Leninism functioned in reality more as an ideology of national development than as an ideology of socialist construction. National development is however essentially an illusory concept within the framework of a capitalist world-economy.[7] It will never be achieved, even in a partial way, by most countries. The reason that Marxism-Leninism is becoming defunct today as an ideology is because all developmentalist ideologies are becoming defunct.

Marxism, however, did not start out as an ideology of national development, and is not doomed to be understood only in this constrictive fashion. There are other possible readings of Marx. And in the coming decades there can be, probably will be, much further thinking and praxis that may permit us to arrive at a new ideological consensus, a new scientific epistemology, a new historiography that will incorporate Marx's fundamental insights and values and, in a Marxist way, go beyond them to a new *Aufhebung* that may permit the construction of a more democratic, more egalitarian world.

---

[7] I argue this in some detail in "Development: Lodestar or Illusion?" *Economic and Political Weekly*, XXIII, 39. Sept. 24, 1988, 2017–23.

7 ❧ The Brandt report

The Brandt Report is a classic document, the kind that future archaeologists of knowledge will read to understand the mentality of the modern world. It is in a sense a quintessential testament to Kantian or Enlightenment liberalism. It touches all the bases, not once but over and over. It talks of moral imperatives, worldwide moral values, and a global civilization. It asserts the objectives of equity and justice. It insists on the moral obligation to survive and wants to bring the world from chaos to order. It asks that we aim at a global community based on contract rather than status, on consensus rather than compulsion. It exhorts us to aim at a global community, or at least a global responsibility. It reminds us that for development to be meaningful, the focus has to be not on machines or institutions but on people.

And throughout the Report, like a litany, comes the refrain that justice and mutual self-interest are, if not identical, at least not contradictory. It argues that what is good or necessary for the poor and very poor nations is good for the better-off areas as well. It admits that the "restructuring" for which it calls will create minor pains but insists it must be done because it will prevent or remedy greater pains.

Nor does the Report merely remain at this level of generality. It is an extraordinary review of virtually every specific issue related to global development that has been analyzed and debated over the past 30 years. No question of any importance has been evaded. On each issue, almost without exception, the Commission comes down on the side of reform, on the side of global liberalism if you will, albeit always in the prudent, rational tones of a patient, persistent advocate. In the welter of specific recommendations, one is often hard-pressed to know from this sober document what are the real priorities. At a few points however the Commission allows itself absolute modifiers, and in these the theme is the same. On page 43, the Commission says: "The South needs, *above all*, finance." And on page 237, it says: "The *most urgent* need is for the programme of large-scale transfer of funds to be stepped up substantially from year to year during the final two decades of this century." And, in its Emergency Programme for 1980–85, the first item on the list is "a large-scale transfer of resources to developing countries," although it adds that such a global transfer forms an interlocking program with three other items – an international energy strategy, a global food program, and a start on some major reforms in the international economic system – the four items being of equal importance.

Who is the audience for a report like this? It is claimed that the Report is addressed to everyone, North and South, the West of the North and the East of the North. But it is clearly not so. The Soviet Union is adjured from time to time to realize that it too must be involved in this process of "restructuring" – as one of the great protagonists in the control of armaments the Commission sees as essential, as a part of the North in North–South negotiations. But these repeated pleas, as well as occasional assertions about the important role China must play, have a perfunctory air about them. The fact is that none of the major thrusts of the report depend on Soviet collaboration; the most they require is the absence of intensive, active hostility – a posture the USSR has already adopted in the discussions concerning the so-called new international economic order.

Nor is the audience the South. To be sure, every once in a while, when the report has called for some specific policy on the part of countries in the North, the Commission adds that the South must do something or other; or else they reassert the right of the South to find original paths to or definitions of development. But these passages read like apologies, to fend off know-nothing critiques in the North about the South not pulling its weight, or angry protests in the South about the paternalism of the liberals of the North.

The report is clearly addressed to public opinion in the North (and, to be more specific, in the West of the North). Indeed the Commission says so in explaining to the leaders of the South why they too must be liberal:

Leaders in the South shoulder the bulk of responsibilities. They should also be aware how important it is that public opinion in the North is convinced that measures of international reform which need support will really affect the living conditions of their people as a whole. (p.17).

Of what is this Commission trying to persuade public opinion in the North? They tell us their problem at the outset: "Many people in government, and elsewhere, may consider this to be the worst possible moment for advocating radical changes" (p.12). But, says the Commission, on the contrary, prolonged recession is the very moment for "bold initiatives." In any case, the Commission reassures us:

Our proposals are not revolutionary; some are perhaps a little ahead of current thinking, others have been on the table for many years. We envisage them as part of a process of negotiated reform and restructuring. And we hope that the understanding of their interrelationships will strengthen the will for change. (p.66).

The Commission is right. Their proposals are not in any way revolutionary. They are determinedly reformist in nature. Quite aside from the question of whether reformism is an appropriate or plausible remedy to the many social dilemmas the Commission describes so clearly, there is the question as to whether this is a moment when reformist measures will in fact be adopted. Does the Commission itself believe their proposed reforms are practical politics? They say they believe it, but permit me to be skeptical.

In a striking self-image, the Commission asserts: "It is not enough . . . to sit around tables talking like characters in Chekhov plays about insoluble problems" (p.47). Yet, speaking about population projections, the Commission remarks: "It is easy to feel a sense of hopelessness at these prospects" (p.106). And, speaking of the history of North–South discussions, the Commission is sober: "We were conscious . . . that many negotiations on these issues had ended in stalemate . . . There is no alternative to dialogue itself and to further negotiation" (p.264). Finally, most wistfully of all, the Commission avers: "Both North and South have an interest in the preservation of hope" (p.77).

Are we in such a bad way then, that we must assert as our objective not the achievement of the good society or the transformation of the world but merely the preservation of hope? So it seems, or so it seems at least to this intelligent, sophisticated, and informed group incarnating world liberalism.

I believe that the next 20 years of North–South negotiations are not going to be more significant or efficacious than the last 20 years, and I believe the evidence for this lies in the very structure of the Report as I have analyzed it. An appeal of the liberals among the powerful to their compeers to make reforms in the interest of equity, justice, and heading off worse has never had any significant effect in the past several hundred years except in the wake of direct and violent rumblings by the oppressed, and it will have no more effect now. Furthermore, I believe the Commission members must know this too.

Nor do I believe that if all the multiple reforms that the Commission advocates were in fact carried out the process of world polarization and ecological and human disaster that has been the *increasing* reality of the capitalist world-economy over its history would in fact slow down. I suspect, in fact, it would increase still further.

Let us look at one of the Commission's casual and orthodox generalizations which is, I believe, profoundly wrong. The Commission says of industrialization that Latin America, Asia, and Africa are today following in the footsteps of Europe and North America, "a development which is already beginning to change the pattern of comparative advantage in the world-economy" (p.172). The Commission further argues that this industrialization "involves a profound transformation of society" and that the "transition from the country to the city and the adoption of new lifestyles and attitudes have far-reaching consequences" (p.173) – consequences which we are led to infer are beneficial.

In fact, the involvement of various parts of the world as peripheral zones of the capitalist world-economy has not been historically beneficial to their populations, and the fact that some of these zones are being restructured today to become "newly-industrializing countries" is no more beneficial and has *not* changed the pattern of comparative advantage in the world-economy. All that has happened is that, in the normal cycle of events, productive activities that once were high-profit, high-wage, and high-technology, like textiles, later steel, later electronics, as they lose this quality, are shuffled off to peripheral zones of the world-economy, while today's core zones are seeking to develop the leading industries of the next era – biotechnology, microprocessors, advanced forms of energy production. Far from reducing unequal exchange, this "new international division of labor" will increase it. And it is very doubtful indeed whether it can be said that the quality of life of the 18–23-year-old girls who staff the factories of the newly industrializing countries is better than that of their mothers 30 years ago.

For a report that was written by a Commission largely composed of political figures, politics is strangely absent from it. Nowhere is there a hint that the world is going through a reshuffling of alliances in the North which, until it is completed and stabilized, doubtless renders politically impossible the realization of the reforms advocated by the Commission, even were they all desirable. And, since this reshuffling is not adumbrated, obviously the Commission could not treat its implications for the North–South division of labor.

Nor does there figure in this report in any way the existence of vast social *movements* – socialist and/or nationalist in character – that have been the motor force of much that has happened in the past 30 years and whose role is bound to increase. One would think from the Report that the "negotiations" are and will be exclusively between states. This seems very poor political prognosis to me.

The Commission seems to know this but wishes it were not so. Speaking of the "search for increased self-reliance and economic independence," the Commission asserts: "This thrust does not imply that the South wants to dissociate or 'delink' itself from the North" (p.134). No doubt this is true for some in the South, but surely not for many others. The Commission must obviously have been talking to different persons from the South than I, but I have heard a lot of demand lately precisely for "delinking."

This is perhaps why this Report is more than an exercise in Chekhovian futility. It is a message to the West that the ideology of "delinking" – an ideology that is profoundly antisystemic – has in fact been gaining ground over the ideology of "development."

The Commission's "programme for survival" may be that of the survival of the system. But Chekhov was describing a social situation that was in fact resolved (or if not resolved, then profoundly affected) by first disintegration and then revolution. The only program for survival is the creation of a socialist world order, and "negotiations" between North and South will only have a marginal effect upon achieving such a world order.

8 ❧ Typology of crises in the world-system

Crisis in the world-system

The theme "typology of crises" suggests a multiplicity of crises. The argument of this paper, however, is that, in spatio-temporal terms, there is only a single "crisis" which, in structural terms, manifests itself in three different spheres of social action.

One must start, of course, by indicating what one means by "crisis." It is an overused term, appropriated regularly for every downturn in any cyclical curve on any scale. It is also a term with negative connotations. A crisis tends to mean something that one wishes to "overcome" as rapidly as possible, lest dire consequences (often unspecified) result.

This is not, however, what I shall mean by "crisis." I shall use "crisis" to refer to a rare circumstance, the circumstance in which an historical system has evolved to the point where the cumulative effect of its internal contradictions make it impossible for the system to "resolve" its dilemmas by "adjustments" in its ongoing institutional patterns. A crisis is a situation in which the demise of the existing historical system is certain and which *therefore* presents those found within it with a real historical choice: what kind of new historical system to build or create.

Let me review my assumptions here, so that we may be very clear what we are discussing. There are six assumptions hidden in that brief description of a crisis.

(1) The meaningful unit of social analysis is an historical system, an ongoing process of a social division of labor organized

along some fundamental principles (or what is sometimes called a "mode of production"). This entity, the historical system, exists in real space and time which are part of its definition and must be specified. The space, however, is not necessarily the same at all points in time. That is, a system may "expand" (or "contract"). To speak of a "division of labor" implies the existence of a set of structured production processes that are located in some political framework and have some cultural expression, although these do not have to be simple ones.

(2) Every historical system has a life – a beginning, a development, and (eventually) an end. While the length of this life has of course varied, many of the larger-scale systems that have existed (the "world-systems") have had lives of 400–500 years or more. The structures that underlie such historical systems constitute the *longue durée* of Braudel. Within this *longue durée*, there are cyclical processes which constitute the *conjonctures*. Distinguishing between conjunctural and structural processes, that is, between the cyclical rhythms and the secular trends of a particular historical system, is a crucial element in the analysis.

(3) Contradictions exist within all historical systems. Contradictions do not refer to conflicts which, of course, also exist. Contradictions refer to structural pressures that force groups to move in two opposite directions at the same time. Since groups are normally reasonable and self-interested and not schizophrenic, the reason they move in opposite directions at the same time is that their immediate interests conflict with their long-run interests. In order to resolve those immediate problems occasioned by the cyclical rhythms, they engage in behavior that in turn creates secular trends that undermine the viability of the historical system.

(4) Since contradictions are unavoidable, it follows that every historical system will eventually undermine its own ability to survive. That is why we can speak of the inevitable demise of historical systems. However, from the standpoint of individual life cycles, this process is a slow one, and there is only a limited degree to which groups can quicken the pace of this inevitable demise by any sort of voluntaristic "great leap

forward." This is not to say that organized opposition has no function within an historical system. It is rather to say that organized opposition is itself the product of the system, endogenous to it, and therefore part of the same secular development of the system's structures.

(5) When the contradictions reach a certain level of intensity, one can say that the historical system enters into "crisis." That is to say, it becomes relatively clear that the continuing development of the system along the lines it has been going (and indeed will continue to develop) will not be viable for much longer. Demise is in view. The adjustments that continue to be made to resolve the continuing cyclical difficulties have begun so to transform the structure that it begins to disintegrate (somewhat analogously to how a vehicle rattles and eventually falls apart when it climbs over a certain speed level). This period of crisis can also be called a period of transition. In an historical system that has existed for 500 years or more, such a transition may be of a length of a century or more.

(6) While demise is certain, since contradictions are certain, what comes after the transition is historically open. There is no inevitable secular line of human history, which guarantees that every successive phase be progress over every previous phase. Quite the contrary. We know many clear instances where successor systems were morally on a par with predecessor systems, and some where there was outright regression. On the other hand, we also know of instances where there was progress. Progress is very possible; it is merely not inevitable.

  Whereas, within the ongoing structural processes of an historical system, there is little role for voluntaristic "speeding up" of the contradictions, at the moment of crisis or transformation, the role of politico-moral *choice* expands considerably. It is on these occasions that it can be truly said that "man makes his own history . . ."

Given these six assumptions, I am somewhat reluctant to accept the question, "world crisis or world transformation"? Crisis as I have defined it necessarily means transformation. The question rather is, our world crisis is world transformation into what? And will the successor historical system (or systems) be worse, the same, or better? That is, our historical choice is a real one, which is what justifies this project on "new social thought."

My discussion heretofore has been somewhat abstract. I have been discussing how *any* historical system works. But we are not living in any historical system. We are living in a very specific one, the modern world-system or the capitalist world-economy. Let me therefore restate my six assumptions in terms of the specific parameters of this particular historical system.

(1) The modern world-system is a capitalist world-economy. That is a description of its formal structure and its mode of production, the two not being separable. It is a world-economy in that the boundaries of its social division of labor are large and cover multiple cultural arenas (hence, a "world"), and it does not have a single unifying political structure (hence not a "world-empire"). It does however have a political superstructure. That superstructure is the network of "sovereign states," members of and defined by an "interstate system" whose social and political reality and importance is far greater than its extraordinarily thin organizational apparatus might suggest.

This world-economy is capitalist in that it is based on the operation of a "law of value," which involves the distribution of rewards to those who give priority to the endless accumulation of capital. This does not mean that everyone operates on the basis of the law of value, simply that the institutional mechanisms of the world-economy are designed to reward and punish materially on the basis of adherence or not to these principles.

The capitalist world-economy has developed certain systematic cultural pressures designed to further its operation. Those pressures that seek to discipline and channel the work force are those we have come to call racism and sexism. Those pressures that seek to discipline and channel the world's cadres or "middle" strata are those we have come to call rationality or universalism or "science."

This capitalist world-economy is not the first historical system of this variety that has ever existed, but it is the first one of its kind that has survived for any length of time. Therefore it is the first one which has allowed the capitalist mode of production to unfold itself fully and realize its potentialities. The reason why previous world-economies did not survive has to do with the inherent frailty of this organizational form in the face of coexisting world-empires. The reason why this particular instance survived, consolidated itself, and then ultimately absorbed and destroyed all its coexisting world-empires is a complex story that is not relevant to our presentation here.

(2) The modern world-system came into existence in the sixteenth century, primarily in Europe. By a series of processes internal to itself, this world-system expanded continually but not continuously until, by the middle or end of the nineteenth century, it was able to incorporate into its social division of labor all the geographic zones on the earth. It thereby created an historically original situation. For the first time in the history of humanity, only one historical system now existed on earth. This, as we shall see, is one of the several causes of its later "crisis."

This capitalist world-economy is still today in existence and still today includes in its social division of labor all the geographic zones of the earth. Furthermore, there are no states today that are not part of the interstate system, which remains the political superstructure of the capitalist world-economy. The cultural pressures of which we spoke still permeate the social realities of all areas of the globe.

(3) The contradictions of this system are multiple and complex. Still there are two broad contradictions that stand out, one in the economic sphere and one in the political sphere.

In the economic sphere, the basic contradiction lies in the curious double role of the accumulator of capital. On the one hand, the accumulator of capital is in competition with every other accumulator of capital, and therefore perpetually seeks to expand the gap in his own enterprises between his "costs of production" and "sales price in the market." This drives him to engage in cost-reducing behavior (including a constant desire to reduce the costs of labor) and in price-raising behavior (including using political and quasi-political mechanisms to constrain the market in monopolistic directions which favor him). The true capitalist must be a cutthroat capitalist, and both workers and other accumulators of capital are his natural opponents.

On the other hand, the good functioning of the system depends on certain politico-cultural guarantees for the operation of such competitive behavior that push the individual entrepreneur in the direction of creating greater effective demand (including increasing the global share of revenue of working strata) and cooperative action with competitive entrepreneurs to reduce disruption of economic activity (whether because of worker unrest or of inter-state "non-economic" rivalry).

(4) This is a contradiction. The accumulator of capital must both lower the cost of labor and increase it; he must struggle against other accumulators of capital and cooperate with them. In fact, the contradiction works itself out in temporal terms. <u>In the short run, the accumulator of capital is cutthroat. In the middle run he is "cooperative." And, in the long run, the system is undermined.</u> It is undermined because a crucial feature of a capitalist system is that the factors of production – land, labor, capital – are only partially "free" to flow at will on a hypothetical pure market. The "unfree" aspects are not mere survivals or anachronisms; they are mechanisms of reducing real costs and increasing real sales prices, and hence of widening the margin of profit.

In order to solve short-run economic contractions, the accumulators of capital, acting as a class, tend to move in the direction of their middle-run "cooperative" behavior. In particular, they sporadically accede to some redistribution of surplus-value to working strata in order to recreate and expand effective demand, thus permitting renewed expansion. This solves the middle-run problem. However, over the long run, it means a "freeing" of the factors of production, which means a reduction in long-run profit margins.

This is not the only contradiction, although it is itself an enormous one. There are political consequences to the middle-run solutions to short-run stagnations. The economic transformations they bring about push towards the grouping together of oppressed strata as well as the increased visibility of surplus extraction (precisely via the "freeing" of factors of production). Hence, as time goes on, oppressed strata are more and more able to rebel, and more and more ready to do so. By the nineteenth century, the level of possibility and will had reached the point that we began to see the emergence of antisystemic movements in their two classical forms (the socialist movements and the nationalist movements).

This political development threatened the logic of the system –

endless accumulation of capital – in two ways. First, it strengthened the hands of the world's working strata in the constant battle
over the division of surplus-value, and therefore threatened
long-run profit margins. Secondly, in order to counter the
working strata politically, the accumulators of capital have been
forced to turn over an ever-greater share of surplus-value to their
agents and defenders, the cadres or "middle" strata, thereby also
threatening long-run profit margins.

(5) Beginning with the First World War and the Russian
Revolution, and greatly accelerating after 1945, the economic
secular trend to full commodification (as opposed to partial
commodification) plus the exhaustion of external arenas in which
to expand and thereby reduce the overall percentage of commodification on the one hand, and the political secular trend to a
double squeeze on long-run profit margins (as opposed to short-
run ones) on the other hand have combined to create the situation
we can call "crisis" of the capitalist world-economy. In some ways
this is less visible economically than it is politically and culturally.
The worldwide "family" of antisystemic movements has grown
ever stronger, ever bolder, ever more diverse, ever more difficult
to contain. Opposition is pervasive and persistent. To be sure, it
takes different forms in China and the US, in Iran and in El
Salvador. I am not suggesting any crude homogenization of the
multiplicity of forms of dissent – the national liberation movements, the proletarian insurgencies, the civilizational "renais-
sances" and defiances, the countercultures, the renewing of
religiosities. But the sense of "crisis" among the defenders of the
world's status quo reflects their dismay at this flowering of
tendencies which seem on the point of getting out of control.

The only thing the accumulators of capital can really do is more
of the same. They can treat these rebellions as part of the
short-run problems to which there are middle-run solutions,
solutions of "cooptation." And, in the middle run, this continues
to work, even work very well. (Reflect upon the temper of the
world in the period *circa* 1968–70, and the temper some short
fifteen years later.) But this "cooptation" is a process that, in the
long run, attacks both the economic and the political underpinnings of the system (a position long held by ultra-
conservatives, who are correct in their predictions, but incorrect

in believing there are real middle-run alternatives for the ruling strata).

(6) It is thus that we say we are living in the "transition," the period of inevitable decline and "eventual demise" of the capitalist world-economy. But where we are heading? We may be heading towards a "socialist world order." Certainly this is the direction in which a large part of the "family" of worldwide antisystemic movements claim we ought to move. Indeed, most of them assert we are in fact moving, and moving inevitably, in that direction. I beg to differ about the sense of inevitability.

There is a contradiction built into the mode of operation of the antisystemic movements themselves. And there is a contradiction built into the mode of operation of the world's reflective structures, the "sciences." These two contradictions belie the easy optimism of the Enlightenment. They create the reality of our historical choice. It is thus these two "derived crises" – the crisis of the movements and the crisis of the sciences – that ought to be the primary concern of those who wish to transform the world. The basic "crisis," that of the capitalist world-economy, is relatively straightforward and simple. That system will come to an end. But what comes next is a function of how we resolve the crisis of the movements and the crisis of the sciences. And here we have a real voice in the matter.

Crisis in the movements

The "crisis of the movements" is not a mere matter of cyclical ups and downs. Of course, there have always been "moments" or "periods" of relative defeat as well as relative victory for the movements. This is normal. The "crisis of the movements" is the crisis brought about by their victories rather than by their defeats. And the crisis is structural, not moral. That is, it is to be explained primarily not by "betrayals" but by "objective pressures."

The movements, when they began to organize in the nineteenth century, were faced with a very elementary problem: what path of political action promised to be efficacious? It seemed clear to both socialist and nationalist movements that the most available locus of real political power lay in the states, in the governmental structures of the various sovereign states. Or at least this seemed clear to the majority of the activists. If this were true, then it followed logically that the most likely way in which the system could be transformed would be by the obtaining in one way or another control of state power. As Kwame Nkrumah was to put it in the 1950s, "Seek ye first the political kingdom . . ." This political strategy, the primacy of the acquisition of state power, became the accepted and practiced strategy of virtually all the major antisystemic movements and remained so up to very recently. It is still, even today, the accepted strategy of the majority of the movements.

This strategy had its opponents in the nineteenth century. There were some, especially in the early years of the movements, who preached a deep suspicion of state power, even in the prospective hands of the people. They were called "anarchists" or, in another version, "cultural nationalists." This opposing group, however, lost out in the internal antisystemic movements' debate because they could not demonstrate that there was in fact any practical way of transforming the world as long as the apparatuses of "legitimate force" lay in the hands of the defenders of the *status quo*. The choice, said those who advocated the state-oriented strategy, was between obtaining state power and being suppressed. This was a telling argument, and it persuaded the majority of activists.

Once that debate was resolved and, as a practical matter it was resolved by the late nineteenth century, the only remaining strategic question was the path to the acquisition of state power, over the degree to which armed insurrection was an essential ingredient. The argument is famous: between "reform" and "revolution," between the Second and Third Internationals, between constitutional decolonization and protracted guerrilla struggle.

A rapid survey of twentieth-century political history will make clear that, especially since 1945, the antisystemic movements have been remarkably successful in achieving their nineteenth-century objective of state power. In the Western industrialized countries, the Social-Democratic parties have acquired the "right" to govern 50 per cent of the time, more or less. This "right" has meant that they could enact basic legislative changes known generically as the "welfare state" which can be shown to have benefited working strata in those countries in various specific ways.

In a second band of countries running largely from eastern Europe to eastern Asia, movements derived from Third International origins have come to power and created "socialist states." This has meant that they have nationalized means of production and engaged in a program of relatively rapid industrialization. They have also extended social benefits to the citizenry.

In a third band of countries, largely in South and Southeast Asia, the Middle East, Africa, Latin America, and the Caribbean – sometimes called the "Three Continents" or the "South" – nationalist and national liberation movements have come to power in many, indeed in most of them. These movements have achieved political independence where it had been lacking, quite often some "nationalization" of basic resources, some "development" of infrastructure, and some collective political leverage on the world scene. Certainly the "life chances" of the stratum defined by being urban and having some education, at least that stratum, can be said to have benefited from these changes.

Thus, at one level, one could say the movements have been magnificently successful. Furthermore, the pattern is continuing such that even more such "successes" are in prospect in other states. Yet it is no secret that there is great discontent throughout the world with (a) the Social-Democrats in power, (b) the Communists in power, (c) the nationalists in power. I am talking about discontent, not as expressed by conservative forces, but as expressed within the broad ranks of supporters of and militants in antisystemic movements.

The basic complaint is threefold. The first complaint is that whatever the list of achievements of antisystemic movements in power, there are large segments of the population who have been in some sense "left out" of the benefits these achievements have bestowed. Those "left out" are often those defined as socially more "marginal" than the presumed core of the political support of antisystemic movements: ethnic/national minorities, migrant populations, women, "peasants." At first, it could be argued that this phenomenon was temporary. As time went on, many began to wonder if it were not "structural," and therefore the consequence of the basic strategy of the movements.

The second complaint is that the movements have been "coopted," that is, that they are no longer playing a "revolutionary" role, even if they once were. The evidence presented is that the movements in power have toned down, often eliminated, their real solidarity with movements not in power. At first, it could be argued that this phenomenon represented momentary tactical prudence. As time went on, many began to wonder whether this "tactical retreat" was not the necessary condition of the assumption of state power within an interstate system.

The third complaint is that the movements in power, although ruling in the name of the working class or of the people, engaged in behavior that might be considered repressive or exploitative on behalf of a smaller group who shared that power. At first, it could be argued that the repression was directed at "counterrevolutionary" forces. As time went on, many began to wonder if the "repressiveness" was not itself the result of the "cooptation," in turn the result of many persons having been "left out" of the revolutionary process from the outset.

The consequence of the cumulation of complaints has been threefold. In the first place, in each of the three main arenas of the world-system, new movements have arisen whose main target has become the "old movements in power." In the Western countries, these new social movements have taken the form of a panoply of organizations not under a single organizational structure: minority movements, women's movements, antiwar movements, Green and ecology movements, sexual preference movements, etc. In the socialist zone, these new movements have also taken diverse forms: "reform" movements inside the Communist parties (the Cultural Revolution, humanist Communism, even de-Stalinization – and now *perestroika*) and movements outside the party (most notably Solidarność, but also "peace" movements). And in the Three Continents, these new movements have often taken the form of religious renewal movements.

What all these "new" movements have in common with each other is their deep suspicion of the "old" movements that have achieved power, their sense that the movements in power are bureaucratic and governed by the groups whose current objectives are hard to distinguish from those of the defenders of the *status quo* in the world-system.

The second consequence is, therefore, great confusion everywhere, as the "old" lefts are under attack from the multiple "newer" lefts. This has led to a mixture, worldwide, of sudden outbursts of "revolutionary enthusiasm" (for example Iran in the period immediately before and after the fall of the Shah or Poland from 1980 to 1982) and longer periods of relative demobilization, a demobilization that can be sensed among militants of both the older and the newer movements.

The relative demobilizations are a negative consequence. There is however a third, a more positive, consequence. The "confusion" has broken the ideological crust to some extent and has led (or is leading) to some rethinking of fundamental strategy. It is not a question of what should have been done in the 1860s (or even the 1950s), but what ought to be done in the 1990s and thereafter. The question that has been opened, or rather reopened, is whether the *primary* path to the social transformation of the world is via the acquisition of state power by the movements separately in each state.

The problem, of course, is that it is by no means obvious that any clear alternative exists, as debates within such diverse loci as Solidarność, the German Greens, and the Iranian revolutionary groups indicate. These movements, as so many others, have included some who rejected state power as an objective and others who have come, however reluctantly, to embrace it. The question remains, therefore, wide open. There is not yet an alternative collective strategy. I am merely arguing that it is on our agenda.

Crisis in the sciences

The crisis in the sciences is not as different from the crisis in the movements as one might initially think. It has long been accepted that the rise of modern science and the rise of the modern world-system have been coordinate and closely-linked phenomena. Science as we have known it is the prime intellectual expression of "modernity." It seems to have had three fundamental premises. The first is that everything in the real world is knowable. That is to say, every empirical phenomenon is considered amenable to an explanation that would call upon generalized statements of processes. Nor is any empirical phenomenon so occult or mystical that the generalizations one needs to invoke for the explanation could not eventually be discovered, even if not presently known.

The second premise is that the wider the generalization the better, and that ultimately all relevant generalizations can be stated in terms of universal laws, applying without regard to space-time, which in a peculiar sense is seen as a "neutral" container for empirical reality rather than as a part of this empirical reality.

The third premise is that the *only* way one can really "know" the real world is via science and that any other form of purported knowledge is subjective, unverifiable, and irrelevant. It follows from this that the only way one can consciously "manipulate" the real world – and it is further assumed that the world is, in fact, manipulable – is via science.

Each of these premises has been contested, and the battle to make these premises hegemonic was long and fierce, but it is unquestionably the case that the battle was basically won by the mid-nineteenth century. One of the last ramparts of resistance to fall was the application of these premises to that narrow part of the real world that involved human beings most directly – the social organization of human activity. It is only in the nineteenth century that history and the social sciences came to have *droit de cité*. Indeed, it is only then that most of our conceptual terminology, including the very names of the so-called disciplines, was born.

There are two things to be noted about the emergence of what I call the historical social sciences. They were in large part the continuing expression of the *ideological* revolution entailed by the French Revolution as a world-historical phenomenon. They also shared the fundamental ambiguity of the French Revolution as a phenomenon that was a natural development within the framework of the capitalist world-economy, but also the locus of the first serious antisystemic movement in the history of modern capitalism.

The French Revolution was the moment in the historical development of the capitalist world-economy when the formulations in the ideological arena finally were changed to express a by then long-existing reality of capitalism as a mode of production. The new ideology took account of the fact that, in the capitalist world-economy, the political superstructure was not only a social construct (both the sovereign states and the interstate system) but a social construct that was constantly being amended and reconstructed. The terminology in which this reality was clothed was that of "the sovereignty of the people" which was a way of legitimizing the fluidity as opposed to the solidity of political structures. To deal with this fluidity, we were bequeathed the antinomy of society/state, and with it the supposed interaction and/or conflict between society and state which was to constitute the largest focus of the scientific activity of the historical social sciences.

As to the political ambiguity of the French Revolution, we can say that on the one hand it was a moment in which one part of the French upper strata/bourgeoisie sought to update and reconstruct the French state to enable it to play on their behalf a more efficacious role in the world-economy. On the other hand, it marked the uprising of French direct producers against the significant life-deprivations that the intensification of capitalist processes had been imposing on them.

This ambiguity was reflected in the continuing struggle for the control over the definition of the task and domain of the historical social sciences in the nineteenth and twentieth centuries. On the one hand the historical social sciences represented an updating of the ideological superstructure of the capitalist world-economy, offering one that would be a more efficacious mechanism of legitimating that historical system, less for the mass of the world's population than for its cadres who were, along with the thin stratum of large-scale accumulators of capital, its principal beneficiaries. On the other hand, the historical social sciences offered the antisystemic movements the language with which they could clarify (expose) the workings of this historical system, outline its contradictions, and therefore pinpoint its vulnerabilities. This is for example what Marx and Engels were saying when they insisted that what they were writing and doing should be called "scientific socialism."

The movements, we have said, had to make a strategic decision about change, and the option they chose was to invest in the acquisition of state power. Similarly, those historical social scientists who saw their role as contributing to the social transformation of the world had to make a strategic choice as to where they would invest their scientific energies. The fundamental decision was that they would present a model for the analysis of social reality that was strikingly different from that presented by bourgeois or Establishment historical social scientists – one which, they argued, would more correctly or adequately explain this reality, and one that was far more useful in counseling us about how to speed up the social transformation of the world. One such model, no doubt the most important one, was Marxism.

Just as state power as a political strategy was eminently plausible, so was the elaboration of a "countermodel" as an intellectual strategy not only reasonable but efficacious. It did contribute to political mobilization, and it did contribute to the formulation of intelligent tactics in the struggle.

Yet, just as the largely successful acquisition of state power by the movements was not unambiguous in its consequences, so was the largely successful elaboration of a countermodel. The countermodel was so plausible and so powerful that it has even crept inside the elaboration of Establishment social science. In many ways, the world of historical social sciences has been converted to Marxism, even as it denies this and tries to hide it by utilizing non-Marxist terminology to express Marxist ideas. And this "creeping Marxization" has profoundly changed the politics of the world-system in the post-1945 period just as did the coming to state power of so many antisystemic movements.

The other side of this coin, however, is that Marxism has as a result often served as much as a justification for the status quo as a means for its undermining – and a particularly powerful one at that since, in theory, it claims to be an "antisystemic" ideology. Why has this happened? It has happened because of the intellectual strategy that was adopted. Concentrating on the elaboration of a countermodel involved two subordinate decisions: accepting the premises of modern science, and accepting the broad outlines of the dominant historiography, the presumed recounting of "what had really happened."

But the premises of modern science and the dominant historiography were no more neutral than the models. And the chickens have come home to roost in the post-1945 period, as both Establishment social science and Marxist social science found it·

increasingly difficult to explain the real world, that is, to account for the actual trajectory of the historical transition in which we had begun to live. One sees this frequently presented today as a "crisis of Marxism" but that is much too narrow. It is rather a "crisis of the historical social sciences," and beyond that a "crisis of science" itself.

The premises are in question not merely among the historical social scientists but among the physical scientists, the presumed high priests of the religion of modern science. We are being told that the search for eternal laws and symmetry has failed and that what we really find are "evolving particles" and "symmetry-breaking processes." We are being told that "irreversibility is the mechanism that brings order out of chaos," irreversibility and not reversibility. We are being told that the "daring wager with the dominant Aristotelian tradition gradually becomes a dogmatic assertion . . ." We are being told that "irreversibility, the arrow of time, implies randomness." And, we are being told, this leads us back to the central ontological problem, the relation between Being and Becoming, with the conclusion that "Being and Becoming are not to be opposed one to the other; they express two related aspects of reality."[1]

But, if this is all true, then we have to cast out the basic methodology that has informed most of historical social science, including most of Marxist social science, insofar as it has sought eternal laws, symmetry, reversibility and, therefore, the certainty of the future. We may have to let back in that part of the Aristotelian tradition constituted by the search for final causes. We may even have to admit that there is knowledge other than and prior to scientific knowledge. Of course, science as we know it was an invention of our modern world, deriving lines of argument immanent in a certain "Western" philosophical tradition. Insofar as the crisis of the world-system is reflected in the "civilizational project," the world is rediscovering its wealth of alternative formulations of knowledge.

This is equality true of historiography. We have long been warned against "ethnocentric" history. We have been told many times that nineteenth-century history was the story of the rulers as

---

[1] Ilya Prigogine and Isabelle Stengers, *Order Out of Chaos*. New York: Bantam, 1984, pp. 292, 298–99, 301.

seen by the rulers and that it ignored the ruled – the working classes, the non-Western parts of the world. This was, of course, true and is today being remedied. We are being offered also the history of, and as seen by, those who have been ruled – the working classes, the non-Western parts of the world. This is no doubt a very useful corrective to the incredibly narrow perspectives of a mere thirty or so years ago. But insofar as this "new" history shares the basic historical myths of the older history, the widening of our scope of coverage may only compound the problem.

The two basic myths in the telling of the tale of the capitalist world-economy have been that it is the story of a new stratum, the middle classes, who overturned the old feudal aristocracy; and that it is the story of the slowly widening circles of economic activity, the transformation of local economies into national economies which then "met" in an international arena. Alternative myths are now being offered: that the "new" middle classes are and always were an avatar of the old feudal aristocracy; and that the development of the capitalist world-economy has involved the densification and filling in of a world-system rather than its slow creation from an inner core.

The calling into question of scientific premises and dominant historical myths has not caused the crisis in the sciences. It is rather the expression of this crisis, which was caused by the fact that the sciences have come increasingly to be in a cul-de-sac, as they found the changing reality increasingly incomprehensible (whereas by the inner logic of their accepted premises, it should have been increasingly comprehensible).

But challenge has not produced new clarity; it has first of all produced great confusion and great uncertainty. The confusion and uncertainty are closely linked to that found in the movements, and both are products of the crisis in the world-system. All these "crises" are simultaneous, imply each other, and can only be resolved in relation to each other.

Prognosis

The key question is where we go from here, and the first thing to says is that we cannot be sure. Some persons find this profoundly unnerving and others profoundly pessimistic. I find this profoundly reassuring in the long run (if simultaneously immediately frightening). If there is no human choice, why play the game? If there is choice, there has to be uncertainty of outcome, or the choice is being exercised elsewhere. Perhaps it is the ultimate Promethean hybris of humanity to assert the reality, if the rarity, of fundamental choice. But it is, in the end, a view sanctioned by every religious and philosophical tradition that includes the concept of human responsibility. We can only be responsible for that which it is in our power to affect.

Progress is very possible. We may in this social transformation move towards the creation of a socialist world order that is both egalitarian and democratic. It could be an order that would leave greatly increased scope for the multiplicity of cultural patterns that humanity has shown the capacity to create. This order would obviously be based on entirely new institutional structures whose form it is impossible to predict because they have yet to be invented.

Whether or not we arrive at such a world order in the next century will largely be a function in my view of how the two subordinate "crises" – the "crisis in the movements" and the "crisis in the sciences" – will be resolved. That is to say, in my view, the critical battles lie in these arenas, and their outcomes will determine the route of the transformation.

For a somber alternative does exist. The present world-system, the capitalist world-economy, could be transformed into something else, either another singular system or a multiplicity of separate ones which will be neither egalitarian nor democratic. The resulting system(s) could even be worse than the existing system. That, after all, is what happened once before when we made the transition (in Europe) from feudalism to capitalism, which was not only not progress but was in many ways regression.

The way in which transitions can result in non-progress is very simple. The defenders of privilege, in the period of transition, can seize hold of the levers of change, not to prevent change (that is, not to conserve a now declining system impossible any longer to conserve) but to steer the change in the direction of another system that, although quite different in form from the present one, would equally ensconce privilege.

This choice is available and real, as is the other one. That is why the social struggle is real, and why it will take place primarily inside the movements and inside the sciences. That is why the "emergence of new social thought" is not an abstract matter but a matter of deep existential urgency. That is why the question is not world crisis or world transformation, but what kind of transformation can we bring about as the modality by which the "crisis" will be resolved. How we act will in fact determine our collective "civilizational quest."

9 ✖ The capitalist world-economy: middle-run prospects

In the short run, the capitalist world-economy is in some difficulties which may soon get worse. But it will no doubt recover within a decade or so and probably do quite well. In the long run (a century or so), it is destined to come to an end in one way or another. But what about the middle run? What can we estimate may possibly happen in the period 2000–50? Obviously, the most we can do is extrapolate certain trends and make some plausible guesses about this period. Nonetheless, despite the uncertain character of such plausible guesses, it is a worthwhile, indeed salutary, effort to make them. Insofar as intellectuals can contribute anything to the arena of real politics, it is precisely in their ability (their very limited ability, to be sure) to make such assessments as to the real alternatives facing the real world.

I shall therefore start with a review of the major developments in the world-system since 1945, then project the short-run prospects (say to the year 2000), and finally devote my attention to the middle-run future (2000–50).

The world-system, 1945–1988

The economics of the period 1945–88[1] are in broad outline easy to expound. There was a major economic expansion of the capitalist world-economy following the end of the Second World War. It came to an end perhaps in 1967, perhaps in 1973. It was

---

[1] 1988 has no historical significance *per se*. It was merely the year this paper was written and presented.

the greatest single expansion in the history of this world-system going back to 1500 (measured by any of the usual criteria, except that of expansion of land area included within the world-economy). In most ways, this period had all the characteristics of a typical Kondratieff A-period. It was a period fueled by relative monopolies in a few leading products for which the rate of profit was high, and the surplus-value of which was very unequally distributed, socially and geographically.

For all the standard economic reasons, this expansion came to an end and has been followed by an economic stagnation. It came to an end because the relative monopolies were eroded by entry into the world market of a large number of competitors, seeking to get on the bandwagon. It came to an end as well because of declining productivity, caused by rising retention of the surplus-value, both by direct producers and by managerial strata. The result was a severe decline in profit rates. Since 1967–73, the stagnation of the world-economy has also had the characteristics of a standard Kondratieff B-period: relatively high worldwide unemployment of wage workers; acute politicized competition among core countries for the tighter world market; increased economic suffering in many sectors and (at least as important) a sense in many sectors that they are suffering by comparison with the previous A-period; increased world concentration of capital (of which Japanese acquisition of US real estate and the Third World debt crisis are merely two symptoms); geographical relocation of production processes; and a search for product innovations. We are in the middle of this period of global economic stagnation and it may last until *circa* 2000.

It should be noted that A-periods and B-periods are positive and negative primarily in terms of the global rate of profit and hence of the accumulation of capital within the world-economy as a whole. Each period has both positive and negative welfare features, which vary for particular economic sectors or particular social groups. Many sectors and groups do quite well in a B-period, while others do poorly in an A-period. Nonetheless, overall, both for world capital and for the majority of the world population, A-periods are happier periods than B-periods.

The politics of the period 1945–88 correspond quite closely with its economics. The A-period, 1945–67, was the period of US

hegemony in the world-system. Based on its overwhelming productivity edge after 1945 in all major economic sectors, the
United States assumed unquestioned political and military dominance of the world-system and even achieved cultural leadership.

Periods of hegemony are rarer than Kondratieff A-periods but
they are just as certain to be eroded by their internal workings.
The economic recovery of the principal allies of the United States,
turning them by the late 1960s into economic competitors,
undermined US political control. This undermining of US leadership was paralleled by the long-term process of de-Stalinization
and de-satellitization of the countries in the socialist bloc, which
commenced with Khrushchev's secret report at the XXth Party
Congress in 1956. As a result, the tacit bilateral accord on the
status quo into which the United States, and the USSR had entered
at Yalta slowly began to unravel.

After 1945, the Third World emerged as a political force, and
not one to be constrained entirely within the framework of a
cooptative decolonization. The wars in Algeria and Vietnam were
particularly upsetting politically. Finally the worldwide revolution
of 1968 marked a revolt not only against US hegemony but also
against the classical antisystemic movements themselves (both
socialist and nationalist), who were seen as being in tacit collusion
with the system.

In short, the period of economic stagnation has also been a
period of declining political power of the United States (and of
the USSR as well). The inability of the United States to impose its
will in Central America (and of the USSR to do the same in
Afghanistan) is merely the latest example of this changed geopolitical reality.

It should be noted that the cultural arena saw parallel developments. The 1945–67 period saw an incredible expansion of US
cultural influence worldwide, which may be observed in such
phenomena as the universal adoption of the ideology of development, US leadership in the contemporary social sciences and the
arts, and the successful imposition of English as the sole lingua
franca of the world-system. In all these spheres, the opposition of
the socialist bloc was loud, but in practice their conformity was
considerable. However, after 1968, there has been an erosion on
all these cultural fronts. The ideology of development (and

beyond it of both Enlightenment progress and Newtonian science) has come into serious question. The social sciences and the arts are once again becoming pluralist and multicentered. The world-level use of languages other than English is beginning to revive, albeit slowly.

The world-system, 1988 to *circa* 2000

The processes we have described of the post-1967 transformations will continue. It should be noted that hegemonic decline is always highly unsettling. It is resisted by the hegemonic power. It causes a scramble for the succession. It is the source of enormous intellectual confusion, since although everyone is clear about what is under attack, few are clear about what might (or should) replace the institutions under attack, at least in the short run.

This triple discomfort will probably be accentuated in the next decade. US resistance to decline in hegemony has already taken two successive forms. The Nixon–Ford–Carter approach was to adopt a lower profile. They tried flexibility in foreign policy, while reinforcing the essentials – hence, detente, trilateralism, and a distinct lowering of the ideological decibels in the Third World. In 1980, this style was considered in the United States to be a failure, as demonstrated by high inflation in the United States, the Soviet entry into Afghanistan and, above all, the embassy hostage ordeal in Iran.

So the United States switched its policy style. The Reagan approach was one of pandemic *machismo* – *vis-à-vis* the Evil Empire, *vis-à-vis* "terrorists" in the Third World, *vis-à-vis* soft-hearted and economically conniving allies, and *vis-à-vis* the heirs of 1968 at home. After eight years of Reagan, we can say the achievement score of Reaganism, in terms of stemming the decline of US power, is no better than the achievement score of Nixon–Ford–Carter, that is, virtually nil. The United States is probably about to embark on another eight-year attempt to stem the tide. Mr Dukakis promised in effect not to make the mistakes either of Nixon–Ford–Carter or of Reagan. But does there really exist a third possible policy style that has a better chance of stemming US decline?

The picture is little better in the global struggle for succession.

There are only two geographic loci of alternative economic strength: one is Japan, the other Western Europe around its German–French core. Both centers have spent the period of 1967–88 primarily minding their own business politically and concentrating on strengthening their world-market economic "competitivity."

No doubt, Japan has been the great success story in this regard. It has kept world political involvement down to nearly zero, and it has singlemindedly worked hard at conquering world markets while zealously protecting its home market. It has done remarkably well. Western Europe has done less well. It has been less able to keep out of constant involvement in world politics, because of its historic links with its former colonies as well as its historic links with and concern about Eastern Europe. Furthermore, the United States had political claims on Western Europe via NATO that it did not have in the case of Japan. The United States could insist on continued West European involvement, as in the issue of missiles placement. Finally, Western Europe is still not a single political entity, and economic coordination has been difficult and subject to multiple local political pressures.

Can we project more of the same in the decade ahead? Perhaps not. The pressures on Japan, from without and from within, to become a more active participant in the world political arena are sure to grow. And economically, Japan must come to some securer arrangements with its East Asian neighbors (both the so-called NICs and China), if it is not to suffer some economic setbacks. Such arrangements may be difficult to obtain. On the other hand, Western Europe is coming to a symbolic and real crossroads, that of 1992. It seems to be moving more smoothly than anticipated in the direction of the construction of Europe. Thus it may be that whereas, from 1968 to today, Japan's edge on Western Europe was growing, Western Europe will be able to reduce the gap in the last decade of this century. It is probable, in any case, that *vis-à-vis* the United States, both Japan and Western Europe will continue to improve their relative positions.

Finally, there are the intellectual uncertainties. They have occurred at two levels – that of the social movements, and that of the social sciences. The social movements have not yet recovered from the shock of 1968. The period 1945–67 may be seen as the culminating moment of the historic strategy of the antisystemic movements. In the period of approximately 1850–80, these movements, both in their socialist and nationalist varieties, as a result of much internal debate, determined that their intermediate strategy should be the taking of state power in the separate states. Between 1945 and 1967, the heirs of the nineteenth-century movements actually took state power in a large number of states: Second International Social-Democrats in the West, Third International Communists in eastern Europe and parts of eastern Asia, and national liberation movements in the Third World.

The world revolution of 1968 was to an important degree the rebellion against the realities created by these historic successes of the classical antisystemic movements. The organizational consequence of this rebellion was the emergence of a large and variegated skein of "new" movements throughout the world – movements of "minorities," women's movements, ecology movements, etc. These movements sought to invent alternative strategies of social transformation. I say "invent" and not "implement" because one of the most striking characteristics of these new movements since 1968 has been their uncertainty about middle-run strategy. They have been strong on long-run vision and often on short-run tactics, but weak and divided on middle-run strategy.

What can we expect between now and the year 2000? Hopefully, some increasing clarity by the movements on the issues and the beginning of the creation of a new consensus about middle-run strategy to replace the one attacked in 1968, but not yet entirely renounced.

The intellectual uncertainties in the social sciences are as great, perhaps greater, than those in the movements. Once again, the period 1945–67 marked the culmination and moment of triumph of a nineteenth-century strategy. The question posed in the nineteenth century was how to know the changing social world (in large part implicitly in order to control this change). The strategic consensus was that since reality was both "objective" and enormously complex, the way to know it was to seize this reality in small chunks, one at a time, and by careful observation. This viewpoint came in two versions. The idiographic version sent us to the archives as the repository of small-scale objective reality and told us to summarize empathetically and in narrative form what we found there. The nomothetic version pushed us in the direction of studying contemporary quantified data and told us to summarize it in statistical form, from which we could infer the presumably eternal and universal laws of human behavior. Both versions pushed us away from the study of the long-term and the large-scale on the grounds of the lack of verifiable data. Both versions, for different reasons, therefore pushed us away from holistic and systemic realities toward the individual (or its organizational equivalent: the firm, the family, the state) as the appropriate unit of analysis. It has been a case-perfect instance of missing forests for trees.

In the period 1945–67 partisans of both the nomothetic and the idiographic versions of knowing social reality flourished as never before. They asserted optimistically that their intellectual day had finally come, that they were now at last truly able to know social reality with some efficacy. This was argued in parallel ways by both the principal ideological variants of these modes of knowledge: the liberal and the Marxist.

The problem was that these historians and social scientists were coming to know better and better less and less of the real world. The gap between what was "known" by these scholars and what was obviously occurring in the real world was growing larger. One could explain away this gap as the result of anomalies and of the undue persistence of archaisms, but such an explanation became eventually quite tenuous and not very credible.

The world revolution of 1968 thus provided a salutary shock not only for the traditional antisystemic movements but for the Establishment world of the social sciences. The parallel between the two arenas persists into the post-1968 period. The advocates of "new" knowledge, of "new" ways of knowing, were far clearer about what was limited and limiting in nineteenth-century modes of knowledge than they were about what might replace them.

And our projection forward to the year 2000 is also parallel. Perhaps we shall begin to move forward to a new consensus about how we may know social reality to replace the badly wounded but still persisting nineteenth-century consensus.

The middle-run (2000–2050): the possible vectors

I propose to describe four possible vectors of historical occurrences for the period 2000–50, and raise the question of where these vectors might lead the world-system as a whole.

The first vector is that of a cyclical upswing in the accumulation possibilities of the capitalist world-economy. Assuming for the moment that the productive processes will continue to operate in the fashion they have been operating for several hundred years now, we can project that the last decade of the twentieth century will have accomplished by the year 2000 a number of things. The innovations in microprocessors, genetic engineering, and new energy sources will be sufficiently perfected to sustain major worldwide leading industrial sectors. To do this, two elements are crucial. One is that the cost of the new technology be sufficiently low such that the product can be sold at a price high enough for significant unit profit but low enough still to command sufficient demand to guarantee a global net profit that represents a significant contribution to world accumulation. In other words, profit per unit is not the most important element, but rather total worldwide profit for the product as a proportion of total worldwide profit on all productive activity. The second element that is crucial is that production be relatively monopolized, such that this global profit is not too widely shared. While the first element is a function primarily of technology, the second element is a function primarily of political arrangements.

Two further changes must occur if there is to be an upswing. The economically strong countries need to complete their divestment of a large part of erstwhile profitable sectors which are no longer as profitable. This relocalization of a significant portion of the world's steel, automobile, chemicals, and electronic sectors from the core to the semiperiphery, long under way, may well be over by 2000. Even more recently organized and somewhat more profitable sectors, like aeronautics and computers, may be partially relocated by 2000. Finally, there needs to be some expansion of effective world demand for all production via the further proletarianization of a sector of the world's workforce. This has been occurring in a number of semiperipheral countries and may be underway in the socialist countries as well.

With these conditions in place, the upswing could begin. Let us now assume that the technological edge will be located in the hands of a Japan–United States consortium in which, at least at the beginning, the Japanese component will tend to offer the entrepreneurial organizational skills and the US component will offer R & D skills. This should be a very powerful combination. If the consortium can hold on to a market edge for even ten years, it would probably lock it in for 30 more by capturing enough of the market to make any alternative technologies, even more efficient ones, unprofitable.

The Japanese–United States economic consortium would doubtless try to ensure its market edge by enclosing, via political arrangements, those zones where for historic reasons commercial ties are presently strongest. This means East Asia (including China), the Americas (not forgetting Canada), and probably Australasia as well. I would give this vector a strong chance of success and believe it could be the basis of an expansion of the world-economy greater and more "glorious" than the so-called 30 glorious years following 1945. It would probably last for 30 years or so.

The obvious loser in such an arrangement would be Western Europe. Remember I suggested that in the short run, that of 1990–2000, Western Europe might improve its position *vis-à-vis* Japan. This would mean that, as of 2000, Western Europe (by then probably a reasonably unified entity, and possibly one already expanded to include the EFTA countries, or some of them) would present itself as a very strong actor on the world economic scene. Nonetheless, if the Japan–United States consortium achieved the technological edge I suggested it might, and was able to hold on to it for at least ten years, Western Europe could find itself in great difficulty: unable to break into the Japan–United States zone of operation, and fighting off penetration of its own markets as well.

In this case, the second vector I could see is a strong European thrust toward protectionism. The protectionist wave that has never really occurred as feared in the 1980s had been held off by the wise manipulations of a combination of the TNCs and the OECD countries. But the context that has made the required coordination possible has been the continued uncertainty as to who would control the technological edge during the next major expansion. Were this uncertainty to disappear, as I am projecting, the pressures for policy coordination among the dominant forces of the world-economy would quickly take second place to their intra-core struggles. A broad protectionism would be the obvious first major move.

I say a broad protectionism because I am thinking of a zonal division limited to two zones: the sphere of the Japan–United States consortium, and the other zone. That is, I expect that Western Europe would seek to include in its zone all areas not clearly in the Japan–United States zone. There are five obvious candidates: east–central Europe, the USSR, the Middle East, Africa, and India.

It is hard to predict the degree of success Western Europe could achieve, since the Japan–United States consortium would doubtless contest the control of these markets in all five zones. There are different political problems in each particular zone. Without reviewing the details of each instance, one might say that Western Europe has a political edge over the Japan–United States consortium in all five zones, but not so large a one as to make the outcome unquestionable. However, even if Western Europe were to organize, probably belatedly, all five of these zones within its economic "sphere of influence," this might not be enough to overcome a Japan–United States lead. At most, it might enable Western Europe to resist the juggernaut in its home base.

The third vector is the North–South projection. The renewed expansion of the world-economy would necessarily involve an expanded involvement of Third World zones in the commodity chains of the world-economy. And the price of this increased involvement would almost surely be, as it has been in the past, a seriously expanded exploitation of the periphery. The last redoubts of partial non-involvement in the world-economy might well disappear. And with it might well disappear the last zones that have not yet been ecologically ravaged.

If one combines this ecological deterioration with the greatly increased needs of the North for waste disposal (the price of which the Third World is already beginning to pay), 30 "glorious" years of renewed expansion of the world-economy might well be more than the Third World states would be politically able to bear. The Third World's peoples learned well the efficacity of anti-North political mobilization during the 1945–1967 expansion. It is not stretching the imagination too much to suggest that a later generation would revive this tactic under the projected even worse conditions after 2000.

One might ask why they have not done this during the current B-phase. The answer is in part the fact that they have had less with which to menace the North, given the worldwide stagnation and the absence of a truly polarized North. By contrast, I am projecting for the period after 2000 both worldwide expansion and the renewal (along new lines) of intra-North bifurcation.

Where will this lead? There may be massive unrest, or one variety or another of revolution – in Indonesia or Nigeria, in Pakistan or Mexico – who can say? It is quite clear from the post-1945 experience of the world-system that, once such unrest in the South gains momentum, it is quite difficult for forces in the North to bring it under control. The Vietnamese war and the Iranian revolution surely stand as monuments to that elementary truth. It might be harder to "turn off" or "tune down" Third World agitation after 2020 than it was after say 1975, precisely because of the still greater momentum it might have achieved between 2000 and 2030.

The fourth vector then would be the renewal of the world revolution of 1968. I think of this renewal in both of the arenas which I previously discussed: the movements and the (social) sciences.

There are two major issues for the movements to resolve in this period. One is whether the "old" and the "new" movements – in the West, in the socialist countries, in the Third World – can arrive at some new consensus about the middle-run strategy of social transformation of the world-system. My guess is that they will, although I believe it is not yet at all clear what this strategy will be. If they do arrive somehow at this renewed consensus, it will have important organizational consequences which, on a world scale, will be more centripetal than centrifugal.

The second major issue is whether, even with a new consensus, the net result of the activities of the antisystemic movements will in fact be antisystemic. Here I am sufficiently uncertain that I decline even to suggest in which direction the vector runs. I think this is one of the truly big question-marks of the period 2000–50. It is in this sense that one can say that the outcome of the process of world transformation depends on the struggle that will occur *within* the antisystemic movements.

Once again, the correlation between the movements and the social sciences will, I believe, prove to be strong. For the social sciences face two major issues that are rather parallel to those faced by the movements. The first is whether or not its practitioners – if you will, the "old" and the "new" – can agree on a new consensus to replace (or, rather, sublate) the nineteenth-century consensus. If they can, and I am somewhat optimistic that they will do so, it will have clear organizational implications, and probably involve a wholesale reorganization of the university system.

But even if this occurs there remains the second major issue of the social sciences. Will the new consensus of the renewed historical social sciences in fact be a critical social science – that is, a social science grounded in the realities of its social world but serving as its intelligent critic? This is, as all of us know, a very hard row to hoe, since the leverages of short-run social control of intellectuals by the power structures – the direct leverages and the more subtle ones – are extremely powerful. And the temptation of playing the philosopher-king is always there to divert those most apt to be the advocates of critical social science. Once again, I decline to project the vector.

What then do the four vectors add up to? Suppose all four vectors turn out to be correctly estimated, and we see a new expansion of the world-economy based on a Japan–United States consortium, the creation of a countervailing "heartland" zone led by Western Europe, an acutely politicized and rambunctious South, and new consensuses among both the worldwide family of the antisystemic movements and that of the historical social sciences.

I see three quite different possible scenarios. All three depend on one assumption that I should make explicit. In the world-economic expansion following 2000 the capitalist world-economy will use up its last margin of rectification. It will come close enough to the asymptotes of total commodification and total polarization (not merely quantitatively but socially), such that it will have exhausted its ability to maintain the cyclical rhythms that are its heartbeat. It will give out. But what form will this demise take?

The first scenario is that, following the classic pattern of the three previous hegemonic cycles, the struggle for hegemony, pitting Japan (allied with the United States and China) against Western Europe (allied with the USSR), will result by, say, 2050 in a "world war." We have had three such world wars in the history of the modern world-system – 1618–48, 1792–1815, 1914–1945 – and structurally there is no reason we should not have a fourth. The only problem, as we are all aware, is that this one would be a nuclear disaster of incredible proportions. Still, as we all know, it is one possible scenario.

The second scenario is that the world, faced with the exhaustion of the existing world-system and the fear of a nuclear disaster, will consciously reorganize the world-system into something else. The question in this scenario is who will be doing this reorganizing. The implementation of a sort of Rousseauian general will has never heretofore been very democratic once we got beyond the village level, as even Rousseau recognized. Self-conscious reorganization of the world-system has the strong possibility (but not, of course, the certainty) that it would be manipulated by those who currently hold privilege to recreate a new structure of inegalitarian privilege.

The third possible scenario is the least popular in both senses of the word. It is the one least frequently predicted, and it is the one with the lowest level of anticipatory approbation. The third possible scenario is that of a crumbling away of the world-system. Such a crumbling away would be anarchic, generating massive experimentation but also massive insecurities. It would be social chaos. It is all very well to assert that the whole universe represents a process of constantly recreating "order out of chaos," to use the English title of the book by Prigogine and Stengers. Nonetheless, in the middle of the chaos, life may be very difficult. Generally speaking, we all have a low tolerance for social chaos, and we generally work very hard to make it disappear very quickly. Too quickly, no doubt! But in my middle-run scenario, I project the possibility that it might not be possible immediately to halt the chaos, that this time the chaos would have to run its course until a truly new order were created. It should be clear that my own bias, with some trepidation, lies with this third scenario as the one most likely to lead us to a relatively egalitarian, relatively democratic world order.

I end on the question, what may we do? You will have noted that, of my four vectors, I was most uncertain and least willing to predict about the fourth – what in shorthand I call the "renewal of 1968." The answer to the political and moral question lies there. It is, in my view, the two internal struggles that will determine our future: the struggle internal to the world family of antisystemic movements, and the struggle internal to the world family of historical social sciences. And the two struggles are, of course, linked to each other but not identical. Hence they have to be fought separately but each with an eye to the other.

Part II
Geoculture: the underside of geopolitics

10 ✤ National and world identities and the interstate system

with PETER D. PHILLIPS

> Though not in substance, yet in form, the struggle of the proletariat with the bourgeoisie is at first a national struggle. The proletariat of each country must, of course, first of all settle matters with its own bourgeoisie . . . The workingmen have no country. We cannot take from them what they have not got. Since the proletariat must first of all acquire potential supremacy, must rise to be the leading class of the nation, must constitute itself *the* nation, it is, so far, itself national, though not in the bourgeois sense of the word . . . . Workingmen of the world unite!
>
> Marx and Engels, *Communist Manifesto*

No document better illustrates the central ambivalence of the modern world concerning national and world identity than this quintessential document of the antisystemic movements. The statement highlights the continuing tension between nationalism and internationalism, between universality and particularity, whch has been a constant feature of the political and intellectual landscape of capitalist development. This tension is reflected historically not only in the strength of the separate yet contending claims of class and nation as appeals to action in the political struggles of the modern world, but also in the various organizational attempts to go beyond the limits imposed on political action by the division of the world-economy into multiple nation-states.

We believe that these broad politico-cultural currents of the capitalist world-economy are fundamentally expressions of the structural constraints imposed by the character of the global capital accumulation process. In particular, they derive from the antinomy that is constituted by the existence of multiple states within the bounds of a single social division of labor, the capitalist world-economy. This condition of the modern world-system sets it apart from previously existing world-empires with their elaborate all-embracing redistributive political structures, as well as from the small pre-modern autonomous mini-systems oriented toward "subsistence" production. A central feature of this modern world-system, which originated in Europe in the sixteenth century, has been the tendency towards the state (or nation-state) to become the general political form and towards the global extension of the interstate system consecrated by the Treaty of Westphalia (1648) in the wake of the Thirty Years War.

Thus, although the continuous drive towards the accumulation of capital, which is the main characteristic of the system, has proceeded on the basis of a single global division of labor, political activities within the system have largely been oriented around the nation-state. Historically these states have interfered with the workings of the world market and have functioned as centralized apparatuses for the domination of labor in the service of capitalist production. Equally, however, states within the capitalist world-economy have been constrained by the limitations of their existence within an interstate system. One consequence of this has been that no single state, or group controlling any state, has been totally free to transform relations within its boundaries as it pleased. Accordingly the antisystemic forces engendered by the functioning of the world accumulation process, in an effort to maximize their effectiveness, have not only sought to intervene in the operation of these processes at the level of the nation-state, but also to reach beyond the state and embrace the "supra-national" or global level.

States, for their part, may be differentiated in terms of their capacity for market intervention, itself a function of the range of economic activities which fall within their respective jurisdictions. States with a concentration of core-like activities within their boundaries tend to be stronger, while those areas which remained confined to peripheral activities have been weak states. Over time, the logic of the system's development has been to reproduce the parallel hierarchies of core and periphery within both the world-economy and the interstate system. More specifically, in terms of the interstate system, the result has been to define coexisting tendencies increasingly in terms of "balance of power" and "imperium." The "balance of power," referring primarily to relations between competing core-states, consists of sets of policies that seek to ensure that no single one of these states should attain overwhelming supremacy. On the other hand, imperial or colonial policies have typically been mechanisms for the political subordination of peripheral areas to core states; they have characteristically been central to the processes of unequal exchange and the creation of a proletariat which have been at the heart of the processes of capitalist development.

Both nationalism and internationalism have resulted from the historical tendencies of capitalist development. They have served both to undergird the objectives of those who have power in this world-system and to rally forces of resistance to this system. Consequently, the sense of identity which has sustained these ideological currents has not been a primordial given; rather it has been the outcome of conscious pressures of political forces occupying particular roles and seeking specific objectives within the development of the world-system.

The "peoples" of the modern world have not always been there. They have been created. And, while some were created, potential others were smashed or distorted or submerged. It was indeed a long time before "peoples" emerged at all as a focus of political sentiment. In most cases, it was the establishment of a state that was the single strongest force in creating a people (and suppressing potential others). Even in the case of those "peoples" created in opposition to states as they existed at a given moment (i.e. when the "people" preceded the state), such "peoples" sought statehood as the essential element in consolidating their sense of peoplehood.

If peoples have not always been there, even less have states always been there. All our states have been creations of the modern world, even if some could make a plausible claim to cultural linkage with pre-modern political entities. And least of all, has the interstate system always been there. The interstate system is the political superstructure of the capitalist world-economy and was a deliberate invention of the modern world. It is the relationship of this interstate system with the multiple national identities, through the structure of the state, that is the focus of this paper.

The growth of the concept of the nation-state has had the effect of centering the ideological and political struggles generated by capitalist development upon the state which has become the main object of concern and contention. We have already noted the ambiguity on the part of the antisystemic forces in their disposition towards the state. On the one hand, a leading demand has been for the strengthening of the state apparatus; it was indeed the most explicit demand of national movements. On the other hand, the claims of internationalism have been for the abolition of the state. Traditionally a line of demarcation has been sharply drawn between these two political currents. Lenin, for example, argued:

Bourgeois nationalism and proletarian internationalism, these are the two irreconcilably hostile slogans that correspond to the two great class camps throughout the capitalist world, and express two policies (nay the two world outlooks) in the national question.[1]

On the other hand, the same Lenin argued:

The aim of socialism is not only to end the division of mankind into tiny states and the isolation of nations in any form, it is not only to bring the nations closer together but to integrate them. And it is precisely in order to achieve this aim that we must, on the one hand, explain to the masses the reactionary nature of Renner's and Otto Bauer's idea of so-called "cultural and national autonomy" and, on the other, demand the liberation of oppressed nations in a clearly and precisely formulated political programme that takes special account of the hypocrisy and cowardice of socialists in the oppressor nations, and not in general nebulous phrases, not in empty declamations and not by way of 'relegating' the question until socialism has been achieved. In the same way as mankind can arrive at the abolition of classes only through a transition period of the dictatorship of the oppressed class, it can arrive at the inevitable integration of nations only through a transition period of the complete emancipation of all oppressed nations, i.e. their freedom to secede.[2]

Lenin's insistence on the historical inevitability of the principle of nationality and his insistence on the right of nations to self-determination against the opposition of many of his leading contemporaries testifies to his vision of the strength of the political appeal of nationalism among popular forces.

Lenin's support for bourgeois nationalist movements exemplifies a further political dimension of capitalist development. It is evident that nationalism and internationalism have historically been the focus of appeals of both capital and labor, through the successive phases of development of the capitalist world-economy.

[1] V.I. Lenin, "Critical Remarks on the National Question," in *National Liberation, Socialism and Imperialism*, New York: International Publications, 1968, 19.
[2] V.I. Lenin, "The Socialist Revolution and the Right of Nations to Self-Determination: Theses," in *National Liberation, Socialism and Imperialism, op. cit.*, 114.

Thus it is not purely fortuitous, for example, that the first assumption of state power on the part of an "internationalist" socialist movement coincided with the "internationalism" of the "new diplomacy" enunciated by Woodrow Wilson and subsequently embodied in the League of Nations. Rather than representing simply abstract ideological expressions, then, nationalism and internationalism represent political and ideological tendencies with a variable class content which is derived from the continuous efforts on the part of capital and labor to respond to the structural conditions engendered by capitalist production.

Provisionally we may distinguish three major periods in the history of the interstate system (within the framework of the developing capitalist world-economy). The first period, from *circa* 1450 to perhaps 1815, is one in which a series of states were created in Western Europe (usually though not always by means of some variant of absolutism); these states came to relate to each other in terms of (to be constrained by) the interstate system that linked the states and, in fact, defined their juridical and moral existence. In this period we had "statism" but virtually no "nationalism." In the nineteenth century, nationalism began to replace statism as the ideological cement of the political entities, but it was also the period in which the class struggle first took an organized and overtly political form. Finally, the antagonistic co-operation of nationalism and class struggle became far more intense in the period after 1914–17 as antisystemic forces blended the social movement and the national movement while conservative forces used the very same blend to support the *status quo*.

The state-building of the first period involved the dissolution of the political arrangements of feudal Europe – the unity between monarchy and church and the complex system of decentralized and parcellized sovereignties. These arrangements were replaced by a system of territorially bounded sovereign states, administratively centralized and possessing a virtual monopoly of the available means of coercion. To be sure, this process occurred unevenly in both space and time. The establishment of strong centralized authority necessitated the elimination, subordination, or the co-optation of rival (often previously established) claimants to political power. As may well be expected, these activities absorbed much of the energies of sixteenth- and seventeenth-

144   Geopolitics and geoculture

century states in Europe and triggered widespread resistance and civil war throughout this period.[3] Despite the widespread nature of these struggles, however, it is nonetheless true that, right up to the French Revolution, the populations within Europe (as opposed to certain elite groups) did not for the most part organize themselves on a statewide basis, but rather confined themselves to local bases of mobilization.

In any case, overall consolidation of the system of nation-states in the sixteenth and seventeenth centuries was the function to some extent of the specific conditions prevailing within Western Europe: in particular its relative cultural homogeneity, marked by a considerable convergence of linguistic, family, legal, religious, economic, and political practice. This condition facilitated the spread of this form of state organization within the area and aided the easy relocation of population and territory between states. Likewise the emergence of this system of states was dependent upon the increase in capitalist activity (mercantile and industrial) during the period, and on the resources which were thereby provided to allow for the development of new administrative mechanisms and forms of political control. Accordingly, the emerging centralized bureaucracies developed a strong interest in reinforcing the tendencies towards capitalist development which were in motion in Europe.

Already in this period the emerging cultural and political ambiguities of the world-economy may be observed. Only tenuously established, and as yet only vaguely defined, its form was nonetheless apparent. The claims of "universalism" became increasingly voluble in the philosophical and intellectual developments of the Enlightenment with its commitment to the "immutability and unity" of Reason which was seen to be "the same for all thinking subjects, all nations, all epochs and all cultures."[4] At the same time, however, the effect of capitalist development was the generation of specific tendencies as demonstrated in the consolidation of territorially distinct nation-states and the attendant doctrines of sovereignty; their purpose was to impress the uniqueness and the specificities of the claims upon the respective

[3] See the overview in Charles Tilly (ed.) *The Formation of National States in Western Europe.* Princeton: Princeton University Press, 1975, chapter 1.
[4] Ernest Cassirer, *The Philosophy of the Enlightenment.* Boston: Beacon Press, 1955, p. 6.

populations and territories within the world-economy. By the end of this period also, the foundations of the social sciences were laid. The publication by Montesquieu of *L'Esprit des Lois* and Adam Smith's *The Wealth of Nations*, to mention but two of the seminal intellectual works of this period, were clear indications of the tone of this period. For both of them the striving for the universality of meaning expressed in different social situations is their paramount concern. It is in this period, too, that there developed the precepts of international law and the doctrine of natural rights which had as their object the specification of the rights and obligations governing the relationships between and within states. Modern international relations thus effectively date from this period, when international law first took shape and the patterns for international intercourse and of warfare assumed their modern shape.[5]

The tension between the "universal" and the "particular" was to become even more clearly defined in the second of our periods. The effect of the turbulence and violence experienced in Europe between 1789 and 1815 was to shatter and transform the bases of authority established in the previous two centuries. For example, the absolutist view that the authority of the state was embodied in the person of the sovereign came to be replaced by the view that sovereignty resided in the people of the nation. Equally disrupted by these upheavals were the interstate arrangements forged during the previous period. The Congress of Vienna of 1815 was intended to restore this system and, in particular, to consecrate the balance of power arrangements among the great powers – England, Prussia, Austria, Russia, and France – whose interlocking policies had provided the pivot to the interstate system before 1789.

The nineteenth century witnessed the beginnings of the surge of nationalist movements which were to gather increasing force subsequently as the capitalist world-economy and its accompanying interstate system were extended across the globe. Nationalism first emerged as the response to the universalizing imperialism of the revolutionary power, France, and then as a response to the conservative reaction represented by the settlements imposed

---

[5] See the discussion in E.H. Carr, *Nationalism and After*. London: Macmillan, 1945.

upon post-Napoleonic Europe by the Congress of Vienna. This resistance to the lack of popular consultation and to the imposition of rulers on the local populations culminated in the blossoming of nationalist movements to unify Italy and Germany, and to divide up and regroup the Balkans.[6]

Of course, nationalism was not the exclusive form of popular antisystemic mobilization during the period. For the nineteenth century was also the period that saw the emergence of an "internationalist" working-class movement. The founding of the International Workingmen's Association in 1864, its demise in 1876, and the subsequent creation of the Second International on the centenary of the French Revolution, were indicative of a more comprehensive set of historical transformations taking place in the organization of the labor force as a consequence of capitalist development. Advances in industrialization in Europe led to the consolidation of an increasingly concentrated and urbanized labor force prone to increasingly militant industrial struggles. At the same time the nineteenth century was, as we have noted, the age of nationalism within Europe, and the nascent labor movement was very much caught up in it. For example, the formation of the First International was in large measure brought about by the common support among English and French labor leaders for Polish independence.[7] Equally the tension between nationalism and internationalism lay at the heart of the disputes on strategy and tactics within the European labor movement and accounts to a considerable degree for the dissolution of the precarious unity of the First and even more of the Second International.

Beyond this, the nineteenth century was also the period of massive European expansion in Asia and Africa. The territorial division of these continents during this period had been foreshadowed in the earlier European colonial expansions of the sixteenth and seventeenth centuries. There were important differences between the two episodes, however. The colonialisms of the earlier epoch were essentially expansions of population into areas with a low population density in which the indigenous population was largely eliminated. Arrighi has argued that we

[6] See Elie Kedourie, *Nationalism*. London: Hutchinson University Library, 1962.
[7] See George Lichtheim, *A Short History of Socialism*. London: Praeger, 1970, p. 171.

should think of them as constituting "the effective expansion of a nationality,"[8] although this concept ignores the extensive importation of African slave labor as part of this process. The political form of the colonial extensions of the nineteenth century were rather different, consisting much more of the simple, direct, and coercive extension of the European state, constituting over-rule in "foreign" territories. By the close of the century the division of the world between the competing "imperialisms" of European powers (including the United States) was truly complete, and the pattern of a hierarchy of states which is most extreme in the colonial system of government was firmly and most definitely inscribed as a central part of the interstate system. Certainly, however, the colonial arrangement was not the exclusive form in which the patterns of imperium were expressed. It is clear, too, that the increased prevalence of the colonial form in the late nineteenth century, as against the "Free Trade imperialism" of an earlier period, was bound up with the challenges to British hegemony by the United States and Germany. Our concern here, however, is not so much with the origins of the "new imperialism" as with its effects on the increasingly well-defined antithesis between nationalism and internationalism in the world-economy.

For the period as a whole, there was a marked extension of the geographical boundaries of the world-economy and of the parallel domain of the interstate system. This territorial extension, based upon the deepening and widening of the patterns of imperium within the interstate system, was both cause and consequence of the growth of antisystemic forces throughout the system as a whole. Increasingly, too, the issues of nationalism and internationalism came to represent one main ideological and political focus of the prevailing social conflicts, although the intensity of widespread resistance waged by local populations to their incorporation into the capitalist world-economy should also be recognized.

In the realm of ideas and ideology, the internationalism of the dominant forces took the face of positivism whose "cult of facts" presumed not only a highly segmented view of social reality but

[8] Giovanni Arrighi, *The Geometry of Imperialism*. London: New Left Books, 1978, p. 37.

also a strong faith that universal laws of social behavior were knowable, and indeed that knowing them was the prime object of social enquiry. For the intellectuals of a triumphant Britain, the fundamental philosophical questions relating to the nature of history itself seemed beyond dispute, the doctrine of natural harmonies appeared to be self-evident and, under the influence of the Darwinian revolution in biology, the notion of a linear scheme of socio-historical evolution from primitive to complex social forms seemed particularly attractive and justificatory in a period of widespread colonial expansion. As Carr points out, the Darwinian revolution in "equating evolution with progress" opened the way to a grave misunderstanding "by confusing biological inheritance, which is the source of evolution, with social acquisition, which is the source of progress in history."[9] The record is clear in this respect: the nineteenth century saw the development of elaborate doctrines of racism which were to come to dominate thinking about the non-European world. In the prevailing world of Spencerian social thought and of Darwinism, there was little to restrain the predilection to identify things European as intrinsically progressive, and conversely to label the non-European as innately primitive. Indeed this was the explicit purpose underlying the works of Gobineau and Houston Stewart Chamberlain and, while these extreme views might not have been dominant during the period, racialism was indeed a quite acceptable intellectual trend, perhaps the dominant trend, within academia.[10]

Again these developments were marked by considerable unevenness and contradiction. By the late nineteenth century substantial challenges were developing to the facile conceptions of the dominant positivism. Marxism, for example, developed as a distinctive intellectual tradition in this period, as did the German historical school associated with *Staatswissenschaften*. In both cases the challenge was directed against universalizing the tendencies towards sectorialization and the penchant for historical generalizations associated with the dominant positivist outlook.[11]

[9] E.H. Carr, *What is History?* New York: Alfred A. Knopf, 1961, p.150.
[10] See Louis Snyder, *The Idea of Racialism*. New York: Van Nostrand, 1962.
[11] See Immanuel Wallerstein, "The Tasks of Historical Social Sciences," *Review*, I, 1, 1977, 3–7.

The outbreak of war in 1914 effectively marked the end of the nineteenth-century interstate political arrangements which had preserved the peace among the Great Powers since 1815. Indeed only after two world wars was any comparable "stability" re-established, this time under the hegemony of the United States. The specificities of the period, however, go beyond that simply denoted by the extension of conflict and the intensification of interstate conflict and revolutionary upheaval. The transformations of the interstate system were an expression of only one aspect of a wider set of historical transformations taking place within the capitalist world-economy.

The changes underlying and reflecting the instability and conflict characteristic of the new political and ideological environment may be explained in terms of the changed economic conditions resulting from the challenge to British economic dominance mounted by the U.S. and Germany: the extension of nationalism within Europe and beyond to the colonized regions of Asia and Africa, and the growing politicization of questions of international politics, reflected in the new forms of union between nationalism and socialism.[12]

In fact the strains in British hegemony and in the "imperialism of free trade" had already been apparent in the latter part of the nineteenth century. The foundation of the international economic order was the universal gold standard, which ensured Britain's pivotal role as the leading international banking center. This system continued essentially unchanged up to 1914. The outbreak of war, however, exacerbated the tendencies towards protectionism which had been gaining increasing strength, and unleashed a period of financial chaos which failed to yield to subsequent post-war attempts to reimpose an order based on the previous arrangements and understandings.

The renewed protectionism which resulted from the failure of the various plans for international reform did in fact contribute directly to the onset of the Great Depression.[13] These problems were, furthermore, intertwined with a wider set of political initiatives centering upon the League of Nations which were

---

[12] See, for example, Carr, *What is History?*, pp. 19ff.
[13] See Fred L. Block, *The Origins of International Economic Disorder*. Berkeley: University of California Press, 1977, chapter 1.

aimed at a general reconstruction of a relatively viable system of international political and economic arrangements. At root the League experiment represented an attempt to grapple with the substantially altered and more complex international environment which emerged after the First World War. No longer, for example, was the "charmed circle of Great Powers" restricted to the leading European states or dominated by European preoccupations. The definitive inclusion of Japan and the United States among the Powers and the extension of the nationalist movement in eastern Europe had decisively changed the context and form of world diplomacy.

Not only had the number of recognized sovereign states increased but the general acceptance of the principle of national self-determination became a "standing invitation to secession," providing encouragement for the increasingly widespread national movements which had by this time taken root in Asia and were stirring in Africa. Though the potential strength of nationalism in the periphery had become evident in the nineteenth century, its overriding political significance only became clear after 1914. Indeed major political initiatives and debates on both the left and the right were directed during this period to the issues of national self-determination. The simultaneous advocacy in both Washington and in Petrograd of a "new diplomacy" based upon the rejection of secret diplomacy, annexations, and trade discriminations, and in support of national self-determination, in a word, the rejection of the old diplomatic traditions, was indicative of the political force and attention generated by the nationalist currents of the period. Simultaneously however, the extension of nationalist demands was accompanied by and often expressed through political initiatives focused more directly on the structures of the interstate system. Such was the case, for example, of the Pan-African Congresses, the first of which was convened in Paris in 1919 with the distinct purpose of influencing the deliberations and settlements taking place among the victorious Allied powers.[14] Indeed the League experiment as a whole, within its espousal of the principle of collective security and collective responsibility for peace-keeping, and involving as it did the

---

[14] See George Padmore, *Pan-Africanism or Communism?* London: Dennis Dobson, 1956.

establishment of an International Labor Organization with responsibilities for overseeing the working conditions of labor globally, implied the devolution upon the "supranational" bodies of responsibilities which had hitherto remained within the exclusive purview of the nation-states. The reality of political practice, however, did not completely support the claims enunciated by the proponents of internationalism in the doctrine of the sovereign equality among nations. The very structure of the League was hierarchical, providing for the representation of the Great Powers as permanent members of the Council and for the establishment of a system of mandates whereby territories "which are inhabited by peoples not yet able to stand by themselves under the strenuous conditions of the modern world" would be placed under the tutelage of "advanced nations" who were accordingly deemed to act on behalf of the League.

Overall then, the thrust of the historical developments of the period was a contradictory one. It involved on the one hand the attempt at the elaboration of a supranational political apparatus implying a limitation on state authorities, and on the other the extension of nationalist demands and of the principle of national self-determination. The rise of "internationalist" political movements implicit in the activity of the Third International and in the increasing strength of the various pan-movements was also destined ultimately to be swept away by the nationalist tide. The early Bolshevik vision of world revolution succumbed to the demands of "socialism in one country" and nowhere during the period did the pan-movements achieve any notable successes in their challenge to the nation-state as the fundamental political unit of the world-economy.

The outbreak of war among the Great Powers in 1939 was the last of a series of failures on the part of the League of Nations and marked its ultimate demise. Nonetheless, its basic organizational form was to be re-established in 1945, this time, however, with the critical inclusion of the United States and in a significantly different global, political, and economic context. In this later period too though, the tension between nationalism and internationalism persisted. The Second World War dealt the final blow to the imperial administrations of the European powers. The extension of nationalist demands throughout Asia and Africa resulted in the almost total spread of the nation-state form globally, by the mid-1960s. At the same time supranational forms of political organization were made more elaborate. This is evident not only in regard to the progressively more complex United Nations system but is apparent also in the proliferation of increasingly institutionalized multinational organizations ranging from OPEC to the various regional integration movements, all of which imply some limits to the unimpeded exercise of "sovereignty" on the part of the respective individual states comprising these organizations.

More than that, however, the persistence of the parallel hierarchies of the axial division of labor and of the interstate system provided the material basis for the continuation of the politico-ideological conflicts between imperium and resistance forces operating in both national and "extra-national" domains within the world-economy. The successes of the nationalist movements in Asia and Africa in achieving national independence has induced the emergence of new arenas of nationalist struggle and has changed the form of their ideological representation. The struggle against colonialism has been replaced by the struggle against neo-colonialism, and within the interstate system there has been the emergence of the movement of nonaligned states, the Group of 77 in UNCTAD, and other similar organizations. The ideology of national liberation moreover has continued to be critically relevant throughout the period in situations where formal colonial apparatuses have long been demolished. (Note, for example, Nicaragua.)

All in all then, hierarchy has persisted, albeit under changed conditions. Formal colonial mechanisms were replaced by informal ones, this implying in turn the emergence of new arenas and forms of struggle. A further matter complicates the issues as we move towards the end of this most recent period. It appears as a complicating factor because to some extent it involves prediction. This concerns the purported decline in the hegemony of the United States, a matter which has been the subject of some academic and journalistic attention. Without here hazarding any precise prediction, it suffices to say that the challenges to US hegemony, presaged by the decline of absolute military superiority and the vulnerability of the dollar as the pivotal reserve currency, implies crucial alterations to the fundamental institutional supports of the post-war political order. How crucial is not yet clear.

In terms of scholarly debate, the sequence of developments has been markedly similar. American social science was particularly preeminent in the early years after the Second World War. It introduced the concept of modernization as a means of theorizing the processes of social transformation in the peripheral areas of the world-economy. Proponents of this theory sought universality in their claim that all countries proceed along an essentially similar path *en route* from traditionalism to modernity. Somewhat paradoxically, in view of the clear assumption within modernization theory that the processes of social change are best analyzed at the level of the nation-state, this approach nonetheless maintained its intense striving for universally applicable propositions.

The pitfalls of ahistoricism inherent in such an approach were pointed out by critics, who questioned the ideal-typical dichotomy between "tradition" and "modernity" as being too narrow and arbitrary in its proposed range of historical possibilities for change. In response to these perceived weaknesses, alternative theoretical formulations were advanced, initially from Latin America, which sought to emphasize the specificities of the peripheral areas of the world-economy, while at the same time emphasizing the unity of the processes of social change which are registered within the respective national units as (national) development or underdevelopment. The theorists who led the main attack against modernization theory thus sought to emphasize the specific condition of the "Third World" areas as expressed in their dependent and subordinate position within the world-economy.

We have seen then that the historical pattern of capitalist development has resulted in the spread of the nation-state as the typical unit of political organization within the capitalist world-economy, and in the progressive geographical extension and institutional elaboration of an interstate system which operates to limit the freedom of action of the constitutive states. Characteristically, too, the processes of the interstate system have involved successive patterns of hegemony and rivalry among competing core states seeking to maximize their strength and influence within the world-economy. Simultaneously, however, capitalist development has involved the extension of imperium, whether by means of direct colonial rule, or by way of less formalized mechanisms.

Partly as a consequence of the persistence of this system of multiple states within an integrated totality, antisystemic movements generated by the processes of capitalist production have historically remained ambivalent with regard to the state or to their struggle against the interstate system. At the political and ideological levels this ambivalence has been reflected in a continuing tension between nationalism and internationalism as organizing principles for the various social and political movements generated during the course of capitalist development.

The ambiguities concretely reflected in the field of political struggle can likewise be seen in the various theoretical efforts that have been made to comprehend the historical dynamic underlying the rise and persistence of nationalism as a political force. Marx and Engels were themselves notably sparse and undecided in their writings about the burgeoning nationalism within Europe in the mid and late nineteenth century.[15] Nonetheless, Marxism has developed a coherent corpus of writings on the subject. Essentially this centered on the notion that the "nation" was an "historically transitory phenomenon", that is to say, that the nation-state was essentially an expression of the historical requirements of the bourgeoisie. As such then "the workingmen have no country" but rather are the bearers of an alternative internationalist order. The nation and nationalist struggles are thus to be evaluated in terms of their contribution to the "proletarian revolution." The ambivalence was clear, however. While generally supportive of the nationalist movements of 1848 which were aimed at dissolving the archaic imperial structures of the Austro-Hungarian Empire, Marx and Engels seemed most of the time to be willing to favor the absorption of small and presumably backward nations by the more powerful. Nor were the founders of Marxism entirely free from the racist sentiments which were becoming increasingly pervasive in nineteenth-century Europe. Thus, in respect of the effects of the Opium Wars on the Chinese,

---

[15] See V.G. Kiernan, "On the Development of a Marxist Approach to Nationalism," *Science and Society*, XXXIV, 1, 1970, 93–98.

for example, Marx's judgement was: "It would seem as though history had first to make this whole people drunk before it could rouse them out of their hereditary stupidity."[16]

By the time of Lenin's writings the issue of nationalist struggle had assumed immense strategic significance. Imperialist expansion in Asia and in Africa, in addition to the immediate exigencies of political struggle in the context of a multi-national Russian state, highlighted the practical political significance of nationalism. In recognition of this, Lenin favored "the full right of all nations to self-determination," though somewhat ambiguously he also proclaimed nationalism anathema. Fundamentally, Lenin's support for nationalist movements stemmed from his view of their progressive role in capitalist development as sweeping away archaic pre-capitalist social forms, and from his recognition that "capitalism's broad and rapid development of the productive forces calls for large, politically compact and united territories."[17] With respect to the anti-colonial struggle, however, Lenin departed from the orthodox conceptions of a sequential political development which had been drawn from the European experience. In Asia, the character of uneven development was such, he felt, as to require the proletariat to assume a leading role in the vanguard of the anti-imperialist struggle.

Essentially, despite Lenin's overall and unequivocal support for the right of self-determination, both he and Marx are united in their acceptance of the idea of fundamental contradiction between nationalism and internationalism in the modern world. For both of them, nationalism and internationalism are conceived of as antithetical, theoretical and ideological principles essentially derived from different historical epochs, the expectation being that the transition to socialism necessarily involved the "withering away" of the nation-state and the "amalgamation of nations" in a higher "internationalist" unity. Nevertheless, contemporary polit-

---

[16] "Revolution in China and Europe," in *New York Daily Tribune*, 14 June, 1853 reprinted in Karl Marx and Frederick Engels, *Collected Works*, Vol. 12, New York: International Publications, 1979, p. 94. But in this same article Marx argues: "It may seem a very strange and a very paradoxical assertion that the next uprising of the people in Europe, and their next movement for republican freedom and economy of government, may depend more probably on what is now passing in the Celestial Empire – the very opposite of Europe – than on any other political cause that now exists" (p.93).

[17] V.I. Lenin, "Critical Remarks on the National Question," p. 38.

ical developments suggest at a minimum that the process is neither so simple nor so straightforward. We have suggested that both nationalism and internationalism represent politico-ideological responses to the structural conditions implicit in the capital accumulation process. In particular, we have argued that they derive from the persistence of the structural antinomy between the unity of the world-economy and its division among multiple states. It should be emphasized further that the histori-cally determined tension between nationalism and interna-tionalism should be seen as only one aspect of a wider set of historical developments, involving the conflict and tension between particularity and universality as organizing principles within the modern world. This tension, manifested in wider cultural and intellectual areas as well as in the more narrowly political spheres of social activity, has become increasingly well defined over time, even though the form and locus of the struggles generated have shifted.

Despite the distinctness of each of the respective arenas of struggle, they nonetheless derive an underlying unity from the character of the capital accumulation process. Here, in particular, we have indicated the extent to which this is premised upon complementary and homologous patterns of hierarchy which operate in terms of the global division of labor and its political correlate, the interstate system. Historically, it would appear that nationalism as an ideology and the general emphasis upon the specific regional or cultural claims have received sustenance particularly from the successive waves of struggle taking place in the semiperipheral areas of the world-economy. Correspond-ingly, the claims of universality have been strongest among the dominant bourgeoisies located in the core states.[18]

Finally, it should be clear that only by proceeding in this way to locate contemporary political and ideological expressions in terms of the historically defined context of a single global capital accumulation process, can we begin to get to grips with current concerns regarding the demise of the nation-state and the con-struction of a socialist community of nations or peoples. While a

[18] See Tom Nairn, "The Modern Janus," *New Left Review*, No. 94, Nov–Dec, 1975, 3–29.

detailed discussion of these issues is beyond the immediate purview of this essay, it is clear nevertheless that the contradictory imperatives behind the historical expressions of internationalism and nationalism continue to operate with considerable force. Thus, for example, we see a continuing pressure towards the amalgamation of national units into larger regional groupings, as is the case in the European Community and in regional integration movements in the Third World. These developments are simultaneously the focus of concern and organization on the part of both ruling-class forces worldwide and of antisystemic forces. Furthermore, these very efforts at regional integration themselves tend to engender resurgent nationalisms that resist them.

In any event, the resolution of the competing claims of national or world identity will ultimately depend on the political capacities of the contending forces operating at both the level of the individual states and of the interstate system and, in particular, on their respective capacities to fuse the currents operating in these complementary spheres of activity. Unfortunately, however, the limited state of our theoretical knowledge continues to act as a major impediment to effective intervention for the realization of a socialist world order.

11 ✎ Culture as the ideological battleground of the modern world-system

It is not our human nature that is universal, but our capacity to create cultural realities, and then to act in terms of them.   Sidney W. Mintz[1]

I

Culture is probably the broadest concept of all those used in the historical social sciences. It embraces a very large range of connotations, and thereby it is the cause perhaps of the most difficulty. There is, however, one fundamental confusion in our usage which I shall address.

On the one hand, one of the basic building stones of social science's view of the world, most explicitly emphasized by the anthropologists, is the conviction that, while all persons share some traits with all others, all persons also share other traits with only some others, and all persons have still other traits which they share with no one else. That is to say, the basic model is that each person may be described in three ways: the universal characteristics of the specie, the sets of characteristics that define that person as a member of a series of groups, that person's idiosyncratic characteristics. When we talk of traits which are neither universal nor idiosyncratic we often use the term "culture" to describe the collection of such traits, or of such behaviors, or of such values, or of such beliefs. In short, in this usage, each "group" has its specific "culture." To be sure, each individual is a member of many groups and, indeed, of groups of very different kinds – groups classified by gender, by race, by language, by class, by nationality, etc. Therefore, each person participates in many "cultures."

[1] Sidney W. Mintz, *The Power of Sweetness and the Sweetness of Power*, 8th Duijker Lecture Deventer, NL: Van Loghum Slaterus, 1988, 14.

In this usage, culture is a way of summarizing the ways in which groups distinguish themselves from other groups. It represents what is shared within the group, and presumably simultaneously not shared (or not entirely shared) outside it. This is a quite clear and quite useful concept.

On the other hand, culture is also used to signify not the totality of the specificity of one group against another but instead certain characteristics *within* the group, as opposed to other characteristics within the same group. We use culture to refer to the "higher" arts as opposed to popular or everyday practice. We use culture to signify that which is "superstructural" as opposed to that which is the "base." We use culture to signify that which is "symbolic" as opposed to that which is "material." These various binary distinctions are not identical, although they all seem to go in the direction of the ancient philosophical distinctions between the "ideal" and the "real," or between the "mind" and the "body."

Whatever the merits of these binary distinctions they all go in a quite different structural direction from the other use of culture. They point to a division within the group rather than to the unity of the group (which, of course, is the basis of division between groups). Now, this "confusion" of the two tonalities of the concept, "culture," is so long-standing that it cannot be a mere oversight, especially given the fact that the discussion of culture in general and of its definition in particular has been so voluminous throughout the nineteenth and twentieth centuries.

It is safest to presume that long-standing intellectual confusions are deliberate and the fact of the confusion should itself be the starting-point of the analysis. Since this voluminous discussion has in fact taken place largely within the confines of a single historical system, the capitalist world-economy, it may be that not only the discussion but the conceptual confusion are both the consequence of the historical development of this system and reflect its guiding logic.

The philosophical distinctions between the "ideal" and the "real" and between the "mind" and the "body" are very ancient, and have given rise, broadly speaking, to two perspectives, at least within the context of so-called Western philosophy. Those who have promoted the primacy of the "ideal" or of the "mind" have tended to argue that the distinction points to an ontological reality, and that the "ideal" or the "mind" is more important or nobler or in some way superior to the "real" or the "body." Those who have promoted the primacy of the "real" or the "body" did not, however, take the inverse position. Instead, they tended to argue that the "ideal" or the "mind" are not distinct essences but rather social inventions, and that only the "real" or the "body" truly exist. In short they have tended to argue that the very concept of the "ideal" or the "mind" are ideological weapons of control, intended to mask the true existential situation.

Let us thus designate as culture (usage I) the set of characteristics which distinguish one group from another, and as culture (usage II) some set of phenomena which are different from (and "higher" than) some other set of phenomena within any one group. There is one great problem about culture (usage I). Who or what has such a culture? It seems that "groups" have. But if "culture" is the term in our scientific vocabulary that has the broadest and most confusing usage, "group" is the term that has the vaguest usage. A "group" as a taxonomic term is anything anyone wishes to define as a group. There exists no doubt, to follow the *ultima ratio* of such a term, a "group" which consists of all those who are of a given height, or who have a certain color hair. But can such "groups" be said to have "cultures"? There would be a few who would claim so. Obviously, it is only certain "groups" then that have "cultures."

We could try this exercise starting from the other direction. To what kinds of groups are "cultures" (usage I) normally attributed? Nations are often said to have a national culture. "Tribes" and/or "ethnic groups" are often said to have a culture. It is not unusual to read about the "culture" of "urban intellectuals," or of the "urban poor." More rarely, but frequently, we might read of the "culture" of "Communists" or of "religious fundamentalists." Now what those "groups" presumed to have "cultures" (always usage I) share in common is that they seem to have some kind of self-awareness (and therefore a sense of boundaries), some shared pattern of socialization combined with a system of "reinforcement" of their values or of prescribed behavior, and some kind of organization. The organization may be quite formalized, as in the case of a nation-state, or it can be quite indirect, as for example the shared newspapers, magazines, and possibly the voluntary associations, which act as communication networks between "urban intellectuals."

However, as soon as I raise the question of who or what has a culture, it becomes immediately obvious how slippery is the terrain. What is the evidence that any given group has a "culture"? The answer is surely not that all presumed "members" of any of these groups act similarly to each other and differently from all others. At most, we could argue for a statistically significant relationship between group "membership" and certain behavior, or value-preferences, or whatever.

Furthermore, if we press the matter a little further, it is quite clear that our statistical findings would vary constantly (and probably significantly) over time. That is to say, behavior or value-preferences or however one defines culture is, of course, an evolving phenomenon even if it is a slowly evolving one, at least for certain characteristics (say, food habits).

Yet, on the other hand, it is surely true that people in different parts of the world, or in different epochs, or in different religious or linguistic communities do indeed behave differently from each other, and in certain ways that can be specified and fairly easily observed. For example, anyone who travels from Norway to Spain will note that the hour at which restaurants are most crowded for the "evening meal" is quite different in the two countries. And anyone who travels from France to the US will observe that the frequency with which foreign strangers are invited to homes is quite different. The length of women's skirts in Brazil and Iran is surely strikingly different. And so on. And I have only cited here elements of so-called everyday behavior. Were I to raise more metaphysical issues, it would be easy, as everyone knows, to elucidate group differences.

So, on the one hand, differences are obvious — which is what the concept of culture (usage I) is about. And yet the degree to which groups are in fact uniform in their behavior is distressingly difficult to maintain. When Mintz says that we have a "capacity to create cultural realities and then to act in terms of them," I cannot but agree. But I then wonder how we can know who the "we" are who have this capacity. At that point, I become skeptical that we can operationalize the concept of culture (usage I) in any way that enables us to use it for statements that are more than trivial. The anthropologists, or at least some of them, have argued convincingly that the concept of "human nature" cannot be used to draw meaningful implications about real social situations. But is this not equally true of their proposed substitute culture?

This then is where I begin. Culture (usage I) seems not to get us very far in our historical analyses. Culture (usage II) is suspect as an ideological cover to justify the interests of some persons (obviously the upper strata) within any given "group" or "social system" against the interests of other persons within this same group. And if, indeed, the very distinction of "ideal" and "real," "mind" and "body" were acknowledged to be an ideological weapon of control, then the confusion of the two usages of culture would be a very logical consequence, since it would no doubt add to the process of masking the true existential situation. I would like, therefore, to trace the actual development of the "culture" (in either or both usages) over time within the historical system which has given birth to this extensive and confusing use of the concept of culture, the modern world-system which is a capitalist world-economy.

II

Let us begin by reviewing some of the realities of the evolution of this historical system, as they have affected the way its participants "theorized" it. That is, I am concerned with the degree to which this historical system became conscious of itself and began to develop intellectual and/or ideological frameworks which both justified it, and impelled its forward movement, and thereby sustained its reproduction. I shall mention six such realities which have implications for the theoretical formulations that have come to permeate the system.

(1) The capitalist world-economy is constructed by integrating a geographically vast set of production processes. We call this the establishment of a single "division of labor." Of course, all historical systems are based on a division of labor, but none before was as complex, as extensive, as detailed, and as cohesive as that of the capitalist world-economy. The political framework within which this division of labor has grown up has not however been that of a world-empire, but instead that of an interstate system,

itself a product of the historical development of this system. This interstate system has been composed of, and given birth and legitimacy to, a series of so-called sovereign states, whose defining characteristic is their territorial distinctiveness and congruence combined with their membership in and constraint by this interstate system. It is not the interstate system, however, but the separate states that control the means of violence. Furthermore, their control is, in theory, exclusive within their respective jurisdictions. Although such total control is a myth, state preemption of violence is at least massive, if never exclusive.

This organization of social life where the predominant "economic" pressures are "international" (a bad term, but the one in common use), and the predominant "political" pressures are "national" points to a first contradiction in the way participants can explicate and justify their actions. How can one explain and justify them nationally and internationally simultaneously?

(2) The capitalist world-economy functions, as do most (perhaps all) historical systems by means of a pattern of cyclical rhythms. The most obvious, and probably the most important, of these rhythms is a seemingly regular process of expansion and contraction of the world-economy as a whole. On present evidence, this cycle tends to be 50–60 years in length, covering its two phases.

The functioning of this cycle (sometimes called "long waves," sometimes Kondratieff cycles) is complex and I will not review it here.[2] One part, however, of the process is that, periodically, the capitalist world-economy has seen the need to expand the geographic boundaries of the system as a whole, creating thereby new loci of production to participate in its axial division of labor. Over 400 years, these successive expansions have transformed the capitalist world-economy from a system located primarily in Europe to one that covers the entire globe.

The successive expansions that have occurred have been a conscious process, utilizing military, political, and economic pressures of multiple kinds and, of course, involving the overcoming of political resistances in the zones into which the geographic expansion

---

[2] I have spelled out the mechanism of these cyclical rhythms in various places. One such explanation is to be found in my "Crisis as Transition," in S. Amin et al., *Dynamics of Global Crisis.* New York: Monthly Review Press, 1982, esp. pp. 12–22.

was taking place. We call this process "incorporation," and it too is a complex one.[3] This process points to a second contradiction which the populations of each successively incorporated zone faced. Should the transformations that were occurring in their zone be conceived as changes from a local and traditional "culture" to a worldwide modern "culture," or were these populations rather simply under pressure to give up their "culture" and adopt that of the Western imperialist power or powers? Was it, that is, a case of modernization or of Westernization?

(3) Capitalism is a system based on the endless accumulation of capital. It is, therefore, a system which requires the maximum appropriation of surplus-value. There are two ways to increase the appropriation of surplus-value. One is that workers work harder and more efficiently, thereby creating greater output with the same amount of inputs (other than human labor-time). The second way is to return less of the value that is produced to the direct producers. In short capitalism by definition involves a pressure on all direct producers to work more and to be paid less.

This requirement however runs afoul of the logic of the individual's pursuit of his/her own interest. The most obvious incentive for hard work is higher recompense. One can substitute coercion for higher recompense but, of course, coercion also has a cost and thereby its use also reduces surplus-value. It follows that, unless one can substitute (at least partially) some other motivation for work other than recompense or fear, it is very difficult to obtain simultaneously the twin goals of harder work and lower pay. How can one think about this system in such a way as to achieve this objective?

(4) Capitalism as a system requires movement and change, at least formal change. The maximal accumulation of capital requires not only goods and capital to circulate but manpower as well. It requires in addition a constant evolution in the organization of production in terms both of the nature of the leading sectors and of the sites of production. We usually analyze these phenomena under two labels – that of economic innovation and that of the rise and fall of nations.

[3] For a discussion of the complexities, see Terence K. Hopkins and Immanuel Wallerstein, "Capitalism and the Incorporation of New Zones into the World-Economy," *Review*, X, 5/6 (Supplement), Summer/Fall, 1987, 763–79.

One principal consequence of this reality is the enormous emphasis placed within the modern world-system on the virtues of "newness." No previous historical system has ever been based on a theory of progress, indeed a theory of inevitable progress. But the emphasis on newness, and its constant implementation (at least at the level of form) raises precisely the question of legitimacy – legitimacy of the historical system in general; legitimacy of its key political institution, the various sovereign states, in particular. From Bodin to Weber to Mao Zedong the question of legitimacy has been constantly debated and seen as an extremely knotty issue to resolve. It is particularly difficult because the very advocacy of the virtues of newness undermines the legitimacy of any authority, however laboriously the legitimacy was achieved.

(5) The capitalist system is a polarizing system, both in its reward pattern and in the degree to which persons are increasingly forced to play socially polarized roles. It is, however, also an expanding system and therefore one in which all the absolute parameters have taken the form of a linear upward projection over time. Since its outset, the capitalist world-economy has had ever more productive activity, ever more "value" produced, ever more population, ever more inventions. Thus, it has had ever more outward signs of wealth.

And yet, if it has been a polarizing system, it must at the least be true that this increase of wealth has been going to only a small proportion of the world's population. It might even be the case that real consumption per world capita has not been keeping pace. For example, it is surely the case that there is less physical space per capita and fewer trees per capita now than 400 years ago. What does this mean in terms of that elusive but very real phenomenon, the "quality of life"?

The contradiction, therefore, that needs to be handled is that between "progress" and deterioration, between visibly increasing wealth and very real impoverishment. The only way to defuse the resulting angers may well be denial, but how is it possible to deny phenomena that are so public, and whose public character is indeed one of the exigencies of the system? That is, the endless accumulation of capital requires as one of its mechanisms a collective orientation towards consumption.

(6) Finally, the capitalist world-economy is an historical system.

And, being historical, it has a life cycle and, as any other such system, must at some point cease to function as the consequence of the aggregated results of its eventually paralyzing contradictions. But it is also a system which is based on a particular logic, that of the ceaseless accumulation of capital. Such a system, therefore, must preach the possibility of limitless expansion.

Limitless expansion can seem euphoric, as in the image of wafting upward into heaven, or disastrous, as in the image of hurtling downward into space. In a sense, both images constrain action since there seems to be little an individual can do to affect the pattern. The mundane reality, however, is more complex, more unsettling, but also more subject to human will.

As systems move towards their natural demise they find themselves in "transition" to uncertain futures. And the very uncertainty, which at one level is liberating, is also disconcerting. Thus we are faced with the dilemma of how to think about such transformation, whether to deny the process of systemic "death" or instead to welcome the process of systemic "birth."

III

The "culture," that is the idea-system, of this capitalist world-economy is the outcome of our collective historical attempts to come to terms with the contradictions, the ambiguities, the complexities of the socio-political realities of this particular system. We have done it in part by creating the concept of "culture" (usage I) as the assertion of unchanging realities amidst a world that is, in fact, ceaselessly changing. And we have done it in part by creating the concept of "culture" (usage II) as the justification of the inequities of the system, as the attempt to keep them unchanging in a world that is ceaselessly threatened by change.

The question is, how is this done? Since it is obvious that interests fundamentally diverge, it follows that such constructions of "culture" are scarcely neutral. Therefore, the very construction of culture becomes a battleground, the key ideological battleground, in fact, of the opposing interests within this historical system.

The heart of the debate, it seems to me, revolves around the ways in which the presumed antinomies of unity and diversity, universalism and particularism, humanity and race, world and nation, person and man/woman have been manipulated. I have previously argued that the two principal ideological doctrines that have emerged in the history of the capitalist world-economy – that is, universalism on the one hand and racism and sexism on the other – are not opposites but a symbiotic pair. I have argued that their "right dosage" has made possible the functioning of the system, one which takes the form of a continuing ideological zigzag.[4]

It is this zigzag which is at the base of the deliberate confusions inherent in the two usages of the concept of "culture." I should like to illustrate the issues by analyzing some comments made by a political intellectual in Jamaica, Rex Nettleford, in a speech he gave in 1983 to a political party meeting, a party that calls itself the People's National Party. The speech itself, when reprinted, bore the title "Building a Nation, Shaping a Society." Nettleford wished to emphasize the importance of a "sense of history" in building a nation against those who "teach our young that they have no history worth studying, only a future which . . . they are expected to conquer." Here is what Nettleford said:

"Black" does not merely mean skin in the history of the Americas. It means culture – a culture woven out of the encounters between the millions of West Africans brought as slaves and the millions of Europeans who came as masters, settlers or indentured labourers. In Jamaica and the Caribbean the substance of a truly indigenous life, for all its texture, has been forged in the crucible of the black majority's early efforts to come to terms with the new environment and to survive. That was a struggle of a fundamental and elemental kind, and it is that struggle which is being denied its proper place in the economic, social and cultural ethos of this society. I sense a *deblackening* of the ethos, a persistent contempt in official and cocktail circles for the fruits of our people's labours, and a hypocritical refuge is being taken in our national motto by those who prefer to emphasize the word "many" since to them the "one" may mean the majority. "Out of many one people" becomes "out of many one." So we keep the country pluralist and divided with the marginalized majority remaining marginal, and a privileged few (with many "roast breadfruits" among them) holding on to the economic, social and cultural power in the land.

The real truth is that our people are better than we like to think: we are not that unsophisticated to be racist, but we are not that foolish not to be race conscious. And on that delicate balancing of sensibilities rests the unusual

---

[4] See "The Ideological Tensions of Capitalism: Universalism versus Racism and Sexism," in J. Smith et al., eds., *Racism, Sexism, and the World-System*. Westport, CT: Greenwood Press, 1988.

sophistication of the mass of this population. It is that sophistication which misleads not only our own leaders, but those from outside who say they want to help us. Our people who have gone through centuries of struggle know that "what is pertinent today is not simply freedom from foreign oppression (which in our own primitive way we can deal with), but the creation within this country of socio-economic and political frameworks which accord high values to the human personality." We are very uptight about our personae, about our personal recognition and status, and we hold suspect any class of people inside or outside our nation, who would agree with a once influential Jamaican private sector leader who, in criticising the policies of a certain regime in the recent past, said that during the seventies "our rich national culture had been reduced, shrunken to fit into the narrow concept of a vigorous black culture." She was saying this in a country where the vast majority are hopelessly of that "culture." Anything that expresses the image of the majority is a "reduction" and a "shrinking"! We are not likely to shape a society or build a nation with such beliefs in place, and especially if they are to be found among those in the power structure; and so I implore this forum to think seriously on these things.[5]

Notice in this analysis that the definition of a culture is central. Nettleford wants to build and shape an entity he calls a nation or a society. This is of course standard language and seems to refer to culture (usage I), a usage which presumably emphasizes the ways in which Jamaicans are alike. But he proceeds to observe that others, "found among those in the power structure" of this same Jamaica, also claim they wish to do the same.

The two groups seem to be using the national motto "out of many one people" to mean opposite things. Those who Nettleford calls the "privileged few" emphasize "pluralism" within and unity without ("freedom from foreign oppression"). Nettleford says this neglects entirely the "black majority" who are "marginalized" and who are seeking "the creation within [Jamaica] of socio-economic and political frameworks which accord high values to the human personality" (which presumably means an increase in economic and social equality).

How are the privileged few doing this? By "a *deblackening* of the ethos," by hypocritically emphasizing the "many" in the national motto, by failing to teach a fact (one that is a fact however not of the history of Jamaica, but of the history of the Americas, and therefore of the world-system). This fact is that "millions of West Africans [were] brought as slaves" while "millions of Europeans . . . came as masters, settlers or indentured laborers." The

[5] Rex Nettleford, "Building a Nation, Shaping a Society," in J. Wedderburn, ed., *A Caribbean Reader on Development* (Kingston, 1986), 9–10.

historic encounters of these two groups "in Jamaica and the Caribbean" forged the "texture" of a "truly indigenous life." "Black" is the term of the resultant "culture," which is "vigorous" and not a "reduction" or a "shrinking."

So, in the end, what is being said is that the assertion of "blackness" as constitutive of the national "culture" of Jamaica (culture here in usage I) is the mode by which the "marginalized majority" can hope to protect themselves against the claims of the "privileged few" to represent a higher "culture" (usage II). Thus what seems particularist at the level of the world-system ("blackness") serves as an assertion of a universalist theme ("high values to the human personality"). This, says Nettleford, is being "race conscious" but not "racist," which he admits requires a "delicate balancing of sensibilities." In this complicated reasoning, which seems to me correct, the more "blackness" that Jamaica would exhibit, the more colorblindness (or humanist values) it would exhibit.

Yes, you may respond, perhaps so, but where does this argument end? At what point do we cross the line from "race consciousness" to "racism"? For there are clearly many, many cases across the world where the assertion of the particularist "culture" of the (national) "majority" to the exclusion of the minority or minorities could be seen as oppressive. Have Bretons no "cultural" claims in France, Swedes in Finland, Ainu in Japan, Tamils in Sri Lanka, Kurds in Turkey, Hungarians in Romania?

Nettleford might agree – I do not know – that all these latter groups have legitimate claims to their "cultural" assertion, and still argue that the situation is historically different in Jamaica. Why? Essentially because in Jamaica it is the majority that has been historically "marginalized" and not the various "minorities." And, as long as that remains true, then Negritude or any similar particularism may serve as the negation of the negation, as Sartre argued in "Black Orpheus."[6]

What the Nettleford quote does is to demonstrate how tangled is the skein of cultural debate in the capitalist world-economy, but also how covered with nettles, and therefore how careful we need to be if we wish to understand and evaluate this ideological battleground.

---

[6] Jean-Paul Sartre, "Orphée noir," *Situations*, III, Paris: Gallimard, 1949, 229–288. He calls negritude "antiracist racism" (p.237).

IV

I would like to take each of the six contradictions of the capitalist world-economy and show how the ideologies of universalism and of racism-sexism help contain each of the contradictions, and why therefore the two ideologies are a symbiotic pair.

(1) Since the capitalist world-economy is a world-system, and for some time now one that has expanded to cover the entire globe, it is easy to see how universalism reflects this phenomenon, and indeed this has been one of the most explicit explanations of the ideologists. Today we have a network of United Nations structures, based in theory on the Universal Declaration of Human Rights, asserting the existence of both international law and values of all humanity. We have universal time and space measurements. We have a scientific community who assert universal laws. Nor is this a phenomenon merely of the twentieth century. Universal science was already being proclaimed in the sixteenth century, and indeed far earlier. Grotius was writing about a universal "law of the seas" in the first half of the seventeenth century. And so on.

At the same time, of course, we have been erecting a network of "sovereign states" with clear territorial boundaries and with national laws, assemblies, languages, passports, flags, money, and above all citizens. The entire land area of the globe is today exhaustively divided into such units, which now number over 150.

There are two ways we can consider these 150 or so sovereign states. We can see them as very strong institutions whose *raison d'être* is to limit the validity of universal rules. Sovereignty means in theory the right to do within the frontiers of the country whatever the internal (and constitutionally appropriate) authorities decide to do. But, of course, at the same time, these 150 or so units are an immense reduction from the number of political authorities (to use a vague term) which existed in the world, as of say 1450. Almost every one of the 150 or so units comprises an area that in 1450 included more than one political authority. Thus most of these sovereign states face the issue of how they are to treat this "coming together" historically of what were previously separate entities. All of them, without any exception, do it on the principle of citizenship, a principle which today usually asserts that all persons born in that state are citizens (plus certain others) and that all such citizens enjoy equal rights. (The most notorious exception, South Africa, which as a state refuses to acknowledge the legitimacy of this theory of citizenship, is considered for that very reason a world scandal.) Thus, each state is proclaiming the universality of the equality of citizens, and virtually all states are accepting this principle as a sort of universal moral law.

We can assert, if we wish, that the principle of universalism both on a worldwide scale and within each of the sovereign states that constitute the interstate system is hypocritical. But it is precisely because there is in reality a hierarchy of states within the interstate system and a hierarchy of citizens within each sovereign state that the ideology of universalism matters. It serves on the one hand as a palliative and a deception and on the other as a political counterweight which the weak can use and do use against the strong.

But racism-sexism as an ideology equally serves to contain the contradiction involved in creating sovereign states within an interstate system that contains a single division of labor. For racism-sexism is precisely what legitimates the real inequalities, the always existing (if continually shifting) hierarchies both within the world-system as a whole and within each sovereign state. We know that the peoples of color were subjected to formal colonization as well as to slave labor during the history of this world-system. We know that there exist many formal discriminations concerning the movements of peoples. And we know that these phenomena have been justified by racist theories, sometimes based on pseudo-science (thereby deferring to the ideology of universalism) and sometimes based on unmitigated prejudice, as in the talk of a Yellow Peril which was so widespread in the White areas of the world in the beginning of the twentieth century.

At the state level, the phenomenon of justification by racism of an internal political, economic, and social hierarchy is so familiar that it is scarcely worth recounting. I would only point out two things. Where internal hierarchies cannot be based on skin color, they can always be based on other particularist criteria, as say in Northern Ireland. Secondly, everywhere – in all the states individually, and in the interstate system as a whole – the racist ideology takes the same form. It is argued that one group is genetically or "culturally" (note here, culture in usage II) inferior to another group in such a way that the group said to be inferior cannot be expected to perform tasks as well as the presumably superior group. This is said to hold true either eternally or for a very long period into the future (pending, in another deference to universalist doctrine, some very long-term educational process).

So racism is used, as we all know, to justify these hierarchies. But sexism? Yes, sexism too, and in two ways. First, if one examines racist terminology, one will find that it is regularly clothed in sexist language. The superior "race" is considered to be more masculine, the inferior one to be more feminine. It is as though sexism was even more deeply rooted than racism. Whereas a purely racist ideology might occasionally fail to persuade, the ideologues can find their clinching argument by adding the sexist overtones. So we hear arguments that the dominant group is more rational, more disciplined, more hardworking, more self-controlled, more independent, while the dominated group is more emotional, more self-indulgent, more lazy, more artistic, more dependent. And this is, of course, the same set of characteristics that sexist ideology claims distinguish men from women.

There is a second way in which sexism doubles with racism. The dominated racial group, because it is said to be more self-indulgent, is thereby thought more aggressive sexually (and more pan-sexual as well). The males of the dominated group therefore represent a threat to the females of the dominant group who, although women and not men, are somehow more "self-controlled" than the males of the dominated group. But since they are nonetheless physically weaker, because they are women, they therefore require the active physical protection of the males of the dominant group.

Furthermore, we can turn this sexist argument around and still justify world hierarchies. Now that, as a result of recent political developments, women have gained more rights of various kinds in Western countries, the fact that they have not yet done as well politically in some Third World countries, say those countries in which Islam is strong, becomes itself a further justification of racist ideology. The Moslems, it is argued, are not culturally capable of recognizing the same universal principles of man-woman relations that are said to be accepted in the Western (or Judeo-Christian world) and from this it is said to follow that they are also not capable of many other things.

(2) We have noted that the historic expansion of a capitalist world-economy originally located primarily in Europe to incorporate other zones of the globe created the contradiction of modernization versus Westernization. The simple way to resolve this dilemma has been to assert that they are identical. Insofar as Asia or Africa "Westernizes," it "modernizes." That is to say, the simplest solution was to argue that Western culture is in fact universal culture. For a long time the ideology remained at this simple level, whether it took the form of Christian proselytization or of the famous "mission civilisatrice" of France's colonial empire.

Of course, this sometimes took the slightly more sophisticated form of arguing that only Western civilization, of all world civilizations, was somehow capable of evolving from a pre-modern form to modernity. In a sense, this is what Orientalism as a discipline clearly implied. Clothed in the legitimation of particularism – Islam or India or China represented complex, high cultures which a Westerner could only appreciate after long, difficult, and sympathetic study – the Orientalists also suggested that these high Oriental cultures were historically frozen and could not evolve, but could only be "destroyed" from without. Various versions of anthropological theory – the search for the pristine pre-contact culture, but also the universalist distinction of structuralist anthropology between cold and hot cultures – led to the same conclusions. The West had emerged into modernity; the others had not. Inevitably, therefore, if one wanted to be "modern" one had in some way to be "Western" culturally. If not Western religions, one had to adopt Western languages. And if not Western languages, one had at the very minimum to accept Western technology, which was said to be based on the universal principles of science.

But at the very same time that the universalist ideologues were preaching the merits of Westernization or "assimilation," they were also (or others were also) preaching the eternal existence and virtue of difference. Thus a universalist message of cultural multiplicity could serve as a justification of educating various groups in their separate "cultures" and hence preparing them for different tasks in the single economy. The extreme version of this, and an explicitly theorized one, is *apartheid*. But lesser versions, perhaps less coherently articulated, have been widespread within the system.

Furthermore, racism and sexism can be justified by a rejection of Westernization which can take the form of legitimating indigenous ideological positions (a so-called revival of tradition) that include blatantly racist and sexist themes. At which point, we have a renewed justification of the worldwide hierarchy. It becomes legitimate to treat Iran as a pariah nation, not only because Iran uses "terrorist" tactics in the international arena, but because Iranian women are required to wear the *chador*.

(3) The problem of getting workers to work harder at lower pay is inherently a difficult one. It runs against the grain of self-interest. The question therefore is whether there can exist an ideological motivation that might help achieve this contradictory objective of world capital. Let us see in what ways universalism and racism-sexism can serve this end.

Universalism can become a motivation for harder work insofar as the work ethic is preached as a defining centerpiece of modernity. Those who are efficient, who devote themselves to their work exemplify a value that is of universal merit and is said to be socially beneficial to all. This is true not only at the individual level but at the collective level. Thus states that are low in the hierarchy of the world-system, groups that are low in the hierarchy of states are adjured to overcome the handicap of lower status by joining in the universal ethos. By becoming "competitive" in the market, individuals and groups may obtain what others already have, and thus one day shall achieve equality. Until then, inequality remains inevitable.

Thus, the universal work ethic justifies all existing inequalities, since the explanation of their origin is in the historically unequal adoption by different groups of this motivation. States that are better off than other states, groups that are better off than other groups have achieved this advantage by an earlier, stronger, and more enduring commitment to the universal work ethic. Conversely, those who are worse off, therefore those who are paid less, are in this position because they merit it. The existence of unequal incomes thus becomes not an instance of racism-sexism but rather of the universal standard of rewarding efficiency. Those who have less have less because they have earned less.

But racism and sexism complement this universalizing theorem very well. Racism and sexism, when institutionalized, create a high correlation between low group status and low income. Thus, those at the lower end of the scale are easily identifiable by what may then be termed cultural criteria (culture, that is, in usage II). Culture (usage II) now becomes the explanation of the cause. Blacks and women are paid less because they work less hard, merit less. And they work less hard because there is something, if not in their biology, at least in their "culture" which teaches them values that conflict with the universal work ethos.

Furthermore, we can enlist the dominated groups in their own oppression. Insofar as they cultivate their separateness as "cultural" groups, which is a mode of political mobilization against unequal status, they socialize their members into cultural expressions which distinguish them from the dominated groups, and thus into some at least of the values attributed to them by racist and sexist theories. And they do this, in a seeming paradox, on the grounds of the universal principle of the equal validity of all cultural expressions.

(4) Modernity as a central universalizing theme gives priority to newness, change, progress. Through the ages, the legitimacy of political systems had been derived from precisely the opposite principle, that of oldness, continuity, tradition. There was a straightforwardness to premodern modes of legitimation which does not exist anymore. Political legitimacy is a much more obscure objective within the realities of the capitalist world-economy, yet states of course seek constantly to achieve it. Some degree of legitimacy is a crucial element in the stability of all regimes.

Here is where culture (usage I) can be very helpful. For, in the absence of the personalized legitimacy of monarchical-aristocratic systems, where real power normally defines the limits of legitimacy, a fictionalized collectivity with a collective soul, a hypothetical "nation" whose roots are located in days of yore is a marvelous substitute. Few governments in the history of the capitalist world-economy have failed to discover the power of patriotism to achieve cohesion. And patriotism has quite often been reinforced by or transformed into racism (jingoist chauvinism, opposition of the citizen to the stranger or immigrant) and sexism (the presumed martial nature of males).

But in the real world of the capitalist world-economy with its regular rise and decline of nations, a multifarious set of patriotisms offers little in the way of explanation, especially for the losers in the cyclical shifts. Here then legitimacy can be restored by appealing to the universalizing principles of appropriate political and social change which, by a change in state structure (a "revolution") will make possible (for the first time or once again) national development. Thus, by appealing to culture (usage II), the advanced elements of the nation can place the state in the line of universal progress.

Of course, such "revolutions" work to restore (or create) legitimacy by seeking to transform in some significant way the position of the state in the hierarchy of the world-system. Failing that, the revolution can create its own tradition about itself and link this self-appraisal to a perhaps revised but still fictive history of the state. Thus, if culture (usage II) is inefficacious or becomes so, one can fall back on culture (usage I).

(5) The capitalist world-economy does not merely have unequal distribution of reward. It is the locus of an increasing polarization of reward over historical time. Here, however, there is an asymmetry between the situation at the level of the world-economy as a whole and that at the level of the separate sovereign states which compose the interstate system. Whereas at the level of the world-system, it seems clear that gap of income between states at the top and the bottom of the hierarchy has grown, and has grown considerably over time, it does not necessarily follow that this is true within each state structure. Nonetheless, it is also the case that one of the moral justifications of the capitalist world-economy, one that is used to justify hard work at low pay (the issue just discussed in the previous section), is that inequalities of reward have been diminishing over time, that such inequalities as exist are transitory and transitional phenomena on the road to a more prosperous, more egalitarian future.

Here, once again, we have a blatant discord between official ideology and empirical reality. How has this been contained? The first line of defense has always been denial. The rising standard of living has been a central myth of this world-system. It has been sustained both by arithmetic sleight of hand and by invoking the paired ideologies of universalism and racism-sexism.

The arithmetic sleight of hand is very straightforward. At the world level, it consists first of all of talking about the numerator and not the denominator, and ignoring the dispersion of the curve. We talk about the numerator when we recite the expanded world volume of production, or total value produced, while failing to divide it by world population. Or we analyze quality of life by observing some linear trends but failing to count others. Thus we measure age of mortality or speed of travel but not average number of hours of work per year or per lifetime, or environmental conditions.

But the real sleight of hand is to engage in national rather than global measures, which involves a double deception. First of all, in an unequal and polarizing world-system, there is geographical dispersion. Hence, it is perfectly possible for real income, as measured by GNP per capita say, to rise in some countries while going down in others and in the system as a whole. But since the countries in which the rise occurs are also those most extensively studied, observed, and measured, it is easy to understand how facile but false generalizations take root. In addition, despite the better statistical systems of such core countries, it is undoubtedly the case that they do not measure adequately the non-citizen component of the population (often illegally in residence). And since this is the poorest component, the bias is evident.

Still, misperception of reality is only a first line of defense, and one that is increasingly difficult to sustain. Hence, in the last 50 years, a worldwide schema of "developmentalism" has been erected and propagated which legitimates the polarization. By this point you will realize how repetitive is the pattern of ideological justification. First of all, there is the universalist theme. All states can develop; all states shall develop. Then come the racist themes. If some states have developed earlier and faster than others, it is because they have done something, behaved in some way that is different. They have been more individualist, or more entrepreneurial, or more rational, or in some way more "modern." If other states have developed more slowly, it is because there is something in their culture (usage I at the state level, usage II at the world level) which prevents them or has thus far prevented them from becoming as "modern" as other states.

The seesaw of ideological explanation then continues into the hypothetical future. Since all states can develop, how can the underdeveloped develop? In some way, by copying those who already have, that is, by adopting the universal culture of the modern world, with the assistance of those who are more advanced (higher present culture, usage II). If, despite this assistance, they are making no or little progress, it is because they are being "racist" in rejecting universal "modern" values which then justifies that the "advanced" states are scornful of them or condescending to them. Any attempt in an "advanced" state to comprehend "backwardness" in terms other than wilful refusal to be "modern" is labeled Third-Worldism, or reverse racism or irrationalism. This is a tight system of justification, since it "blames the victim," and thereby denies the reality.

(6) Finally, let us turn to the contradiction of limitlessness and organic death. Any theory of limitless expansion is a gambler's paradise. In the real world, it is not possible. Furthermore to the limited extent that the theory has seemed to accord with the existential reality of the capitalist world-economy as a world-system, it has not seemed to accord with the realities of the separate states. Even the strongest and the wealthiest of states, *especially* the strongest and wealthiest, have risen and declined. We are currently living the beginnings of the long-term relative decline of the United States, only recently still the hegemonic power of the world-system.

Thus the world-system as a whole must deal with the problem of its eventual demise and, within the ongoing system, the strong states must deal with the problem of their relative decline. The two problems are quite different, but regularly fused and confused. There are basically two ways to deal with demise or decline: to deny them or to welcome the change.

Once again, both universalism and racism-sexism are useful conservative ideologies. First of all, racism-sexism serves to sustain denial. Demise or decline is at most a temporary illusion, caused by momentarily weak leadership, because by definition it is said it cannot occur, given the strength or the superiority of the dominant culture (usage II). Or, if it is really occurring, it is because culture (usage II) has ceded place to a deceptive world humanism in the vain hope of creating a world culture (usage I). Thus, it is argued the demise or decline which it is now admitted may really be occurring, is due to insufficient emphasis on culture (usage II) and hence to admitting "lower" racial groups or "women" to political rights. In this version of ideology, demise or decline is reversible, but only by a reversion to a more overt racism-sexism. Generally speaking, this has been a theme throughout the twentieth century of what we today call the extreme, or neo-fascist, right.

But there is a universalizing version to this exercise in denial. The demise or decline has perhaps not been caused, or not primarily caused, by an increased political egalitarianism, but much more by an increased intellectual egalitarianism. The denial of the superiority of the scientific elite, and their consequent right to dictate public policy, is the result of an anti-rationalist, antinomian denial of universal culture (usage I) and its worldwide culture-bearers (usage II). Demands for popular control of technocratic elites is a call for "the night of the long knives," a return to pre-modern "primitivism." This is the heart of what is today called neo-conservatism.

But if the overtly "conservative" versions of the ideologies are inadequate to the task, one can put forward "progressive" versions. It is not too difficult to "welcome" the "transition" in ways that in fact sustain the system. There is the universalizing mode, in which progressive transition is seen as inevitable. This can lead on the one hand to postponing the transition until the equally inevitable "preconditions" of transition are realized. It can lead on the other hand to interim measures whose reality is the worsening of conditions on the grounds that this "speeds up" the realization of the preconditions. We have known many such movements.

Finally, the "welcoming" of the transition can have the same conservative effect in a racist form. One can insist that it is only the presently "advanced" groups that can be the leaders of the next presumed "advance." Hence, it is only on the basis of presently-realized culture (usage II) that the transition to a new world will be realized. The more "backward" regions must in some way wait on the more "advanced" ones in the process of "transition."

V

The paired ideologies of universalism and racism-sexism then have been very powerful means by which the contradictory tensions of the world-system have been contained. But of course, they have also served as ideologies of change and transformation in their slightly different clothing of the theory of progress and the conscientization of oppressed groups. This has resulted in extraordinarily ambivalent uses of these ideologies by the presumed opponents of the existing system, the antisystemic movements. It is to this last aspect of culture as an ideological battleground that I should like now to turn.

An antisystemic movement is a movement to transform the system. An antisystemic movement is at the same time a product of the system. What culture does such a movement incarnate? In terms of culture (usage I), it is hard to see how the antisystemic movements could conceivably have incarnated any culture other than that of the capitalist world-economy. It is hard to see how they could not have been impregnated by and expressed the paired ideologies of universalism and racism-sexism.

However in terms of culture (usage II) they have claimed to have created a new culture, a culture destined to be a culture (usage I) of the future world. They have tried to elaborate this new culture theoretically. They have created institutions presumably designed to socialize members and sympathizers into this new culture. But, of course, it is not as easy to know what shall be the culture, a culture, of the future. We design our utopias in terms of what we know now. We exaggerate the novelty of what we advocate. We act in the end, and at best, as prisoners of our present reality who permit ourselves to daydream.

This is not at all pointless. But it is surely less than a sure guide to appropriate behavior. What the antisystemic movements have done, if one considers their global activities over 150-odd years, has been essentially to turn themselves into the fulfillers of the liberal dream while claiming to be its most fulsome critics. This has not been a comfortable position. The liberal dream – the product of the principal self-conscious ideological *Weltanschauung* within the capitalist world-economy – has been that universalism will triumph over racism and sexism. This has been translated into two strategic operational imperatives – the spread of "science" in the economy, and the spread of "assimilation" in the political arena.

The festishism of science by the antisystemic movements – for example, Marx's designation of his ideas as "scientific socialism" – was a natural expression of the post-1789 triumph of Enlightenment ideas in the world-system. Science was future-oriented; it sought total truth via the perfectibility of human capacities; it was deeply optimistic. The limitlessness of its ambitions might have served as a warning-signal of the deep affinity of this kind of science to its world-system. But the antisystemic thinkers interpreted this affinity to be a transitory misstep, a surviving irrationality, doomed to extinction.

The problem, as the antisystemic movements saw it, was not that there was too much science but too little. Sufficient social investment in science was still lacking. Science had not yet penetrated into enough corners of economic life. There were still zones of the world from which it was kept. Its results were insufficiently applied. The revolution – be it social or national or both – would at last release the scientists to find and to apply their universal truths.

In the political arena, the fundamental problem was interpreted to be exclusion. The states were the handmaidens of minorities; they must be made the instrument of the whole of society, the whole of humanity. The unpropertied were excluded. Include them! The minorities were excluded. Include them! The women were excluded. Include them! Equals all. The dominant strata had more than others. Even things out! But if we are evening out dominant and dominated, then why not minorities and majorities, women and men? Evening out meant in practice assimilating the weaker to the model of the strong. This model looked suspiciously like Everyman – the man with simple but sufficient means, hard-working, morally upright and devoted to family (friends, large community).

This search for science and assimilation, what I have called the fulfillment of the liberal dream, was located deep in the consciousness and in the practical action of the world's antisystemic movements, from their emergence in the mid-nineteenth century until at least the Second World War. Since then, and particularly since the world cultural revolution of 1968, these movements, or at least some of them, have begun to evince doubts as to the utility, the reasonableness of "science" and "assimilation" as social objectives. These doubts have been expressed in multiple forms. The green movements, the countercultural movements have raised questions about the productivism inherent in the nineteenth-century adulation of science. The many new social movements (of women, of minorities) have poured scorn upon the demand for assimilation. I do not need to spell out here the diverse ways in which this has been manifested.

But . . . and this is the crucial point, perhaps the real triumph of culture (usage I), the antisystemic movements have hesitated to go all the way. For one thing, the priorities of one kind of antisystemic movement have often been at odds with that of another kind (e.g. ecologists vs. Third World liberation movements). For another thing, each kind of movement itself has been internally divided. The debates within the women's movements or Black movements over such questions as political alliances or the desirability of "protective" legislation for the "weaker" groups are instances of the tactical ambivalences of these movements.

As long as the antisystemic movements remain at the level of tactical ambivalence about the guiding ideological values of our world-system, as long as they are unsure how to respond to the liberal dream of more science and more assimilation, we can say that they are in no position to fight a war of position with the forces that defend the inequalities of the world. For they cede, by this ambivalence, the cultural high-ground to their opponents. The advocates of the system can continue to claim that scientism and assimilation represent the true values of world culture (usage I) and that their practitioners are the men of culture (usage II), the high priests of this culture (usage I). And, as long as this remains true, we are all enveloped in the paired ideologies (and the false antinomy) of universalism and racism-sexism.

The cultural trap in which we are caught is a strong one, overlain by much protective shrubbery which hides its outline and its ferocity from us. Can we somehow disentangle ourselves? I believe it is possible, though at most I can only indicate some of the directions in which, if we moved along them, I believe we might find ways to disentangle.

Beyond scientism, I suspect there lies a more broadly defined science, one which will be able to reconcile itself dramatically with the humanities, such that we can overcome what C.P. Snow called the division of the two cultures.[7] (Note the term again, here in usage II.) I suspect we may have to reverse the history of science and return from efficient causes to final causes. I think, if we do, that we may be able to scrape away all that is contingent (that is, all that is Western) to uncover new possibilities.

This will make possible a new rendezvous of world civilizations. Will some "universals" emerge out of this rendezvous? Who knows? Who even knows what a "universal" is? At a moment of world history when the physical scientists are at last (or is it once again?) beginning to talk of the "arrow of time," who is able to say that there are any immutable laws of nature?

If we go back to metaphysical beginnings, and reopen the question of the nature of science, I believe that it is probable, or at least possible, that we can reconcile our understanding of the origins and legitimacies of group particularisms with our sense of the social, psychological, and biological meanings of humanity and humaneness. I think that perhaps we can come up with a concept of culture that sublates the two usages.

I wish that I saw more clearly how this could be done, or where it is leading. But I have the sense that in cultural terms our world-system is in need of some "surgery." Unless we "open up" some of our most cherished cultural premises we shall never be able to diagnose clearly the extent of the cancerous growths and shall therefore be unable to come up with appropriate remedies. It is perhaps unwise to end on such a medical analogy. Medicine, as a mode of knowledge, has only too clearly demonstrated its limitations. On the other hand, the art of medicine represents the eternal human response to suffering, death, and transition, and therefore incarnates hope, however much it must be tempered by an awareness of human limitations.

[7] C.P. Snow, *The Two Cultures and the Scientific Revolution.* New York: Cambridge University Press, 1959.

12 ❧ The national and the universal: can there be such a thing as world culture?

The very concept of "culture" poses us with a gigantic paradox. On the one hand, culture is *by definition* particularistic. Culture is the set of values or practices of some part smaller than some whole. This is true whether one is using culture in the anthropological sense to mean the values and/or the practices of one group as opposed to any other group at the same level of discourse (French vs. Italian culture, proletarian vs. bourgeois culture, Christian vs. Islamic culture, etc.), or whether one is using culture in the *belles-lettres* sense to mean the "higher" rather than the "baser" values and/or practices within any group, a meaning which generally encompasses culture as representation, culture as the production of art-forms.[1] In either usage, culture (or a culture) is what some persons feel or do, unlike others who do not feel or do the same things.

But, on the other hand, there can be no justification of cultural values and/or practices other than by reference to some presumably universal or universalist criteria. Values are not good because my group holds them; practices are not good because my group does them. To argue the contrary would be hopelessly solipsistic and force us either into an absolutely paralyzing cultural relativism (since the argument would hold equally for any other group's values and/or practices) or into an absolutely murderous xeno-

---

[1] I have elaborated on the distinction between these two usages of "culture" in a previous paper, "Culture as the Ideological Battleground of the Modern World-System," chapter 11.

phobia (since no other group's values and/or practices could be good and therefore could be tolerated).

I

If I have chosen as the theme "the national and the universal," that is, if I have chosen the national as my prototype of the particular, it is because, in our modern world-system, nationalism is the quintessential (albeit not the only) particularism, the one with the widest appeal, the longest staying-power, the most political clout, and the heaviest armaments in its support.

My query is, can there conceivably be such a thing as a world culture? This may seem an absurd question, given two facts. First, for thousands of years now, some people at least have put forward ideas which they have asserted to be universal values or truths. And secondly, for some 200 years now, and even more intensively for the last 50 years, many (even most) national governments as well as world institutions have asserted the validity and even the enforceability of such values or truths, as in the discussion about human rights, concerning which the United Nations proclaimed in 1948 a Universal Declaration.

If I insist that the paradox is gigantic, it is because it is not only a logical paradox but an historical paradox. The so-called nation-states, our primary cultural container (not our only cultural container by any means, but today our primary one), are, of course, relatively recent creations. A world consisting of these nation-states came into existence even partially only in the sixteenth century. Such a world was theorized and became a matter of widespread consciousness even later, only in the nineteenth century. It became an inescapably universal phenomenon later still, in fact only after 1945.

Side by side with the emergence of such nation-states, each with frontiers, each with its own invented traditions, the world has been moving, so it is said, towards a world consciousness, a consciousness of something called humanity – a universal persona beyond even that of the so-called world religions which, in practice, tended to include inside their universe only those who shared the religion.

And, to top off this dual track – the historical creation of the particular nations side by side with the historical creation of universal humanity – we find a very curious anomaly. Over time, the particular nation-states have come to resemble each other more and more in their cultural forms. Which state today does not have certain standard political forms: a legislature, a constitution, a bureaucracy, trade unions, a national currency, a school system? Few indeed! Even in the more particularistic arena of art forms, which country does not have its songs, its dances, its plays, its museums, its paintings, and today its skyscrapers? And are not the social structures that guarantee these art forms increasingly similar? It is almost as if the more intense the nationalist fervor in the world, the more identical seem the expressions of this nationalism. Indeed, one of the major nationalist demands is always, is it not, the obtaining of some form that more privileged countries already have?

This is in part, no doubt, the result of cultural diffusion. The means of transport and communication at our disposition are ever better. We all know more about what are for us the far corners of our earth than did previous generations. But it should also lead us to reflect on what pressures exist which cause us to assert our cultural differences and exclusions in such clone-like fashion?

Let us deal with two opposite modes of explaining this phenomenon that have been put forward repetitively. One is the thesis of the linear tendency towards one world. Originally, it is argued, the globe contained a very large number of distinct and distinctive groups. Over time, little by little, the scope of activity has expanded, the groups have merged and, bit by bit, with the aid of science and technology, we are arriving at one world – one political world, one economic world, one cultural world. We are not yet there, but the future looms clearly before us.

The second explanation suggests a rather different course but the outcome predicted is more or less the same. The historic differences of all groups, it is argued, have always been superficial. In certain key structural ways, all groups have always been the same. There have, no doubt, been several different such structures, but they make up a patterned sequence. This is, of course, the stage theory of human development, so popular in modern social science since its onset. Since, in this mode of theorizing, all "societies" go through parallel stages, we end up with the same result as in the theory of a secular tendency towards one world. We end up with a single human society and therefore necessarily with a world culture.

But can there be a world culture, I have asked? Not should there be one – I will return to that question – but can there be one? There seems clearly to be some deep resistance to the very idea. It takes the form on the one hand of the multiple political chauvinisms which constantly seem to resurface around the globe. It takes the form as well of the multiple so-called countercultures which also seem to surge up constantly, and whose rallying-cry, whose *cri de coeur*, always seems to be the struggle against uniformity.

I do not think that either of the two classic explanations – the secular tendency towards one world, or the stage theory of human development – are very helpful models. No doubt both capture some elements of the empirical reality we think we know, but both also disregard some very visible phenomena. And both require leaps of inference (leaps of faith?) that seem quite hazardous.

I would rather start with a model of successive historical systems in which what is certain is only that there has been and will be a succession of systems, leaving quite open what both its content and its form might be.

My basic reason for an initial skepticism about the concept of a world culture stems from the sense that defining a culture is a question of defining boundaries that are essentially political – boundaries of oppression, and of defense against oppression. The boundaries must necessarily be arbitrary in the sense that the case for drawing the boundaries at one point rather than at another is seldom (perhaps never) logically tight. Who is an Arab? What is good music? Or even what is music? Is Confucianism a religion? It is clear that the boundaries depend on definitions, and that these definitions are not universally shared, or even consistent over time. Furthermore, of course, at any given time, all Arabs do not speak Arabic, all Englishmen are not individualists, some Jews and some Moslems are atheists. That is to say, it is clear that however a culture is defined, not all members of the designated group hold its presumed values or share its presumed practices. Hence, in what sense does such a group share a culture? And why are the boundaries drawn where they are drawn?

Let me begin the discussion with an example from the tenth century. At that time, a change in the social relations of production was occurring in Western Europe which historians call *incastellamento* (from the Italian word for castle). It involved the building of a castle by a powerful person, who sought to use this castle as a base to force the juridical and economic submission of the local peasantry – both the freeholders and the tenant-farmers – to the seignior of the castle. These seigniors successfully asserted their right to command, to constrain, and to apprehend these peasants. What is interesting in terms of this discussion is that, as part of this process of social transformation, the terminology changed.

It seems that by the eleventh century these rights that the seigniors had basically usurped by force in the tenth century were being officially termed "usages" and "customs."[2] Thus we see, in this case at least, that the word "custom," a basic term in cultural discourse, was used to describe what we know to have been a power that was usurped only a relatively short time before. In effect, calling this practice a custom was a way of legitimating it, that is, of reducing the amount of current force required to enforce it. Calling it a "custom" was an effort to transform it into a "right." The effort presumably succeeded, more or less.

No doubt, not every peasant internalized fully the idea that the dues to the seignior were the latter's "right," but many did, and most children were thereupon being socialized into this culture, even as they were also learning a given language, identifying with particular religious practices, and being taught to consider certain objects beautiful. A perceptive visitor traveling from one region to another could have described how the cultures of different regions varied. This same traveler no doubt might have noticed as well boundary uncertainties, where one culture's reach blurred into that of a neighboring culture. The more foreign the visitor the larger the arena he may have considered to constitute the boundaries of a single culture. What may have seemed a "Chinese" cultural zone to Marco Polo may have been visualized as a series of smaller zones to a merchant born within Marco Polo's "Chinese" cultural zone.

---

[2] See Isaac Johsua, *La face cachée du Moyen Age*. Paris: La Brèche, 1988, p. 21.

What might be called the fluidity of culture has always been a social reality, and can only have become intensified with the increasing density of human settlement. Perhaps, in 100,000 BC, when humanity may have consisted of a series of small bands living distantly from each other, each such band was relatively culturally homogeneous. But it makes no sense whatsoever today, or even for the period of so-called recorded history, to conceive of ourselves as living in culturally homogeneous bands. Every individual is the meeting-point of a very large number of cultural traits. If one imagined a series of groups consisting of all persons who held each of the particular traits found in a single individual, each such group would be composed of a different list of persons, although no doubt there would be substantial overlapping. Still, it means that each individual is in effect a unique composite of cultural characteristics. To use a metaphor of painting, the resulting collective cultural landscape is a very subtle blending of an incredibly large number of colors, even if we restrict ourselves to looking only at a relatively small unit (small spatially, small demographically).

In this sense, the history of the world has been the very opposite of a trend towards cultural homogeneization; it has rather been a trend towards cultural differentiation, or cultural elaboration, or cultural complexity. Yet we know that this centrifugal process has not at all tended towards a Tower of Babel, pure cultural anarchy. There seem to have been gravitational forces restraining the centrifugal tendencies and organizing them. In our modern world-system, the single most powerful such gravitational force has been the nation-state.

In the unfolding of the capitalist world-economy, the nation-states that were coming into existence were a very special kind of state. For they defined themselves in function of other states, together with whom they formed an interstate system. The nation-state had boundaries that were fixed not merely by internal decree but just as much by the recognition of other states, a process often formalized in treaties. Not only did the nation-state have boundaries but there was a very strong tendency to bound the states such that all their parts were contiguous to each other, in which case the outer boundaries of the state were constituted by a single continuous line, hopefully not containing enclaves within it. This is, of course, a purely formal consideration of political geography, but it would be a mistake not to notice how forceful and how constant has been the pressure to comply with such a morphology.

There were some additional *de facto* rules in the creation of the interstate system. There were to be no no-man's-lands, no zones that were not part of some particular state. And all these resultant states were to be juridically equal, that is, they were each to be "sovereign." This presumably meant that the authorities in any state had not only full but also exclusive authority within the boundaries of the state, and that no one escaped the authority of some state.

Of course, it took several hundred years to include all parts of the globe within this system, to make each part share the same formal characteristics, and to have the volatile boundaries settle down. We are not really altogether there yet. But, compared to say 1648, when the Treaty of Westphalia was signed, consolidating the then existing European state-system, the post-1945 era of the world-system (the era of the United Nations) is a model of juridical clarity and stability.

The system as it developed was not only a system structuring state-units but also one defining the relationship of each individual to the nation-states. By the nineteenth century, the concept of "citizen" was widespread. Every individual was presumed to be a participant member of one sovereign unit, but only of one. To be sure, we have wrestled ever since with the problem of "stateless persons" as well as with that of "double nationality," but the trend pattern has been clear.

Thus were created a series of clearly bounded entities of contiguous territory with a specified list of member-individuals. There remained the issue of how one acquired citizenship. And this issue posed itself at two moments in the life cycle: at birth, and later in life. At birth, there are really only two non-arbitrary possibilities: one acquires citizenship genetically (via the parents) or geographically (via the location of the birthplace). Though which of these methods is to be used has been a matter of constant passionate political debate, the overall trend has been from reliance on genetic inheritance to reliance on geographic rights. Later in life, there are also only two possibilities: either it is possible legally to change citizenship, or it is not. We have moved from impossibility to possibility, and the latter doubly: possibility of acquiring a new citizenship; possibility of relinquishing an old one. The codification of all of this has been complex, and the process is still not completed, but the direction has been clear.

If we take these political processes as given, then it is clear that they have posed incredible "cultural" problems. Every individual belongs juridically to one unit only, and each such unit is called upon to make a series of cultural decisions, most of them legally binding. Modern states have official languages, school systems with specific curricula, armies that require specific behavior, laws about migration across boundaries, laws about family structures and property (including inheritance), etc. In all of these arenas, some decisions must be made, and one can see why states in general should prefer uniformity whenever it is politically possible. In addition to these arenas where decisions are inescapable, there is a further arena where states could theoretically remain neutral but in practice are pressed to make political decisions. Since the state has become the major mechanism of allocating social income, the states are pressed to offer financial support to both the sciences and the arts, in all their multiple forms. And since the money available is inherently limited, the state must make choices in both the sciences and the arts. Clearly, in any given state, after 100 years of making such decisions, it is very clear that a "national" culture will exist even if it didn't exist at the outset. A particular past, a heritage is institutionalized.

But there is a second reality, which is economic. Our modern world-system is a capitalist world-economy. It functions by giving priority to the ceaseless accumulation of capital, and this is optimized by the creation of a geographically very wide division of labor, today a division of labor that is worldwide. A division of labor requires flows – flows of commodities, flows of capital, flows of labor; not unlimited or unrestricted flows, but significant ones. This means that the state boundaries must be permeable, and so they are. At the very moment that one has been creating national cultures each distinct from the other, these flows have been breaking down the national distinctions. In parts, the flows have broken down distinctions by simple diffusion. We talk of this when we speak of the steady internationalization of culture, which has become striking even in realms where it seemed least likely – in everyday life: food habits, clothing styles, habitat; and in the arts.

However, all has not been smooth in this diffusion process. People cross frontiers regularly, and not merely as temporary visitors. People move in order to work, but they do this in two different ways, or at two different levels. At the top of the occupation scale, people move regularly from rich countries to poor ones, and such persons are normally sojourners, rather than emigrants. They neither "assimilate" nor wish to assimilate; nor do the receiving states wish them to assimilate. Culturally they tend to form relatively discrete enclaves in their country of sojourn. They often see themselves as bearers of world culture, which means, in fact, bearers of the culture of dominant groups in the world-system.

The bigger issue is the other kind of migration, of persons at the lower end of the occupational scale, going from poorer countries to richer ones. These persons are in cultural conflict with the receiving country. They often stay permanently, or try to stay. When they wish to assimilate into the national culture of the receiving country, they are often rejected. And when they reject assimilation, they are often required to assimilate. They become, usually quite officially, a "minority."

"Minorities" are not rare today; quite the opposite. Every country has one or several; and they have them more and more. So just as there is a dialectic of creating simultaneously a homogeneous world and distinctive national cultures within this world, so there is a dialectic of creating simultaneously homogeneous national cultures and distinctive ethnic groups or "minorities" within these nation-states.

There is, however, one critical difference in the two dialectics. In the two parallel contradictions – tendency to one world vs. tendency to distinctive nation-states, and tendency to one nation vs. tendency to distinctive ethnic groups within each state – it has been the states which have had the upper hand in both contradictions. The states have had this upper hand for one simple reason: they have controlled the most physical force. But the states have played opposite roles in the two contradictions. In one case, they have used their force to create cultural diversity, and in the other case to create cultural uniformity. This has made the states the most powerful cultural force in the modern world and the most schizophrenic. And this is true of the states, whether we are referring to the relatively powerful, like the USA, France, or the USSR, or to the relatively weak, like Ecuador, Tunisia, or Thailand.

II

Culture has always been a weapon of the powerful. That was what I sought to illustrate with my very brief reference to medieval Europe. But culture has always cut both ways. If the powerful can legitimate their expropriations by transposing them into "customs," the weak can appeal to the legitimacy of these same "customs" to resist new and different expropriations. This is an unequal battle to be sure, but not one that has had no effect.

What is striking about the political history of the modern world-system, as it has historically developed, is the ever more frequent and ever more efficacious utilization by oppressed elements of what might generically be called cultural resistance. Of course, cultural resistance is an eternal theme. There have long been relatively stable popular cultures which have asserted their values and their forms against elite cultures. And there have long been conjunctural countercultures in the sense of groups who have deliberately sought to withdraw from the control systems to which they were subjected. This has often been linked with production in the arts in the form of bohemias, or with production of utopias in the form of new religions. But the conjunctural countercultures have regularly been recuperated, losing their bite. And the very stability of popular cultures has been their weakness as well as their strength. They have more often led to social anesthesia than to social revolution.

What is new in cultural resistance today is the result of the sociological invention of antisystemic movements in the nineteenth century, having the key idea that opposition must be organized if it is to succeed in transforming the world. Cultural resistance today is very often organized resistance – not spontaneous or eternal, but planned.

Planning cultural resistance is like planning political resistance:

its efficacity is also its fatal flaw. When an antisystemic movement organizes to overthrow or replace existing authorities in a state, it provides itself with a very strong political weapon designed to change the world in specific ways. But, by so organizing, it simultaneously integrates itself and its militants into the very system it is opposing. It is utilizing the structures of the system to oppose the system which, however, partially legitimates these structures. It is contesting the ideology of the system by appealing to antecedent, broader ideologies (that is, more "universal" values) and, by so doing, is accepting in part the terms of the debate as defined by the dominant forces. This is a contradiction which a movement of political resistance cannot escape, and with which it must cope as best it can.

The same thing is true of organized cultural resistance. This is not surprising since cultural resistance is part and parcel of political resistance. If we deliberately assert (or reassert) particular cultural values that have been neglected or disparaged in order to protest against the imposition of the cultural values of the strong upon the weaker, we are, to be sure, strengthening the weaker in their political struggles, within a given state, within the world-system as a whole. But we are then pressed to prove the validity of our asserted (or reasserted) values in terms of criteria laid down by the powerful. Accused of being "uncivilized," the proclaimers of the (re)asserted cultural values suggest that it is they who are truly "civilized." "Civilization" (or some equivalent term) thereupon becomes the universal criterion by which one judges particular cultural acts – whether these are acts of artistic performance, or acts of religious ritual, or acts of the esthetic utilization of space and time. The planners of cultural resistance, in planning the assertion of some particular culture, are in effect (re)legitimating the concept of universal values.

The systemic cooption of cultural resistance occurs in two opposite ways, which combine to deprive the cultural resistance of its *raison d'être*, resistance. On the one hand, the powerful of the world seek to commodify and thereby denature the practices of cultural resistance. They create high market demand for the forms of avant-garde (and/or exotic) artistic production. They create high-tech market networks for the distribution of previously artisanal or illicit production of the means of everyday life;

that is, they transform a private domain into a semipublic one. They assign public space, delimited public space, to the non-standard linguistic, religious, even juridical forms.

But it is more than a matter of mere cooption, of a kind of cultural corruption. It is as much the fact that any movement of cultural resistance that succeeds, even partially, in mobilizing a significant support must deal with the consequences of what Weber called the "routinization of charisma." There are, it seems to me, only two ways to deal with the routinization of charisma. One can reduce the difference of substance to a difference of form. Thereby one may guarantee the survival of the organization that originally promoted the resistance, but at the sacrifice of the quality of its "resistance." Or one can reassert the quality of its resistance by shifting from a policy of self-assertion to a policy of proselytization. This too may enable the organization to survive, but only as a protagonist of some universal. It is the shift from proclaiming an alternative art-form, an alternative religion, an alternative epistemology to proclaiming a singular truth that deserves to be imposed.

Thus the case of cultural resistance involves the same dilemmas as resistance at the level of political power in the narrow sense. The contradictions of planned resistance are inescapable, and the movements must cope with them as best they can.

Of course, one can try to take a different tack. One can move in the direction of anarchy or libertarianism as a strategy. One can argue that the only mode of cultural resistance, the only mode of cultural assertion, that is of value is that of the *franc-tireur*, of the individual against the mass (all masses, any mass). And surely this has been tried, time and again – whether in the form of so-called art for art's sake, or in the form of withdrawal into small communes, or in the form of nihilism, or in the form of schizophrenia. We should not dismiss these diverse modes of resistance out of hand.

There are enormous advantages to these modes of cultural resistance, to which one might give the label "individualist." They are easy to pursue in the sense of not requiring the effort of organizing them, or at least requiring less effort. They are relatively spontaneous and need less to take account of dominant values. They become, therefore, somewhat more difficult for the authorities to control, and thereupon to coopt. They do not seek *organizational* triumph, and hence are less likely to breed among those who practice such modes the temptation to justify themselves in the universalistic language of the dominant culture. Individualistic modes of resistance are for all these reasons more total as resistance than planned social modes.

This being the case, such modes, however, create their own difficulties in turn. Because individualistic modes involve so much less social organization, the holders of cultural power can and do treat them either with the disdain that requires no notice, or by severe repression, which is harder to combat precisely because of the relative lack of social organization.

Thus, the individualist forms of cultural resistance have exactly the opposite advantages and disadvantages of the planned forms of cultural resistance. It is not at all clear that the balance-sheet in the end is any more positive. Furthermore, can individual resistance be called *cultural* resistance? If one pursues activities with reference only to one's inner ear, in what sense is one sharing a culture with anyone else, even with other individualist resisters? And, if the answer is that the inner ear is a guide to the true path, is this not an appeal to universalist values with a vengeance, since in this case, the claim to universalism lacks any control whatsoever of social dialogue?

I have never thought, and do not think, that we can successfully escape the contradictions of planned cultural resistance by turning inward. It may be quite the opposite: it is perhaps the case that we can minimize these contradictions (one can of course never escape them entirely) of planned cultural resistance only by a *fuite en avant* of being still more social in our outlook.

III

This therefore brings us to the issue of world culture. World culture, the humanism of many sages, has long been advocated on these grounds, that it alone permits one to overcome the provincialism – hence both the limitations to moral growth, and the obscurantism – of cultural particularisms.

Let us eliminate from our discussion the naïve conceptualizations of world culture, those that barely disguise an attempt to impose a particular culture in the guise of a "mission civilisatrice". Such naïve conceptualizations are, to be sure, commonplace, but they are an easy target of our criticism. Let us take its more sophisticated version, the advocacy of what Léopold-Sédar Senghor has called, in a celebrated phrase, *le rendez-vous du donner et du recevoir*. Can there be such a rendezvous, and what would it look like?

In a sense, the concept of the university is itself supposed to constitute this rendezvous. After all, the words university and universalism have the same etymological root. And, curiously, in medieval European usage, a *universitas* was also the name given to a form of particular cultural community. Was it then that the university in the sense of the universal was being suggested as the meeting-place of the universities in the sense of particular communities? It is certainly doubtful that this is what they have been historically, but it is regularly suggested that this is what they should become today and in the future.

The post-1968 discussion in many universities of the concept of "cultural diversity" (and its implications for curricula) is one more instance of this call. We face the very bizarre situation today of a major debate within US universities between, on the one side, those who advocate a universe of cultures via the promotion of Black studies or women's studies or the extension (if not the elimination) of the so-called canons in literature and, on the other side, those who advocate a universal culture via the promotion of courses in Western civilization. Truly the world is upside down. One arrives, it seems to be argued by both sides, at the universal via the particular (although they differ as to which particular).

Still, is this call for cultural diversity, as Sartre suggested of Negritude, a Hegelian negation of the negation? Will not only the states, but the national cultures, wither away, sometime in the future? And, if they were to wither away, is that the image at last of the good society? Or is it some new hell of robot-like uniformity? Would this be the fulfillment of the old anti-socialist joke: (Orator:) "Comes the revolution, everyone will eat strawberries and cream"; (Worker in audience:) "But I don't like strawberries and cream"; (Orator:) "Comes the revolution, you will have to like strawberries and cream"?

I believe we have too long avoided thinking seriously about the cultural implications of a post-capitalist future, given our quite understandable preoccupation with the difficulties of a capitalist present. Suppose it is true, as I myself believe, that there can be no liberty outside an egalitarian world, and no equality outside a libertarian world, what then follows in the realm of culture – in the arts and in the sciences? Is a libertarian world one in which everyone follows his/her inner ear? Is an egalitarian world one in which we all share equally the same universal values?

And if, as I have tended to argue here, culture is a collective expression that is combative, that requires another, in this putative libertarian–egalitarian world, does "culture" exist?

I could retreat at this point and say I don't know, which is true. I could also retreat at this point and say that, to solve the problems of the present, the answers to these hypothetical questions can wait, but I do not really believe this to be true. It is no accident, it seems to me, that there has been so much discussion these past 10–15 years about the problem of "culture." It follows upon the decomposition of the nineteenth-century double faith in the economic and political arenas as loci of social progress and therefore of individual salvation. Some return to God, and others look to "culture" or "identity" or some other realistic illusion to help them regain their bearing.

I am skeptical we can find our way via a search for a purified world culture. But I am also skeptical that holding on to national or to ethnic or to any other form of particularistic culture can be anything more than a crutch. Crutches are not foolish. We often need them to restore our wholeness, but crutches are, by definition, transitional and transitory phenomena.

My own hunch is to base our utopistics on the inherent lack of long-term equilibria in any phenomena – physical, biological, or social. Hence we shall never have a stable libertarian–egalitarian world. We may, however, achieve a world-system that is structured so as to tend in the direction of being libertarian and egalitarian. I am not at all sure what such a structure would look like. But whatever it might be, I assume that there would also be within its operation a constant tendency to move away from both libertarianism and equality.

In this vision of the best future I can envisage, there would indeed be a place, and a permanent place, for cultural resistance.

The way to combat the falling away from liberty and equality would be to create and recreate particularistic cultural entities — arts, sciences, identities; always new, often claiming to be old — that would be social (not individual), that would be particularisms whose object (avowed or not) would be the restoration of the universal reality of liberty and equality.

Of course, this may not be a description only of a hypothetical future; this may in part be a description of the present we are living.

13 ❧ What can one mean by Southern culture?

In his famous book *The Mind of the South*, published in 1941, W.J. Cash observes: "There exists among us ordinary [people] – both North and South – a profound conviction that the South is another land, sharply differentiated from the rest of the American nation, and exhibiting within itself a remarkable homogeneity. As to what its singularity may consist in, there is, of course, much conflict of opinion, and especially between Northerner and Southerner. But that it is different and that it is solid – on these things nearly everybody is agreed."[1]

Cash goes on to say that "if it can be said there are many Souths, the fact remains that there is also one South."[2] This is the proposition I wish to consider: that there is a cultural entity we may call the South. I shall not be concerned with what this culture is supposed to be, but whether and in what sense it is meaningful to suggest that it exists.

I feel somewhat like Michael O'Brien who, in the introduction to his book *The Idea of the American South, 1920–1941*, thought it imperative to note at the outset:

But it may be wise to caution the reader, especially if he be a Southerner, that the outsider feels no partisanship on the competing moral claims of these various versions of Southern identity; that is a private debate, on which it would be impertinent to intrude. To him, the debate is an interesting problem in intellectual history rather than a matter of social passion projected into history. To him, it does not matter personally whether Southerners are racist baboons or

---

[1] W.J. Cash, *The Mind of the South*. Garden City, NY: Doubleday Anchor, 1954, p. vii.
[2] *Ibid.*, p. viii.

the true heirs of Aristotle, but he is intrigued by how such opinions should have come to pass.[3]

Well, not quite. It does matter to me, but for the moment I put this concern aside.

O'Brien discusses the controversies among analysts and the zigzag of emphasis between social and intellectual history, noting:

> There are great, and complicated, controversies among students of human consciousness and myth that the Southern historian is now obliged to address. Defining what is myth, what is "reality", and where myth can be disentangled from intellectual traditions of perception is not easy. To reduce the difficult to the simple, he is obliged to take up a position in an old dispute: that between philosophical idealism and positivism. In Southern terms, this is a choice between seeing the South itself as an idea, used to organize and comprehend disparate facts of social reality, or viewing the South as a solid and integrated social reality about which there have been disparate ideas.[4]

Since I consider myself neither a philosophical idealist nor a positivist, this choice leaves me somewhat bewildered. It is quite clear the South has been an idea. One has but to note the very large number of books which discuss that "idea" to verify this. It seems likely that the South has been a social reality, if only because there once was an entity called the Confederate States of America, willed into existence, enjoying widespread social support, and destroyed only by the force of arms. But a "solid and integrated" social reality? That depends on what we mean by such adjectives.

The concept of culture has a long and checkered past. Etymologically, it derives from the Latin verb *colere* meaning "to till (the soil)." This root is found in words like *cultivate* and *agriculture* as well. Hence, the word *culture* has had from the beginning the implication of something that grows – and not spontaneously, but as the result of human will. Yet it is frequently used to designate phenomena that are quite the opposite of products of human will. In the literature on economic development, it is used by many as an explanation of why, despite presumably manipulable variables of economic policy, some regions of the world develop more slowly than others. For example, an economist from the South, William Nicholls noted what he considered to be the anomaly that upper East Tennessee "developed" earlier and more rapidly than

---

[3] Michael O'Brien, *The Idea of the American South, 1920–1941*. Baltimore: Johns Hopkins Univ. Press, 1979, p. xi.

[4] *Ibid.*, p. xiii.

other parts of the South. He was puzzled by this. "I was forced to turn to largely non-economic factors, related to this area's markedly different cultural tradition, for a plausible explanation."[5] Thus culture in some sense was defying will.

There is another ambiguity in the use of the word *culture*. As anthropologists have tended to use the term, *culture* is the property of a whole "people." However, in more popular parlance, *culture* refers to particular cultural behavior with regard to the arts, the manners of everyday life, etc., and is usually the property of only some members of the "people." We can get around this ambiguity by calling the latter *high culture*, but this points to a problem. It seems that within a "people" there may be several cultures – a high culture; a low culture; a culture for each class; a culture for each group as defined by religion, language, race, geographic origin of ancestors, etc. In recent decades we have been calling the latter subgroups "ethnic groups" and this practice has now been extended to the South as an American subgroup in such a book as George Brown Tindall's *The Ethnic Southerners*.

There is still another semantic problem of long standing, the relationship of the terms *culture* and *civilization*. In some usages, they are more or less synonymous. For example, Clement Eaton entitled his work on southern culture *The Waning of the Old South Civilization, 1860s–1880s*. For some other writers, however, the two terms are contrasted, as in (*folk*) *culture* versus (*high*) *civilization*. And to compound the looseness, for some, mostly non-English, usages, *civilization* refers to the everyday phenomena while *culture* refers to the highbrow. There is no consistency whatsoever, as any look at the synthetic essays in encyclopedias will reveal. Finally, there is the ambiguity between the use of *culture* (singular) and *cultures* (plural), *civilization* (singular) and *civilizations* (plural).[6]

It will be of little use to engage here in one more definitional exercise. What may be of some use, however, is to discuss the

[5] William H. Nicholls, *Southern Tradition and Regional Progress*. Chapel Hill: University of North Carolina Press, 1960.
[6] I have discussed the importance of the distinction between singular and plural usage in "The Modern World-System as a Civilization," Chapter 14.

utility of the concept in any guise. I will begin by simply reporting on some of the ways this concept has been used in relation to the South. There seem to me at least three principal ways in which writings on the South have utilized the concept (but of course not writings on the South alone). These three usages have different implications for action.

First, there is culture as a description of a set of traits, culture as "tradition." By culture in this sense is meant some *summum* of institutions and ideas/values that is thought to be long-existing and highly resistant to change. This can be seen as a very negative thing as in Nicholls: "It has become my firm conviction that the South must choose between tradition and progress." For Nicholls, the South is an underdeveloped country (or was, at least, in 1960) with an "agrarian value system." High resistance to change of course does not mean imperviousness to change. Nicholls for example, argues: "Within limits it would be more appropriate to argue that the South has persisted in its agrarian value system because of its lag in industrialization rather than to attribute the latter to its stubborn agrarianism."[7] The practical implication of this is clear. Industrialize, and the benighted tradition will disappear.

Tindall, by contrast, presents tradition more positively:

In this perspective a larger southernism is an unquestionable reality, especially those who have grown up in the South, and the historian can list some of the objective factors that produced it: a distinctive historical experience involving defeat and poverty; the climate and physical setting with their effects on life, tempo, emotion, and character; the presence of the Negro and his pervasive influence on the whole life of the region; the powerful religious heritage and the knowledge of good and evil; and, finally, the persistence of an essentially rural culture with its neighborliness in human relations.

The practical implications are once again quite clear. Tindall is, to be sure, no stick-in-the-mud. He hopes for many kinds of changes: "Wide vistas of opportunity beckon at last, and if a leadership can emerge with the genius to seize the day, the South can exploit a chance that comes to few generations. Reconciliation is not out of reach, the land remains relatively unspoiled, the political system is more open and unrestricted than ever before. It may be something of a cliché now, but it is also a self-evident

---

[7] Nicholls, *Southern Tradition and Regional Progress*, pp. x, 18.

truth, that a region so late in developing has a chance to learn from the mistakes of others."

But the sagacity of a historian conversant with the power of tradition leads him to be skeptical and therefore to warn his readers, in the closing words of his essay: "But before this begins to sound like Henry Grady warmed over and spiced up with a dash of Pollyanna, let us not forget that if experience is any guide, the South will blow it. We will have to make the same mistakes all over again, and we will achieve the urban blight, the crowding, the traffic jams, the slums, the ghettos, the pollution, the frenzy, and all the other ills that modern man is heir to. We are already well on the way."[8]

What should be noted about this idea of culture as a bundle of traits, culture as a tradition, is that it forces one's vision inward. There is some entity we may call the South; it has traits; it has alternatives (either to persist in these traits or to change them); the likelihood of change may be estimated; the desirability of change may be argued; the ultimate moral responsibility lies with the entity.

There is an elementary difficulty with this approach that Richard Current has pointed out: "The South may be eternal, but what 'the South' means is not always clear. Even its boundaries are uncertain."[9] But this difficulty can be handled within the approach as an empirical question. Let us, the scholars, be more precise in our definitions and in our research. We will arrive eventually at a more careful bounding of the entity in question, one that obtains a greater consensus among scholars. The limitations of the use of the concept lie, therefore, not in the concept itself but in its less than optimal manipulation by the analysts.

A second usage of culture in the literature is quite different. Culture represents one-half of a basic human antinomy, that between mind and body, God and Mammon, good and evil. Richard Weaver makes this most explicit in the introduction to his book *The Southern Tradition at Bay*: "I expect to speak of the South therefore as a minority within the nation, whose claim to attention

[8] George Brown Tindall, *The Ethnic Southerners*. Baton Rouge, 1976: Louisiana State Univ. Press, pp. 86, 241.
[9] Richard N. Current, *Northernizing the South*. Athens, Ga., 1983: Univ. of Georgia Press, p. 11.

lies not in its success in impressing its ideals upon the nation or the world, but in something I shall insist is higher – an ethical claim which can be described only in terms of the *mandate of civilization*. In its battle for survival the South has lost ground, but it has kept from extinction some things whose value is emphasized by the disintegration of the modern world."[10] The same view appears less personally, more indirectly, in E. Garvin Davenport's discussion of Southern history as a "regional myth" that has served national needs – that is, as someone else's myth. In discussing the nineteenth-century version of this myth, he says:

The imaginative history of the post-Reconstruction period of the South is directly related to the central body of myths by which the national community defined itself in the nineteenth century. Henry Nash Smith has noted that most Americans defined the distinctive national uniqueness which separated them from Europe in terms of a nature vs. civilization dichotomy. The United States represented a state of nature, while the Old World represented historical civilization. Thomas Jefferson believed that the majority of Americans, because they were yeoman farmers, could be free individuals – free from restraint by social institutions or traditions; free to live in harmony with nature's laws. This meant, for Jefferson, that Americans, unlike Europeans, could live in a state of innocence rather than corruption because power would be virtually absent from a community of free and equal men. In such a social and economic condition, there would be no rulers and no ruled . . .

The democratic yeoman farmer, therefore, became the symbol of the ideal American citizen. And it was against that ideal that the myth of the Southern Cavalier was contrasted. Yeoman vs. Cavalier represented democrat vs. aristocrat, nature vs. civilization, American culture vs. European, innocence vs. corruption. Ultimately these symbols seemed to find dramatic confirmation in the Civil War when the yeoman democracy of the North, according to national mythology, successfully defended national innocence against the conspiratorial effort of the undemocratic Cavaliers to impose the corruption of the institution of slavery on the entire nation. It was viewed as a righteous war led by the yeoman figure Abraham Lincoln against the sinister plans of the Cavalier, Jefferson Davis.

Davenport sees the Southern agrarians as retaining the mythical story and simply inverting the cast of characters:

For while the Agrarians were participating in the continuing national quest for a rehabilitation of agrarian innocence and simplicity, they professed a regional uniqueness . . . The South was the America of Jeffersonian ideals and eighteenth-century agrarianism . . .

This Old South, of which the twentieth-century South is the only remaining manifestation, was seen as a land of small farmers and planters, each group

[10] Richard M. Weaver, *The Southern Tradition at Bay*. New Rochelle, NY: Arlington House 1968, p. 29 (italics added).

serving as a force of moderation on the other. The aristocratic element kept the democratic element from becoming too acquisitive, either politically or economically. The democratic element returned this same favor and, presumably, also helped to keep the albatross from becoming too removed from the virtue-giving soil. Civilization modified the materialism of the frontier; the frontier in turn shed its democratic spirit on civilization.[11]

In this kind of analysis, culture does not refer to the traits of a group but to those of a minority, almost inevitably a beleaguered minority, within some larger whole. This minority could be a regional minority, a class minority, an ethnic minority. Culture as virtue – that is, culture as anti-barbarism – turns out to be much more hidebound in its implications than culture as tradition. Traditions may be less than perfect. There are times and ways in which traditions ought to be changed. But virtue can only be defended. This is the explanation of Tindall's correct observation: "The belief that the South is forever disappearing has a long and honored tradition."[12]

There is a third way to discuss culture: as the expression of a binary relation, South is the counterpart of North. They are defined in relation to each other. This comes out in the almost antithetical titles of two books, John Egerton's *The Americanization of Dixie: The Southernization of America* and Richard Current's *Northernizing the South*. Both books see this binary relationship as changing over time and coming in some sense to an end, something not necessarily positive for either author.

What Egerton means can be seen in his epitaph. He quotes Malcolm X ("As far as I am concerned, [the South] is anywhere south of the Canadian border") and then a Ku Klux Klansman ("The South is going to die . . . [the South is] going the way of the rest of the country"). He concludes his book on this plaintive note: "The South, no less than the nation as a whole, is under the influence of neo-elitism and assimilation, being pulled both toward fragmentation and toward homogenization. If there is a middle ground, an integration of cultures that thrives on both

---

[11] F. Garvin Davenport, Jr., *The Myth of Southern History: Historical Consciousness in Twentieth-Century Southern Literature.* Nashville: Vanderbilt Univ. Press, 1967, pp. 7–9, 57–58.

[12] Tindall, *The Ethnic Southerners*, p. 2. Wayne Mixon, in the introduction to Current, *Northernizing the South*, reminds us that "at the very beginning of the American nation, most of the Founding Fathers from the South not only believed that their region was distinctive but that its interests were threatened by the rest of the country" (p. ix).

unity and diversity, that exalts both relationship and differences, it is not very much in evidence."[13]

Current sees this "Americanizaton of Dixie" in a somewhat more positive light than Egerton. He observes that there have been many different analyses of the ways in which the South has been northernized: "Whatever the process, the result to be anticipated has been, in reality, not so much a South resembling the North as a South conforming to the modern world. Northernization has generally been synonymous with modernization." Nonetheless, he too ends his book on a plaintive note: "And so, after two hundred years the idea of Northernizing the South, as a project to be either welcomed or resisted, continued to live on. Whether the South itself still lived on – the South as a basically and truly distinct entity – was another question."[14]

On closer look, culture as a reflection of a binary relationship may turn out to be nothing but a variant of culture as the efforts of a minority defending virtue, seeking to hold back the tide of homogenization which is reduction, corruption, the return to the lowest common denominator.

For all of these writers, without exception it seems, culture represents a problem, a concern, a moral element. Culture turns out to be less an analytic concept or analytic construct than a rhetorical flag around which one rallies, a weapon in the larger political battles. This use of the concept of culture as shorthand for a political program is not about to disappear, in the South or anywhere else. But unless we distance ourselves from it just a bit, our vision of social reality risks being obscured. I should like, therefore, to attempt to see how the rhetoric is created and why it is treated as "culture."

Let me start with one more quote. In his book *Social Origins of Dictatorship and Democracy*, Barrington Moore writes: "The South had [prior to 1865] a capitalist civilization, then, but hardly a bourgeois one."[15] While in some sense I can discern what Moore is talking about, I cannot imagine a more infelicitous and mis-

---

[13] John Egerton, *The Americanization of Dixie: The Southernization of America*. New York: Harper & Row, 1974, p. 208.
[14] Current, *Northernizing the South*, pp. 12–13, 117.
[15] Barrington Moore, Jr., *Social Origins of Dictatorship and Democracy: Lord and Peasant in the Making of the Modern World*. Boston: Beacon Press, 1966, p. 121.

leading way of talking about it. Since however, Moore's formulation is in many ways typical of almost all such statements (in form, not of course in content), allow me to dissect it. It hinges around the implicit assumption that there is a smaller entity, the South, and a larger one which Moore does not name but which I call the capitalist world-economy. When he says the South had a capitalist civilization, he refers to its participation in this larger entity, which means that people in the South were subject to certain structural constraints and therefore operated within the norms of a "capitalist civilization." When he says the South did not have a "bourgeois civilization," he means that the socio-political influence of urban industrialists and merchants was relatively less than that of large landowners in this particular part of the world-economy. Both statements are surely true of the *antebellum* South. But if capitalism is a system in which the bourgeoisie dominate the socal arena, the distinction between capitalist civilization and bourgeois civilization makes no sense. It only seems plausible by attributing to both the larger entity and the smaller geographical entity distinctive "cultures" despite the fact that the one encompasses the other.

Of course, as soon as we allot "cultures" to entities within entities, there is no logical end. The West has a culture, the United States has a culture, the South has a culture, Georgia has a culture, and I suppose Atlanta has a culture. In addition, Blacks and Whites in Georgia/the South/the United States have distinct cultures. And so on. Why not each community, each kin network, each household? And why not each generation of each group? The answer is there is no reason why not, and people do speak of cultures at each of these levels. Can we then assume each of these cultures represents some kind of enduring set of behaviors and values that is resistant to change? We can if we want to, but where does that get us?

As soon as we look closely at the smaller-scale entities, we become very conscious of how constantly changing are the sets of practices and values of small groups – within an individual's lifetime, not to speak of over longer periods, and whenever a group or an individual finds itself in a different location.

Furthermore, we know that even if group values remain constant over any period of time, we can never assume that all individuals in that group either affirm those values or engage in behavior consonant with them. At most, the statement of group values is a statistical mean of specific ways of behaving or of professed beliefs with a presumably low standard deviation. As to this presumption, we have in practice virtually zero hard evidence. Perhaps the standard deviation varies from group to group, from time to time. Perhaps? All too probably.

In what is clearly a maelstrom of constantly varying behavior, does it make sense to assume that constancy is the norm and that it is change which is to be explained? Would it not be far more defensible intellectually to assume that variability is the norm and that continuities are to be explained? If so, then perhaps we should set aside the very term *culture* as having quite misleading implications.

What we can say is that all historical systems have structures, and rules/norms/values corresponding to these structures, which are part of their operation. These structures always include some kinds of mechanisms that partially constrain deviance in some fashion. Such an historical system is, for example, the capitalist world-economy, which has its history, its changing spatial boundaries, its culture or "civilization" if you will.

Since this system has a structure that is hierarchical and involves variegated and often spatially distinct groups, the politics of this world-system involves the efforts of these multiple groups (whose existence is the result of a combination of self-definition and other-definition) in struggles over benefits. One of the ways in which groups struggle is by seeking to impose norms and behavioral practices on their members, with middling degrees of success.

Since the world-system is continuously changing, the position and definition of these groups is continuously changing. Hence the "local cultural definitions" that groups find useful is continuously changing. How, then, has it been possible in such a system to talk of things like "the mind of the South"? It has been possible because groups, in seeking to pursue their interests, will be more able to do so insofar as they can persuade their "members" to act in the present in some unified fashion. And a crucial mode of persuading these individuals, who in fact hold multiple group memberships (and, hence from the point of view of any particular group within which they are defined as falling, are individuals of

divergent interest), is to persuade these individuals that the
desired behavior is normal, "traditional," hallowed by time and
therefore expected in the present. The re-creation of an ever-
varying tradition requires the spread of the belief that no change
has in fact occurred.

What we have been calling the culture of a group – say, for
example, that of the South – is thus something far more fluid *and
flexible* than our collective discussion heretofore has made it out to
be. Each writer, each "spokesman," each orator is seeking, when
he talks of this "culture," to create it as a set of rules and priorities.
In the process of doing this, he claims longevity and pervasiveness
as the cachet of his version of the culture. To the extent that his
efforts are consonant with those of some others, he thereby
creates a momentary theoretical justification of actions in the
present. This is why still other persons are always in the business
of reanalyzing and debunking any statement of the key features
of this so-called culture. The extent of the debate that has gone on
in the South about its "mind," about the boundaries of the very
South that is supposed to have a mind, is in fact not significantly
different from comparable debates everywhere else within the
time-space boundaries of the capitalist world-economy. There is
nothing special about the claim to be special. There is nothing
unusual about the ambiguities surrounding all the claims. The
claim to specialness is part of the world-systemic political game,
and it plays a central role in the operation of the system.

Interpreting the specific content of the successive claims
requires looking at the evolving position of particular geographic
zones in the developing world-system. For example, it seems to
me, without in any sense claiming expertise in Southern history,
that the South and therefore its "mind," its "culture," its "civilization" has changed drastically at least several times over the past
350 years.

Before the American Revolution, was there really anything
much to be called "the South"? There were juridically a set of
British colonies, which were agricultural-exporting peripheral
zones of the world-economy, using a good deal of coerced
cash-crop labor. On a world scale, their economic role was not that
different from many other such zones at the time – not only some
Caribbean islands and Brazil, which are often referred to as

comparable areas, but Quebec, Andalusia, Sicily, Poland, and Hungary among others. If one takes a close look at the cultures of these zones, the features which make them different at that time among themselves (and there are of course many – language, dominant religion, historical origins of their local structures, etc.) pale before the striking similarities of the attitudes we associate with "plantation" or "seigniorial" zones of the capitalist world-economy. What we usually think of as feudal values – the combination of the harsh exploitation of labor with paternalism – is in fact less a picture of Europe in the Middle Ages than of these "plantation" zones of the capitalist world-economy.

The basic economic situation did not change after the American Revolution. If anything, the invention of the cotton gin reinforced the pattern. What changed was a theoretically accidental phenomenon. The Southern states found themselves part of the United States, a sovereign state which contained other zones of differing economic role, and in which they were numerically a minority. To pursue their interests, the dominant economic forces in this agricultural export region had to create a cultural entity known as the South. It was an essential weapon. The development of U.S. nationalism led quite logically, given the situation, to the development of Southern nationalism. As John McCardell correctly noted, this nationalism, "as a political movement, did require the exploitation of the proslavery argument."[16] More than that, it required the sense that there were within this one political entity "two distinct peoples, two distinct civilizations, one in the North and the other in the South."[17] I am not saying that the Civil War was inevitable; this would be absurd. What I am saying is that it was not at all surprising given the ways in which the capitalist world-economy operates, and it was not at all exceptional. And I am also saying that the concept of the Old South was a construct useful to many in the world political conflicts of the time. The Old South was in some sense created as a mental construct only a short time before it was historically eliminated as a material construct.

The defeat of the Confederacy changed all that and, most of all,

[16] John McCardell, *The Idea of a Southern Nation: Southern Nationalists and Southern Nationalism, 1830–1860*. New York: W.W. Norton, 1979, p. 49.
[17] Current, *Northernizing the South*, p. 17.

culturally. The U.S. federal state thereafter pursued energetically an economic and political policy geared to transforming the role of the United States in the world-economy. This federal state was not particularly anxious to change too much in how the South operated locally, at least in the following fifty to seventy-five years. Yes, reconstruction and carpetbagging were traumas from the point of view of many persons in the South. But they changed less than we often argue. What they changed most was how the South thought of itself – that is, what political line it was going to follow.

Clearly the old line hadn't worked and had to be shed. Basically two new lines were put forward and their proponents fought for supremacy. On the one hand, there was the line of the New South. The New South was the path of cultural assimilation. It was no different than a hundred variants we see across the globe. Advocates of the New South essentially said that if "we" are behind, it is because "we" are outdated – technologically, to be sure; culturally, at least in part. Let us therefore modify our ways, retaining nonetheless some label so as to make a political claim for "aid," and we will catch up.

The other possible line was that of the Southern agrarians. Catch up to what? was their watchword. We are conceding everything of value in the effort to "catch up," which, even if we try, will never really succeed. Even at the end of the horizon, there will be no true material equality, and our quality of life will have disappeared. Once again, this kind of claim to particularistic "agrarian" virtue has been put forward in every zone of the world-economy undergoing an intensification of its peripheralization.

I am not here to mediate between the proponents of the New South and the Southern agrarians. They are both dead-end positions, and they are also the only two that were really available. What I wish to insist upon is that they were both very different from the Old South and were both claims to create a "culture" – claims at best only partially realized. Neither the New South nor the agrarian idea swept the other from the scene and became the true, the only culture of the South.

When the United States moved into its position as unquestionable world hegemonic power as of 1945, all changed again. It was no longer in the interest of the dominant political forces of the

U.S. federal state to have a "backward" geographical zone, just as it was no longer in its interest to have the denial of political rights to minorities such as the Blacks. The homogenization of America was an urgent political (and diplomatic) need of the U.S. federal state. The industrialization of the South and the Civil Rights Act were all part of a larger picture of "cultural" reorganization. The question was only how various subgroups would react to it. Blacks in the U.S. reacted by asserting, in many ways for the first time, their separate "culture." This is easy to explain, but not our subject here. The South reacted to it, it seems to me, largely by beginning to disappear as a construct.

Perhaps you will not think this is so, and this very forum may be negative evidence – or it may be an effort to stem the tide. Of course, there are people in whose interests it would be to stem that particular tide, but surely not, for example, most of those who have become active in the Republican party, part of whose effort has been for the last thirty years the redrawing of U.S. cultural regional boundaries. This is what they mean by constantly referring to the "new majority." Egerton put forward the argument in 1974 that "it is mostly Southerners with a particular perspective – for want of a better term, it is Southern liberals – who still gather to talk introspectively about their region."[18] One can see why this might be so.

And now that the United States is entering its post-hegemonic phase (despite Mr. Reagan's Canute-like efforts to order the ocean to recede), will there be a place for a Southern mind? Perhaps, but if so, of a very different kind. The decades ahead for the United States are probably decades of increasing internal struggle as the nation adjusts with difficulty to its slow economic and hence geopolitical decline in the world-system. For many Americans this will be the opportunity for new or renewed egalitarian claims; for others, this decline holds the promise of great short-term programs of enrichment.

Many "cultures" will be born or renewed in the decades ahead. The growing worldwide attacks on the capitalist system include attacks on the "universalist" system of values which is used to sustain it. This encourages thereby the reassertion of "particular-

---

[18] Egerton, *The Americanization of Dixie*, p. 15.

isms." We are seeing this throughout the world. Why not the South? But also why in the South? Perhaps rather in Georgia. If we see such new particularisms, you may be surprised what traditions they may begin to invoke in the South – perhaps the ultraradical claims of some threads of early Protestantism. On a worldwide measuring scale, the South may move from being a concept towards the right of the political spectrum to being one towards the left. Or it may not.

Since culture is so fluid and so flexible, it is virtually impossible to make any sensible projections of this. We do better to make projections about the world-economy and the world political system (including the antisystemic movements found everywhere) and assume that the protagonists will make "cultural" claims whose details may vary enormously but whose utility can be analyzed. The point is that if we want to know the traditions of the near future the last place we should look is at the traditions of the near past.

14 ✣ The modern world-system as a civilization

The word civilization, it is well-known, has two rather distinctive meanings, both of which are reflected in the very title of our conference, "Civilizations and Theories of Civilizing Processes." On the one hand, it is a term with very positive connotations which by its logic is grammatically singular, denoting processes (and their results) which have made men more "civil," that is less "animal"-like or less "savage." When French colonialists in the late nineteenth century launched the slogan of "la mission civilisatrice," no one had any doubt about the uniqueness and therefore the universality of the civilization to which they referred.

On the other hand, there is the plural usage, in which *a* civilization refers to a particular concatenation of worldview, customs, structures, and culture (both material culture and high culture) which forms some kind of historical whole and which coexists (if not always simultaneously) with other varieties of this phenomenon. This usage is a bit more "neutral" in tonality than the other, or rather the ideological overtones are more complex and more subtle.

Lucien Febvre starts his discussion of this very concept of "civilization" with the assertion, "It is never a waste of time to write the history of a word".[1] It turns out, on looking into the matter, that the two meanings have been with us almost from the beginning, and reflect two very fundamental developments in the

---

[1] Lucien Febvre, "Civilisation: évolution d'un mot et d'un groupe d'idées," in *Pour une histoire à part entière*. Paris: SEVPEN, 1962, p. 481.

modern world-system as a civilization. That is to say, and let me emphasize this from the outset, the very concept of civilization (a bimodal one) is itself an historical product. But it is the product of a particular civilization. Does it, therefore, by this very fact, call into question one of the usages? Or is it the product of the "civilizing process," thereby calling into question the other?

Before, however, we get lost in this mirror within mirrors, let us review briefly the terminological history. Usage number one, civilization as the (singular) civilizing process, civilization as the opposite of barbarity, appears first in the middle of the eighteenth century in the works of two quintessential Enlightenment scholars – in French with Mirabeau in 1756, in English with Adam Ferguson in 1767. As Raymond Bloch says, the word came at the right moment and corresponded to a notion that had been gradually developing and was destined for a great future, the optimistic and nontheological idea of a continuous progress in the condition of man and society.[2]

In short, the concept reflected the intellectual triumph of "rational and experimental science" expressed by the thinkers of the Enlightenment, for all of whom "civilization remains primarily an ideal – in very large measure, a moral ideal."[3]

The French Revolution occurred precisely in the wake of this triumph. This is not the place to review either the causes or the consequences of this major historical moment in our modern world. Two points, however, are necessary to note for our discussion. First, the French Revolution was not only perceived as a fundamental structural change in "society," a "revolution" – let us not debate whether or not it really was – but it also legitimated the idea of deliberate, manipulated construction and reconstruction of a social order as nothing had before. This legitimation had an intellectual consequence. If it were possible to *construct* a social world, one was led logically to analyze by careful study the alternatives. The ground was thus prepared for the emergence in the nineteenth century of the social sciences.

Secondly, Napoleon's empire first expressed in concrete practice all the ambiguity of a universalizing idea with which we are so

---

[2] Raymond Bloch, "Préface" to A. Soboul, *La civilisation et la Révolution française*. Paris: Arthaud, 1970, p. 11.
[3] Febvre, "Civilisation," pp. 499, 505.

conversant today. On the one hand, the French Revolution and hence Napoleon's armies were seen not only by the French themselves but by other Europeans as the carrier of a universal idea, precisely that of civilization, and were welcomed as such. But, on the other hand, many of the same welcoming Europeans very soon reacted as local "nationalists" against French "imperialism." Indeed, one could argue that the real birth of nationalism as a political concept can be located in this Napoleonic era.

The ground was therefore ripe for the second usage of the word civilization, civilization as a particularity rather than civilization as universality. The *Grand Larousse* cites[4] Guizot in 1828 in this latter sense but Febvre gives prior credit[5] to a book by Ballanche written in 1819, which he says first used civilization in the plural. The two meanings would henceforth remain with us because the antinomy universalism/particularism not only became ever more acute but, as it slowly became clear, was inherently unresolvable within the premises and practices of the modern world-system as a civilization.

The problem is structural. In an historical social system that is built on hierarchy and inequality, which is the case of the capitalist world-economy, universalism as description or ideal or goal can only in the long run be universalism as ideology, fitting well the classical formulation of Marx, that the ruling ideas are the ideas of the ruling class. But if this were all that universalism was, we would not be discussing it today. Universalism is a "gift" of the powerful to the weak which confronts the latter with a double bind: to refuse the gift is to lose; to accept the gift is to lose. The only plausible reaction of the weak is neither to refuse nor to accept, or both to refuse and to accept – in short, the path of the seemingly irrational zigzags (both cultural and political) of the weak that has characterized most of nineteenth and especially twentieth-century history.

Marxism, the great oppositional *Weltanschauung* of the modern world, solved nothing in this regard. In some ways it compounded the problem. As Abdel-Malek has noted quite correctly, Marxism is perceived in the "Three Continents" as "the most advanced

---

[4] Larousse, Pierre, *Grande dictionaire universal du XIXe siècle*, vol. II, p. 750.
[5] Febvre, "Civilisation," p. 507.

critical synthesis of Western civilization and cultures".[6] And therefore what? One response is that of Abdallah Laroui. It is to perceive the existence of two Marxes – Marx the neo-liberal, the "scientist," and therefore the Western ideologue, and Marx the student of "backward humanity," the historicist, the scholar. To the former Marx, Laroui says, "The Third World will always have the reaction that Europe had to Napoleon, the Napoleon of universalization by force of arms, for this abstract universalization by imperialism is a disguised murder." To each his Marxism, he says: the Third World intellectual "will express his own version, born out of the conditions of the world in which he lives".[7]

This problem of the ambiguity of civilization/civilizations is not merely a political problem, if "merely" can be used of such a major issue. It is even deeper than that, since opening up this issue reopens the fundamental issue of the very nature of science, which seems to me to have been the basic building-block of our present civilizational consensus. There is a sense in which this consensus had already been achieved at the dawn of the capitalist world-economy. It was located in the triumph of the so-called Baconian spirit which John Herman Randall defined as follows:

Not power over men, but power over Nature, and that power is the fruit of knowledge. Nature to be commanded must be obeyed; not by the anticipation of Nature in some magic dream, but by the study and interpretation of Nature will there rise the kingdom of man.[8]

This Baconian/Cartesian/Newtonian worldview posed science against magic, anywhere and everywhere, and always. This world-view logically could tolerate the concept of civilization only in the singular. Those imbued with the scientific spirit were civilized and civilizing; all others were not. No doubt many resisted such implications in the name of humanism, or of relativism, or of the concept of original sin, but after five centuries it is hard to contend that science as the "disenchantment of the world" has not

---

[6] Anouar Abdel-Malek, "Marxisme et sociologie des civilisations", in *Marx and Contemporary Scientific Thought*. The Hague and Paris: Mouton, 1969, p. 498.
[7] Abdallah Laroui, "L'intellectuel du Tiers Monde et Marx, ou encore une fois le problème du retard historique", in *Marx and Contemporary Scientific Thought*, p. 281.
[8] John Herman Randall, *The Making of the Modern Mind*. New York: Houghton Mifflin, 1940, p. 224.

come to predominate our intellectual world in ways both obvious and overt and ways more hidden and deep-rooted.

The link between science as "the disenchantment of the world" and capitalism as a civilization based on the "rational pursuit of renewed profits" has been stated many times, and no doubt most influentially by Max Weber. It is a pity his many disciples ignore Weber's own warnings about the dangers inherent in this link as "the rosy blush of [religious asceticism's] laughing heir, the Enlightenment, seems . . . to be irretrievably fading . . ." Weber worries that, of the last stage of this cultural development, it might well be truly said: "Specialists without spirit, sensualists without heart; this nullity imagines that it has attained a level of civilization never before achieved".[9]

Having said this, Weber typically begs off from pursuing the issue on the grounds that he was now talking in the "world of judgments of value and of faith" – implicitly not the world of science. Perhaps the moral is to be a specialist with spirit, but only after hours.

Freud, that other late nineteenth-century genius come to fulfill the Enlightenment, was no doubt bolder than Weber in *Civilization and its Discontents*. The whole point of Freud's essay, after all, is to see civilization as a sacrifice, "built up on renunciation of instinct or renunciation of instinctual gratifications . . . This 'cultural privation' [of powerful instinctual urgencies] dominates the whole field of social relations between human beings."[10]

While Freud sees this as somehow inevitable in general, its particular manifestation in the modern world was not, is not, inevitable in detail, according to Freud. He raises "objections . . . [to] the ethical standards of the cultural super-ego,"[11] since it doesn't take into account the possibilities to obey, the limits to man's ability to control the id. Indeed, Freud concludes:

For various reasons, it is very far from my intention to express any opinion concerning the value of human civilization. I have endeavoured to guard myself against the enthusiastic partiality which believes our civilization to be the most

[9] Max Weber, *The Protestant Ethic and the Spirit of Capitalism*. New York: Charles Scribner, 1930, p. 182.
[10] Sigmund Freud, *Civilisation and its Discontents*. London: Hogarth, 1957, p. 63.
[11] Freud, *Civilisation*, p. 139.

precious thing we possess or could acquire, and thinks it must inevitably lead us to undreamt-of heights of perfection.[12]

But, in the end, he says: "My courage fails me . . . at the thought of rising up as a prophet before my fellow-men, and I bow to their reproach that I have no consolation to offer them."[13] At least, unlike Weber, he does not seek refuge in the value-neutrality of science, but only in his own human fallibility.

Still, one must ask why such keen and wide-ranging intelligences as Weber and Freud, having put their finger at the key dilemma of our civilization (singular or plural usage), quail at going further. No doubt, the sanctity of the Baconian worldview holds a very strong grip on their imaginations. *Fin de siècle* pessimism as counterpoint no doubt was acceptable if melancholic but only if it was self-restrained. Weber and Freud, as we know, gave rise to whole academic industries, but not Nietzsche.

And yet today, within the very inner sanctum of physics, this worldview is being challenged, not with melancholic self-restrained pessimism, but with a sober insistence on the range of human possibility. The challenge, raised by Ilya Prigogine most dramatically, is precisely against the historic self-image of science, accused of reproducing the very sin it claimed to oppose – the divinization of the world:

We echo the complaint that science, and in particular physics, disenchants the world. But it disenchants it precisely because it divinizes it, because it denies diversity and natural coming-into-being, which Aristotle made the attribute of the sublimer world, in the name of an incorruptible eternity alone susceptible of being the object of thought in truth. The world of dynamics is a "divine" world on which time has no impact, from which the birth and death of things are forever excluded.[14]

We are reminded that Kant admired as two inevitable orders the moral law and the eternal movement of the stars, but:

We know that we can no longer guarantee even the stability of the planetary movement. And it is this instability of the trajectories, it is this bifurcation wherein we rediscover the fluctuations of our cerebral activity, which serve us today as our source of inspiration.[15]

[12] *Ibid.*, p. 142.
[13] *Ibid.*, p. 143.
[14] Ilya Prigogine and Isabelle Stengers, *La nouvelle alliance*. Paris: Gallimard, 1979, p. 266.
[15] *Ibid.*, pp. 268–269.

That Prigogine is ready to break the idol in ways that Weber and Freud feared to do is less a commentary on his moral qualities than on the evolution of the real world in the 50–75 years that separate their writings. The basic paradigms of social science which were also the basic paradigms of the social movements were products of a nineteenth-century world-system, itself rooted ideologically in a Baconian worldview that had been firmly elaborated and established by the sixteenth century. If these paradigms can be challenged today it is because the capitalist world-economy as an historical system, what Schumpeter called "the civilization of capitalism,"[16] is in fact in serious historical crisis, and therefore the most basic consensuses are open for discussion for the first time since they were established. Prigogine echoes a complaint whose most visible expression can be read about every day in our newspapers.

An historical crisis is however a major phenomenon, not an everyday event. It involves the coming to an end of one historical system and *therefore* an historical choice, the bringing into being of one or more successor systems. The choice before us is a double one that hinges on the two usages of civilization. Will the successor system(s) be more "civilized" than the present one? What is the relationship of this transition to the existence of multiple "civilizational" processes, and will the successor system(s) have a place for the concept of multiple civilizations?

I will not restate here my views on why the particular historical system which is the capitalist world-economy is in crisis,[17] except to say that the source of the crisis is the cumulation of internal contradictions such that the system will find it impossible, is finding it impossible, to reproduce itself as the same kind of system. These contradictions find their roots in economic processes which lead to solutions of short-run difficulties which create long-run ones and in politico-cultural processes which are the consequence of the increasingly visible strains caused by the economic contradictions, but which in turn create political contradictions.

crisis

---

[16] Joseph A. Schumpeter, *Capitalism, Socialism, and Democracy*. London: George Allen & Unwin, 1943, ch. XI.
[17] Immanuel Wallerstein, "Crisis as Transition," in S. Amin et al., *Dynamics of Global Crisis*. New York: Monthly Review, 1982, 11–54.

We are consequently living in a period of transition in my view. But a transition to what? The only reasonable answer to that question is that the answer is uncertain. That in some sense is always true of crisis-periods/transitions. We can never be sure how they will be resolved. But it is particularly true of this transition, because of an historically new element in the picture.

If we now take the planet Earth over historical time and describe the patterns of coexistence of the three varieties over time, we quickly arrive at a periodization which has only three moments thus far. Moment one is before *circa* 8 to 10,000 BC. At that time there were presumably only multiple mini-systems. We do not know how many, how long-lived a given one was, or even very much about how they operated. Our ignorance is quite large. that the whole is, from both a material and a social standpoint, *de facto* autonomous. A mini-system is simply a small-scale division of labor within which one finds a single cultural and a single political process. World-systems then are the opposite in scale, larger divisions of labor within which multiple cultural processes can be seen to operate. Two types of such larger systems can be observed: the world-empire with an overarching political structure, and the world-economy without one.

If we now take the planet Earth over historical time and describe the patterns of coexistence of the three varieties over time, we quickly arrive at a periodization which has only three moments thus far. Moment one is before *circa* 8 to 10,000 BC. At that time there were presumably only multiple mini-systems. We do not know how many, how long-lived a given one was, or even very much about how they operated. Our ignorance is quite large.

From that time up to *circa* 1500 AD, the three varieties of historical systems seem to have coexisted. That is to say, we could in theory (if not in practice) construct maps for any point of time therein and physically locate a whole series of historical systems, reaching an uncertain total number. The pattern, of course, was constantly changing since each instance of each variety of historical system was mortal. Historical systems came into and out of existence.

During this period, the world-empire seemed to be the "strong form." By that I mean that world-empires seemed to expand and contract largely by a logic internal to them. (I forgo here a discussion of the dynamics of this process.) Also, such world-empires as were "successful" seemed to have a longer life than any mini-system or world-economy, which seemed on the whole more "fragile," due both to their internal dynamics and their vulnerability to outside attack. The history we have written up to now has primarily been the history of the expansion and contraction of these world-empires. Each time a world-empire expanded, it absorbed surrounding mini-systems and world-economies, destroying their autonomous existence. Of course, a world-empire sometimes also conquered part or all of another world-empire, but this was actually comparatively infrequent. When the world-empire contracted, it left a social void in the abandoned zones, within which new mini-systems and world-economies arose.

Somewhere *circa* 1500 a qualitative change in this pattern occurred. For the first time in human history, an instance of a world-economy survived its "fragility" and consolidated itself as a capitalist system. This is the modern world-system we all know and in which we live. Why this qualitative change occurred is not relevant to this discussion, though I have explicated my views elsewhere.[18] When this happened, the world-economy suddenly became the "strong form." That is, now it was this capitalist world-economy which expanded by virtue of its inner dynamic. In the process of its expansion, it incorporated and destroyed the autonomy of multiple mini-systems and world-empires. By the late nineteenth century, its expansion encompassed the whole globe. Now another qualitative change occurred. For the first time, there existed on planet Earth only one historical system. We are still in that situation today. It is out of this new situation, anticipated in the eighteenth century and realized in the nineteenth, that the ambiguous double meaning of "civilization" arose. We can now see to what each meaning structurally referred.

Civilization in the singular was the ideological construct of the proponents of the new all-encompassing historical system. Civilization (singular) implied that the exclusivity of this new system, its all-encompassing nature, were both inevitable and desirable. In

[18] Immanuel Wallerstein, *The Modern World-System*, Vol. I. New York: Academic Press, 1974, chapter 1.

the language that became widespread, the capitalist world-economy represented progress because it was "civilizing." It should be noted that this was the argument not only of the advocates of the system, but also of its major intellectual opposition, Marx and the Marxists. For Marx too (at least in one of his guises) argued that capitalism was progress. He merely added that it was only the penultimate and not the ultimate stage of progress. This was no doubt a crucial modification of the analysis, but it still left civilization as a singular concept.

The concept of civilizations (plural) arose as a defense against the ravages of civilization (singular). The defense was sometimes given a "conservative" tone, sometimes a "radical" tone. It came to the same thing. It was a rejection of the hypothesis that capitalism in its only concrete existing form, a world-economy in fact dominated by the "West," was morally or politically "better" than alternative historical systems. The most concrete alternative historical systems to which reference could be made and was made were the world-empires that had been incorporated into and destroyed by the expanding world-economy.

I have previously referred to the double bind of those opposing the system. To assimilate to civilization (singular) was to acknowledge previous inferiority and acquire at best second-class citizenship. To reject civilization (singular) in the name of civilizations (plural) was to risk immolation in archaisms that may not even have had the virtue of being truly traditional and may further have been crippling because non-growing. There was no solution within the terms of the debate as given. This can be easily verified by looking at the personal and collective trajectories of the various spokesmen of the oppressed strata of our world-system as they tried to utilize the multiple weapons of cultural nationalism (*lato sensu*), weapons which sometimes worked very well against the enemy, but which at other times blew up in their faces.

We are thus before a moral and political dilemma of no mean proportions when we talk about the relevance of the concept of civilization to our current problems in the late twentieth century. It will not do to try to hide the dilemma by abandoning the concept and avoiding the difficult analysis. Rather, let us embrace it as the central issue of our time.

First of all, what are our real choices? Since we now have only one historical system existent, we have, I believe, three main possibilities. One is that the single system break up into multiple historical systems, each again with a separate social division of labor. In short, we could go back in this sense to the pre-1500 situation (or perhaps the pre-8000 BC one). This seems implausible, other than via the route of a nuclear Armageddon, which I do not rule out but which also seems to me eminently preventable. If we go this route our present discussion will prove largely irrelevant.

The other possibilities involve the transformation of the present Earth-wide historical system into a different kind of Earth-wide historical system. This seems to me the more likely. Indeed, I believe we are already in the early stages of that process. But, in this case, we have the question of what alternative futures exist, which are more likely, which more desirable, and what we can do to make the more desirable more likely? I shall address each query in turn.

Which alternative futures exist? In detail, no doubt, the answers are legion. But in basic structure, there are really only two possibilities. We could construct a system that would be, as is our present one and most of our previous ones, hierarchical, inegalitarian, and oppressive. There have, of course, always been persons who argued that *all* historical systems (or at least all complex ones) had to have these characteristics necessarily. Alternatively, we could construct one that was relatively egalitarian and democratic, fulfilling the slogan of the French Revolution. There have long been advocates of such a system. Others, of course, have regarded such advocates as Utopian. If Utopian means socially impossible, I do not agree with this assessment, though any arguments I could bring to bear would necessarily be speculative or deductive, and not based on empirical experience.

If, however, you will provisionally grant that we are talking of two realistic long-term alternative historical possibilities, then the question remains: what can we say about the historical probabilities? The theory of progress in both its liberal and Marxist version has argued the inevitability (if perhaps a slow one) of reaching a democratic, egalitarian reality. I surely reject any concept that this is historically inevitable. I see no evidence for this whatsoever. For one thing, I do not believe that every successive historical system up to now has been more "progressive" than the prior one. I specifically do not think that the capitalist world-economy has represented progress over its predecessors. At best, it has been no worse. It could be argued it has in fact been much worse.[19]

It follows from this premise that we need to examine structural likelihoods. What are the pressures in one direction or another? The main pressures in favor of a democratic, egalitarian alternative are usually thought to be those deriving from mass consciousness and hence mass will in favor of such an alternative. The creation of such mass consciousness in turn has been thought to be a consequence of technological development and its social consequences: increased education, increased communications, increased mass access to instruments of power, and *ergo* decreased advantages of the "elites." You will note here familiar themes of the Enlightenment and the nineteenth century about the "civilizing process." Even the Freudian pessimism about "civilization and its discontents" has been mitigated by the belief that a particular health technology of psychotherapy (defined broadly) could and would contribute to this civilizing process.

Personally, I do not deny any of this. I do believe that these processes all do operate, and do have the suggested consequences, up to a point. The question is whether there are not simultaneously other processes at work, going in an opposite direction. For each simplification that technology has brought (and therefore accessibility to non-experts), have there not been coordinate complexities? In the twentieth century, improved communications has been said to imply Big Brother at least as much as the ability of the working class to organize. Has not the mass access to instruments of power been matched by the high cost and extremely tight access to the most powerful and technologically advanced of such instruments? I could go on, but the point is simple and hard to refute. There is no clearcut case for a technological road to one system or the other. At the very least, we must say that we cannot be sure whether technology will ever have irrefutable implications for this social choice.

Furthermore, I believe we have missed a major process in our

---

[19] See Immanuel Wallerstein, *Historical Capitalism*. London: New Left Books, 1983.

analysis of processes of consciousness. Most of the discussion about consciousness and ideology revolves around a scenario with two stages. In stage A, those who have real power control the mechanisms that form consciousness. They have cultural "hegemony," in Gramsci's phrase. In stage B, by some process or other, the majority acquire a true consciousness of their self-interest. The veils are lifted; the old system collapses, or is reformed. There seems to have been relatively little debate about the possibility that the very same people who created the old veils might construct new ones. But surely this is not all that implausible. Surely this is one way we can describe much of past history, and indeed is one way we do so describe it.

Furthermore, the most obvious technique for the holders of current power to construct new veils would be to take the lead themselves in destroying the old system in the name of constructing the new. I believe this is what happened in the so-called transition from feudalism to capitalism, although I know this is a controversial position.[20] If, however, this is acknowledged to be a structural possibility, then our attention must inevitably shift from the ostensible political foreground of the struggle between anti-systemic movements and the defenders of the existing system to a close look at the history, nature, probable trajectories, and internal struggles of the antisystemic movements themselves.

Before turning to this issue, let us discuss the third query – which alternative future is more desirable? In fact, the modern educational system everywhere in the world preaches on the surface the values of a democratic, egalitarian world. It seems almost gratuitous to defend its virtues. And yet, this preaching is done with such clear and obvious smirking that it is in fact necessary to talk on occasion about these moral fundamentals.

The arguments for the inevitability of social hierarchy derive either from the irreducibility of human differentials (some people are always more intelligent or more competent than others) and/or from the necessity of coordination of all complex processes, coordination in turn requiring hierarchy. It seems to me

---

[20] Immanuel Wallerstein "Economic Theories and Historical Disparities of Development," in *Eighth International History Congress, Budapest 1982*, J. Kocka and G. Ránki, eds., B.I.: *Economic Theory and History*. Budapest: Akadémiai Kiadó, 1982.

that the case is weak on both counts. No doubt there are human differentials, and one might even assume that they contain a biological component resistent to (perhaps even inaccessible to) social determination. But how significant are they? And would they necessarily imply negative consequences for a polity organized in a truly democratic fashion? And even if they have been significant in the past, is not the impact of technological and educational advance such as to reduce their significance? Finally, even if there remained some residual impact on collective decision-making, are there not social mechanisms (for example, structuring delays into decision-making processes to leave more time for collective analysis and reflection) that might reduce the impact still further? I do not propose to write here the disquisition that would answer these queries; merely to pose them, however, indicates, it seems to me, that the spokesmen for the inevitability of hierarchy based on the irreducibility of human differentials have a difficult case to demonstrate.

There is then the second argument against the possibility of an egalitarian world: complexity requires coordination which implies hierarchy. Here the argument is usually an empirical one. It has always been thus; *ergo*, it must aways be thus. But this kind of assessment seems to me to underplay (indeed ignore) the incredible amount of human collective ingenuity that exists, also a lesson to be drawn from past history. We have been inventing institutional structures for at least 10,000 years, and the later ones always were unpredicted in the earlier stages. Human sociability is too young as a biological phenomenon for us to announce grandly that complexity can only be coordinated via hierarchy. We know on a small scale this is not necessarily the case. And the technical difficulties of complex information-gathering, storage, and retrieval are in the process of being enormously simplified these days. Here I make appeal to our knowledge of biological adaptation to assert that it is impossible to rule out that we can create an historical system that is both complex and egalitarian.

Having engaged in this elementary, perhaps simplistic, but nonetheless necessary exercise in arguing the possibility of an egalitarian world, I must then add my moral assertion of its desirability, on the very simple grounds that inequality not only hurts the obvious victims, the oppressed, but hurts as well (if not to an even greater degree) its immediate beneficiaries, by depriving the latter of their human wholeness and their possiblities of self-realization. Privilege is a barrier to self-fulfillment, forcing its holders into activities they would not otherwise choose and constraining their alternatives. Abraham Lincoln said it quite simply: "As I would not be a slave, so I would not be a master."

All that I have written is but a prelude to the important question: if we have a real historical choice before us at this time, and we also have a reason to prefer one alternative to the other, how can we arrive at the preferred social choice? I must start by saying that I cannot give a good answer to that question, nor can any other individual. It is not a matter of mere individual insight, but of social praxis socially arrived at. The locus of this social praxis, it seems to me, lies more in the arena of the antisystemic movements (broadly defined) than in the state mechanisms, the economic area *stricto sensu*, or the cultural-ideological sphere.

It is a matter of envisaging the overall framework of a transition, which might be posed as a choice between a controlled reconstruction or a looser, less structured disintegration. One of the strongest and perhaps least useful heritages of the Enlightenment is the feeling that since change is possible, it is only possible or optimally possible through rational social planning. We have had planned social change ad nauseam, from Jeremy Bentham to the Bolsheviks. And the results have been less than happy. Our rationality has involved rationalization, both in Weber's sense and in Freud's sense. We have had the worst of each sense: the Iron Cage and the self-deception. Perhaps it is time to experiment seriously with alternatives.

Perhaps we should deconstruct without the erection of structures to deconstruct, which turn out to be structures to continue the old in the guise of the new. Perhaps we should have movements that mobilize and experiment but not movements that seek to operate within the power structures of a world-system they are trying to undo. Perhaps we should tiptoe into an uncertain future, trying merely to remember in which direction we are going. Perhaps we should constantly reevaluate whether in fact what we are doing is deconstructing an inegalitarian system or reinforcing it. I know this will seem both vague and naïve, but our hardheaded organizational biases of the past 100 years have not been all that successful.

What is least clear is the role of the multiple civilizations in this process of deconstructing. Surely we have no more interest in re-creating the world-empires of yesteryear than in refurbishing the universalizing domination of a capitalist civilization? These multiple civilizations, however, are indeed the foci of important antisystemic movements. We may deconstruct more rapidly in their wake than without them. Indeed, can we deconstruct without them? I doubt it. In any case, a new social praxis must clearly be built out of a family of movements that encompasses the wisdom and the interests of all sectors that have been put down and marginalized in our present system. An inclusive family of movements will not only be numerically stronger; it will also have the great advantage of experiential variation and hence of increasing the likelihood of discovering correct paths.

It will not be easy to build such a family of movements, and the opposition will be fierce. Norbert Elias ends his book with a citation from Holbach: "la civilisation . . . n'est pas encore terminée."[21] Indeed not, and the obstacles seem to me great indeed. But I take heart from this conclusion of Prigogine and Stengers:

The ways of nature cannot be foreseen with certainty. The elements of accident therein cannot be eliminated, and it is far more decisive than Aristotle himself understood. Bifurcating nature is that in which small differences and insignificant fluctuations can, provided they occur in opportune circumstances, spread out through the whole system and bring into being a new mode of functioning.[22]

The circumstances seem to me opportune. Let us encourage by our actions this bifurcating process and let us try to engender a new mode of functioning in which the distinction between civilization (singular) and civilizations (plural) no longer has a social relevance.

[21] Norbert Elias, *The Civilizing Process*, Vol. II: *Power and Civility*. New York: Pantheon, 1982, p. 333.
[22] Prigogine and Stengers, *La nouvelle alliance*, p. 271.

15 ✤ The renewed concern with civilization(s?)

Civilization is not a term widely used in the literature of the social sciences. I doubt that you would find it in very many sociology textbooks, I'm sure you'd not find it in any economics textbooks, and probably in no political science textbook. The concept was in favor in some pre-1914 anthropology, where it appeared at the end term of a presumed evolutionary sequence: savagery to barbarism to civilization. In that usage, civilization was the name for "us," and its usage was in the singular mode. But that kind of grand-sweep anthropology has more or less disappeared, although it reemerges from time to time in new clothing. Nineteenth-century historians sometimes used the term but in the twentieth century its use has been largely restricted to the grand comparativists (who were often simultaneously doomsayers) like Spengler and Toynbee. However celebrated, these authors were distinctly marginal to the profession of history. Civilization has thrived as a term only in the bastard field of Orientalism, which came to be defined precisely as the study of other "civilizations" (there used in the plural), such as China, India, the Ottomans, the Arab-Islamic world (and analogously classical Antiquity). Orientalism is in poor repute these days, although it still has its advocates. All in all, however, the social sciences have been averse to talking about civilization, either in the singular or in the plural.[1]

---

[1] I have discussed the significance of the distinction between talking of civilization in the singular or in the plural in "The Modern World-System as a Civilization," chapter 14.

Yet here we are in 1987 holding a Thematic Session of the American Sociological Association on the rise and fall of this conceptual stepchild, civilization(s). What is going on? In the real world, it is clear that there are two principal phenomena that account for this renewed concern with the concept. On the one hand, once again there are serious doubts, especially in the wealthier zones of the world-system, about the inevitability of progress and the desirability of its principal modern lodestar, technological advance.

Progress, as we know, emerged as the great moral desideratum of the Enlightenment of the eighteenth century, and became the official dogma of the Western world in the heyday of British hegemony in the world-system in the mid-nineteenth century. It was subsequently subjected to serious skeptical reassessment, first in the *fin de siècle* questioning of the pervasiveness of human rationality, then in the gloom of the 1930s about the spread of fascist ideas, and finally in the widespread fears of the deterioration of the world environment in the 1970s. It is no accident that each of these reassessments occurred during Kondratieff B-phases and each occurred primarily in the core countries of the capitalist world-economy.

If the doubts about progress are stronger today than previously, it is because, in addition to the Kondratieff downturn (after all, B-phases are normally followed by A-phases), there is a second consideration, one of fundamental geopolitical change. The expansion of Europe, which went on essentially unchecked from the sixteenth to the twentieth centuries, has now been reversed. We are living the political rise of the Third World and the cultural decolonization of the world-system. This process may be slower than some wish (and faster than others wish), but it seems quite inexorable.

Faced with a conjunctural Kondratieff downturn and a structural reversal of the expansion of Europe, the Western world (for it is their intellectual ideas which have been placed in question) is trying to understand this new state of things, no doubt hoping that the social changes it implies will turn out to be less unsettling than many fear. Hence the social scientists of Western countries have turned in recent years to dabbling in an historically grounded macrosociology which, however feeble, at least is concerned with explaining this puzzling and anxiety-producing transformation of the real world.

Still, we have only been dabbling in historically grounded macrosociology. We have not collectively been taking it very seriously, because we are afraid. To take seriously the subject of the rise and fall of civilization means to open up a debate about two of the long-accepted premises of Western science: universalism and linearity.

Universalism is dear to the Western heart. It finds its roots in the three great monotheistic religions – Judaism, Christianity, and Islam. It was nourished by the Baconian–Newtonian paradigm of science, and it received its ultimate philosophical imprimatur during the Enlightenment. Universalism has a simple enough premise. It is that human behavior is subject to general laws that can be discovered and clearly stated in verifiable form and which apply across time and space. This is presumably a general scientific premise applied to the human arena. This thesis has been challenged from the outset, in a sort of rearguard way, in the name of humanist values. This humanist challenge denied the existence of any laws governing human behavior on the grounds that human beings are both sentient and conscious and therefore not subject to mechanical laws. Human beings, the humanists have argued, have free will and therefore act in ways that science cannot predict. It is consequently pointless, even counterproductive, to search for such laws. In this view, all particular behavior is said to be idiosyncratic.

This so-called idiographic-nomothetic debate is more than a century old. What is new today is that universalism is being challenged from *within* science, and on scientific grounds. Classical dynamics, that is Newtonian physics, is based on the calculation of linear trajectories which were said to be lawful, determined, and reversible (that is, atemporal). Contemporary science has, however, discovered to its surprise that "such a description is not valid in general . . . [and that] 'most' dynamic systems behave in a quite unstable way."[2] Intrinsic randomness and intrinsic irreversibility (or the arrow of time) are being discovered to be the basis of physical order.

[2] Ilya Prigogine and Isabelle Stengers, *Order Out of Chaos*, New York: Bantam, 1984, p. 263.

Instead of linearity and equilibrium, scientists are saying today that systems move away from equilibrium states and that, when they do, bifurcation replaces linearity, a bifurcation being defined simply as "the appearance of a new solution of the equations for some critical value."[3] Bifurcations imply elements which are deterministic only between bifurcation points. As the bifurcation points are approached, "fluctuations play an essential role,"[4] and there are constant innovations and mutations.

Thus, at the very moment that physical scientists are saying that "bifurcation introduces *history* into physics and chemistry,"[5] and that "there can be no end to history,"[6] at this moment when physical scientists are experiencing a "profound change in the scientific concept of nature,"[7] many social scientists are still clinging to their versions of universalism and linearity, derived from an older view of physical science. The implications for social decision-making are obviously even more immediate and more threatening of established interests than the implications for engineering and technology.

This is what the renewed interest in civilizations is about. The concept of civilization (singular) is a Newtonian idea. The concept of civilizations (plural) is consonant with an understanding that order emerges from chaos, that chaos is itself creative. I have used the phrase "is consonant with" deliberately. This is because the concept of civilizations (plural) has had other connotations in the past which we must clear away if we are to find it relevant for our understanding of human complexity today.

The idea that there have been multiple civilizations has long been tied to a cyclical chronosophy.[8] Civilizations rise and civilizations fall, it is argued. They are presumed to do this following some kind of standard format. Here, under the pretense of cultivating a particularist view of the world, we find a hidden universalism. It is merely a universalism without progress — probably the worst kind. There are fortunately not too many

[3] Ilya Prigogine, *From Being to Becoming*, San Francisco: Freeman, 1980, p. 105.
[4] *Ibid.*, p. 106.
[5] *Ibid.*
[6] *Ibid.*, p. 128.
[7] Prigogine and Stengers, *Order Out of Chaos*, p. 312.
[8] On chronosophies, see K. Pomian, "The Secular Evolution of the Concept of Cycles," *Review*, II, 4, Spring 1979, 563–646.

advocates any longer of this particular usage of civilizations (plural).

There is, however, a derived notion which is logically very similar and which is still popular. It is what I would call the "decline and fall" thesis. The great civilizations "decline and fall" and, when they do, are overwhelmed by the barbarians.[9] This is nourished directly by the Western experience of the fall of the Roman Empire and the invasions of Europe by so-called barbarian tribes. The *leitmotiv* of this theorizing is cultural pessimism, and the message is that, once the American empire has declined, the world will go to pieces. Today, we are even getting movies on this theme, albeit Québecois in origin and sardonic in style. But of course, if the scientific model of birfurcating tells us anything, it tells us that we cannot predict that the outcome will be a pessimistic one.

Finally, the concept of civilizations (plural) can dissolve into a sort of mindless cultural pluralism. Humanity has invented many versions of social order. There is no way of comparing them morally or evaluating them historically. We simply have to accept the reality of past and future variation. This is a sort of ultimate abandonment of rationality, a game I for one am not ready to play.

Is there then a more viable concept of civilizations (plural), one which will help us in our interpretation of human history? I think there is.

I would start by making a distinction between an historical system and a civilization. An historical system refers to an empirical reality. The Tang dynasty in China or the Roman Empire or the Mughal empire were historical systems. A civilization refers to a contemporary claim about the past in terms of its use in the present to justify heritage, separateness, rights.

Chinese civilization, Western civilization, Indian civilization are such contemporary claims, These claims do not have to be based exclusively on verifiable empirical data. These claims are in any case based on contemporary choices about historical boundaries of inclusion. Apparently, neither Chinese "civilization" nor

---

[9] See the debate on "Civilizations and Their Declines," between Johan Galtung, Tore Heistad, and Erik Rudeng on the one hand and Samir Amin on the other in *Review*, IV, 1, Summer 1980.

Indian "civilization" lays claim to a direct heritage from Central Asia but Western "civilization" lays claim to a direct heritage from Greece and perhaps even from ancient Israel. The reasons for such claims cannot be located in what happened in the past but in what is happening in the present. These claims about historical boundaries of inclusion are not subject to empirical verification, except as current ideology. Studying the situation in the past will not throw light on the validity of regarding certain prior time–place structures as part of the "heritage" of a contemporary group. This is because a cultural heritage is non-material and can be appropriated by multiple groups. It can be appropriated by whoever wishes to appropriate it, more or less.

Civilizations have not risen and fallen. Rather, world-empires have come into existence, flourished, and declined. In some geographical zones of the world (China is an excellent example), there have been successive world-empires with overlapping geophysical coordinates. Later world-empires have often (not always) laid claim to a "civilizational" heritage, based on a certain degree of cultural continuity.

The form of continuity can be varied: for example, that of language, or of religion, or of *Weltanschauung*, or of food habits. It is never perfect and sometimes the argument for continuity can be quite strained. Take the link between the contemporary U.S. and Greece of the fourth century BC and reflect upon the degree of closeness of language, religion, *Weltanschauung*, and food habits. There is no doubt some link, but nonetheless . . .

Let us therefore turn to our own historical system and see how the concept of civilizations can be most useful to us. We have to remember that, as empirical reality, the capitalist world-economy in its own process of expansion destroyed other historical systems. They ceased to exist as systems. Their influence remained as civilizational claims, that is, as claims in the present within the existing historical system about heritage, separateness, rights. They are as valid as they are asserted effectively. When we say there has been an Arab *ba'ath*, renaissance, it means that some large group of persons are claiming to be "Arabs" within the modern world-system and therefore are putting forward political demands in cultural clothing. Can Christians as well as Moslems be Arabs? Are Mauritanians Arabs? There is no way of answering this except in terms of contemporary ideology. Today Sephardic Jews in Israel are not Arabs. Tomorrow they could be, however far-fetched this may seem now. These are neither moral questions nor factual ones; they are primarily political questions.

We know two things principally about our existing capitalist world-economy. One, it is approaching a bifurcation point. And two, one of the elements of this process is what I have called the cultural decolonization of the world-system. The latter is manifested in two ways: political renaissance of civilizational claims, and concerns of historical social scientists with concepts like "civilization."

The process of bifurcation is going forward. Its results are unpredictable. That does not mean that they are unamenable to human decision-making. Quite the contrary. Because the constraints of determined outcome are lifted in situations of bifurcation, even small changes of the input can create great changes of the output. To translate that into everyday language: it is now that it really matters what we do collectively. There is real historical choice precisely because the process is stochastic and non-linear.

We may therefore, should therefore, pursue our desired objectives, our fulfillment of human potential as we can imagine it. To do this well, we must draw upon the widest range of options. Civilizational claims widen our range of options, provided that they are done in the spirit of Senghor's "rendez-vous du donner et du recevoir." The decline of the West, the decline of the American empire, the decline of capitalism – however we wish to word it – are not occasions for cultural pessimism. But they are equally not occasions for cultural optimism. They offer the possibility – but only the possibility – of creating a new and better historical system, provided we judge well (with care, with imagination, with courage). Studying the operations of past historical systems without the distorting lens of linear universalism may well be an essential element in the struggle.

❧ Index

242   Index